in the
shadow
of the
rainbow

in the
shadow
of the
rainbow

LESTER VENTER

Heinemann

www.heinemann.co.za

© Heinemann Publishers (Pty) Ltd

PO Box 781940
Sandton 2146
Johannesburg
South Africa

First published 2001

2004 2003 2002 2001
10 9 8 7 6 5 4 3 2 1

ISBN 0 79620 170 6

Cover design by Comet Design
Cover photograph by C & D Heierli Photography
Production by Comet Publishing
Typesetting by Zebra Publications

Printed and bound in South Africa by
CTP Book Printers

Dedication

This book is for:
- Bonni, whose strengths of character and of mind have triumphed;
- Thandi, whose elevated task is the construction of consciousness;
- Louise, whose serenity has transcended;
- Christoph, whose achievement is to do what others only teach.

Acknowledgements

In the text I have tried, through footnotes and other means, to indicate the sources of ideas and material. This is to aid readers who might like to follow trails that I have found interesting to pursue. However, there are many sources that do not lend themselves to being credited in this way, yet have played an enormous role in shaping my thoughts — and in the production of this book. I am mainly indebted to Lindsay Norman, my agent, for the firm and unflappable way she guided the book … and me. Her steady hand has been a source of great reassurance. As a publisher, Garry Rosenberg has been tolerant, insightful, and creative. I expect he will bring to the book a success greater than it may deserve; any ignominy that attaches to it will have to be borne by me. I am grateful to my colleagues in The Tuesday Group — Carl Albrecht, Michael Gillis and, until recently, Pieter Kritzinger — for our many joint explorations, for their great knowledge in their fields, and for the provocative rounds of email discussion. Many conversations, ongoing, with Charles Marais, who is an adventurer at the frontiers of science, have extended my horizons considerably. Lisa McNamara withstood the pressures of last minute research and fact checking. Nic Jooste produced a cover design that captured the essence of the book before there even was one, and gave art direction with a skilled hand. Christoph and Diane Heierli made a cover picture that enhanced the mood and may be the best of me because it shows the least of me. Lastly, but mostly, my wife and companion explorer, Madeline, edited the text, curbed my excesses and polished my roughness, and brought into my life not only an excellent reference library and two dogs, but a lamp to light the shadows.

About the Author

Lester Venter started describing the passing human show as a journalist. He became familiar to South Africans as a commentator on television and radio during South Africa's transition to democracy. He has visited many places and worked among many people in different phases of social evolution and intent on different destinations — in Africa and in the West. He lives now in the village of Simon's Town, from where he writes and coordinates The Tuesday Group, which focuses on analysis of the future, and the investment climate in biotechnology and information technology. He is the author of *When Mandela Goes,* an analytic account of South Africa's future, and a history of Namibia, called *History Makers.* The unfolding stories of the human experience have not finished, and nor has he.

Contents

Contents

Return to the Present

Importing hindsight from the future

The best view you can get of the present is from the future. Think about it. It's hard to understand what's happening in the present for the very reason that it's still happening. Things have not yet run their course. Without a conclusion of sorts, we cannot say how far along that course we are now. Things have not yet become what they have set out to be. So it is difficult to know their nature, or even recognise them for what they truly are. It's not surprising we seldom try.

When we really want to understand what's happening we pause and look back. That helps make the past comprehensible — but still leaves us with the fragmentary present. So, imagine this: suppose we could somehow leap out of the kaleidoscope of the present into the future ... and look back from there. Then we could see the present in perspective and in focus, and a lot of it would make a lot more sense than it does now.

It's no big trick. I know that when I look back on my youth it makes a lot more sense than it did to me at the time. I also see the things that were genuinely important, the things that would endure and dog me into the years I live now. I see, further, the things that seemed important at the time and that they weren't at all. They were the things that preoccupied me but were destined to wither and fall by time's wayside. I see, too, the things I didn't see then. The life of a nation is no different. That's why we have history.

So here's the trick. If we fast-forward into the future, then we would be afforded all the advantages of perspective, recognition and understanding of the present that are denied us now. We would see what is really important in the present because we would see what is going to stay with us. We would see what is undeserving of serious attention because it's going to fade by itself. We would see what we need to take seriously and what we can safely ignore. Moreover, we would see vital things that we are overlooking right now. And we would be able to fix that.

That's the value of the exercise; and that's the exercise I attempted with the book *When Mandela Goes*.[1] It was a bid to follow the running

---

[1] Lester Venter, *When Mandela Goes: The Coming of South Africa's Second Revolution*, Doubleday, London, 1977.

1

course of events, from the present to the future. It was the first part of an undertaking. What you are reading now is the second part, the return to the present. The assignment now is to examine more closely the nature of present events, having taken that journey of the mind into the future. The route from the present to the future and back again is well travelled and understood. Each of us has been on it many times. Last century's great poet, Thomas Eliot,[2] ends his statement of the metaphysics of our time in the *Four Quartets* with his view that we are compelled to journeys of exploration — and " ... the end of all our exploring / Will be to arrive where we started / And know the place for the first time".

This prologue is meant to act as a passage that allows the outward leg of the journey, undertaken in *When Mandela Goes,* to be followed by this, the return leg. To make the passage meaningful, we will extract in the following pages the main forecasts contained in *When Mandela Goes.* Then we will measure them against events as they have subsequently unfolded. This will allow us to attach value to the predictions and the methods by which they were achieved ... or allow us to discredit those that fail in our scrutiny. Either way we'll learn something. Additionally, we'll be on much surer ground when we embrace the present, and peer once more into the future from where we stand now. We'll discover if Mr Eliot's teaching works for us.

Looking back to see ahead

The ideas that culminated in *When Mandela Goes* evolved along a path that was in part personal, and in the main rooted in the work of others who were developing a growing consensus about how the post-Cold War world was put together, and where it was headed.

I spent two decades as a political reporter and in that time an awareness slowly arose in me: the reasons for people's political behaviour were not the ones they gave in the interviews, speeches, and reciprocal criticisms that I laboured through. Nor did the real reasons for their actions appear in any of the explanations they themselves forwarded. In fact, there seemed precious little to learn about politics by listening to the explanations of politicians. Clearly, there were underlying mechanisms that drove them and their often dismaying show forward. A pattern of determinants undoubtedly existed below the level of public articulation. I can draw no more vivid a picture of this notion than the futurist Michael J Mazarr, a

[2] T. S. Eliot, *Collected Poems 1909–1962,* Harcourt Brace Jonavich, New York, 1971.

research fellow at the Centre for Strategic and International Studies in Washington. He likened the onward rush of people and events, perhaps most fittingly, to columns of ants. Seen through a magnifying glass, the actions of individual ants appear erratic as they dart hither and thither for whatever reason ants dart hither and thither. Seen from some distance, however, the column has a clear form and direction. The randomness of the energy expended by each ant takes on meaning when viewed from above.

Inevitably, it became more interesting to me to observe the direction of the column than the frantic dartings of insignificant ants. We might add straight away: how long could one observe the direction of the column without starting to wonder what its purpose and destination were? But if we did ask, we would be getting ahead of ourselves. Let's stay with the evolution of awareness a little longer.

Naturally, in the early stages of the unfolding awareness, I had no idea what the underlying mechanisms and patterns were. (I would soon discover that the drive to understand these truths was one of the great undertakings of the great minds of our age. I was a Tom Thumb straying into a land of giants. Fortunately, as a reporter, I was brassed with enough cheek not to be bothered by this.)

Whatever the patterns of behaviour were, what was equally as clear as their existence was the fact that they were not confined only to the political class in society. For society as a whole endorsed the behaviour of the political class. True, sometimes it is only a section of society that endorses the behaviour of the political class — as was the case in the South Africa that I grew up in. Nevertheless, as South Africa itself showed, when the rulers are in direct conflict with the ruled, the situation sooner or later corrects itself ... and the society produces a political class it *is* prepared to endorse. This is so no matter how perverse the relationship between the rulers and the ruled may seem at first glance, as it does in the case of societies that submit to tyrants. It's true, tyrants are nearly as effectively endorsed by public acquiescence as other, more amenable, leaders might be through public selection.

Very much part of the process of social endorsement of politicians is the media — which is where I became a direct participant in the patterns of behaviour. In market economies where information is treated as a commodity, the most successful journalists are those that read the market for their product best. "Knowing what the public wants" is a working definition of what constitutes news because, at the heart of it, the people must want what the news organisation produces. If not, the people would not buy the news, and there would be no news organisation.

I rank among the unrepentant who see nothing wrong with this arrangement. What I can tell you, though, is one thing the public does *not* want is the underlying explanation for its willingness to endorse its political class — at least not in its daily news diet. Accordingly, there are no serious attempts on the part of journalists to analyse the public demand they cater to.

How are people's demands for news and information formed? What are the patterns of those demands? Why do the patterns change and what do those changes tell us? (Before World War 1 the preponderance of media news concerned politics, business, the professions and science; by the end of the century entertainers and entertainment made up the media bulk.) In what overall direction are these demands leading us? These are questions journalists never ask. Journalists satisfy demands for news, and they analyse the news. They don't analyse the demands.

Like anything else, the evidence for the patterns' existence proliferates in proportion to the intensity with which you search. Be that as it may, the evidence is undeniable — and I offer two illustrations. The first concerns the eminent American historian, Barbara Tuchman (Tuchman had first been a journalist but I'll let that go, now). In one of her absorbing works, *The March of Folly*,[3] she sets out to show how entire governments, and the societies that tolerated them, pursued courses of action that were patently against their best interests.

Along the way, she joins American President John Adams in observing that government "is little better practised now than three or four thousand years ago". Even so, she sets three criteria for unmitigated folly in the government of society's business: a policy must be perceived as counter-productive in its own time; a feasible alternative course of action must be available; and the policy must be that of a group, not an individual ruler. Tuchman becomes interested when a society and its government, driven by something other than reason, pursue a course of action in the face of her criteria.

No doubt you will now pause to wonder whether you have experienced, or can recall, such government. I know that I, as a South African, have experienced at least one government that is a hand-in-glove fit for the Tuchman test. As it happens, it is in connection with just that government that I offer the second illustration.

[3] Barbara Tuchman, *The March of Folly: From Troy to Vietnam*, Papermac, London, 1996.

On a sunny day early in February 1990 that government turned on a dime. So did the majority of the white electorate, which had voted that government into power for an unbroken run of more than four decades. The day before, the government and its supporters were locked in a mind set that had been constructed and propounded over many years. Apartheid was held to be the only sensible way to order a multi-ethnic society, the world's moral norms were a parade of hypocrisy, the African National Congress (ANC) was bent on the destruction of the white man, the South African Communist Party personified the anti-Christ and equal votes for all were a ticket to doom. The following day, apartheid was a mistake and an abomination, vilified by all who had sworn by it not 24 hours previously. The ANC was now a party of legitimate political aspirations. The communists were actually quite nice when you got to know them; a harmless bunch of idealists, really. A democracy structured round the land's black majority was a noble ideal that represented whites' best prospects for survival.

It was an about-turn matched in modern times only by the amazing haste with which communism was abandoned by its adherents and followers in the disintegrating Soviet Union of the late 1980s.

No satisfactory account has since then been forwarded by F W de Klerk, then president, whose pivotal speech to parliament occasioned the South African turnaround, or by anyone else, of the profound change of views and beliefs that the Afrikaner leader went through. Of course, it may have been as much a change of strategy, and a recognition of diminishing options, as it was a change of views and beliefs, but that's another story. The point is that the acceptance of the turn-around by his followers both in and outside government was immediate and all-embracing. They dropped one set of principles and hoisted another without visible hesitation. Preparation, reason, insight, persuasion, debate, introspection, enlightenment … none of these played any role whatsoever. In the unforgettable jibe of the poet Breyten Breytenbach, the ruling elite did an about-turn "in mid goose step".

It struck me at the time — as it did so many others — that I had witnessed an extraordinary episode in history. It seemed proof conclusive that my fellow citizens' political behaviour was dictated by something other than reason, insight, persuasion, debate, introspection or enlightenment.

Flights of the futurists

Let's pause to size up. I couldn't look for explications of politics within politics itself. Surrounding society couldn't help because it was locked into the deal with politics — the one was an expression of the other. The media was just that — a medium through which society and politics talked to themselves. There was some critical distance in the media, but not enough. Whichever way you cut it, looking for answers here was like asking one of the trees to describe the forest.

I began to read, and I sought out a particular kind of reading. I had been told that in the natural sciences a theory became accepted when it could predict that given results would arise from given conditions. So I looked for writers who looked for similar cause-and-effect relationships in the social sciences.

The first I encountered was the most popular of the futurists, Alvin Toffler (Toffler, too, had been a journalist ... but I said I'd let that go). At the time he was writing — the late 1970s — Toffler accurately anticipated the development of a knowledge-based economy, then in its early stages of formation. Like most successful futurists, Toffler's achievement lay in being among the first to see and describe something that had already started happening.

Toffler was a good place to start because he works from a historical base. In *Future Shock*[4] and *The Third Wave*[5] he showed how the knowledge economy was an evolution of what had gone before. In doing this Toffler illuminated one of the most important factors in understanding the future — knowing the past. For the present is no more than an arbitrary, shifting point in the continuum of events. The present is wherever we happen to be as events flow from their origins to their destinies. The present is an on-going culmination of the past, and being able to embrace and comprehend the momentum up to now is to be best able to make sense of where it is likely to go from here.

From Toffler I moved on to James Dale Davidson and William Rees-Mogg. They made vivid predictions of impending fortune and misfortune in the postmodern economy in their books *Blood in the Streets: Investment Profits in a World Gone Mad*[6] and *The Great Reckoning*.[7] Davidson and Rees-Mogg were bold and challenging ... and often quite wrong. From them I learned something else about futurism: being right is not all it's

---

[4] Alvin Tofler, *Future Shock*, Bantam, New York, 1991.

[5] Alvin Toffler, *The Third Wave*, Pan, London, 1981

[6] James Dale Davidson & William Rees-Mogg, *Blood in the Streets: Investment Profits in a World Gone Mad*, Pan Books, London, 1987.

[7] James Dale Davidson & William Rees-Mogg, *The Great Reckoning: How the World will Change before the Year 2000*, Pan Books, London, 1994.

about. Sounds dodgy, I know. But, again, think about it for a moment. The value lies in extricating oneself from immersion in the present to examine what's happening and to explore its consequences. It's a way of living more intensively in the present, with greater awareness of the worth or silliness of what you're involved in. Also, you then have a better idea of where to place your bets. Not a definitive idea, mind you, just a better one. That's what Rees-Mogg and Davidson were aiming at. (Incidentally, Rees-Mogg had earlier been the editor of *The Times*, which means that he, too ... uh, okay, I promised.)

The problem with Toffler and Davidson and Rees-Mogg was that they were popular and successful, which meant that the academic establishment regarded them with sniffy condescension. That's not a serious problem, because I know as well as you do that nine out of ten of those academics would have written a bestseller like snap if they only knew how.

Still, I did want to know what the real heavyweights had to say. That meant reading Paul Kennedy, the Yale historian. Kennedy's great works were *The Rise and Fall of the Great Powers*[8] and *Preparing for the Twenty-First Century*.[9] In them Kennedy revealed the deep science of the futurist. He parted the obscuring veils of current affairs to expose the forces that shaped society in the last century and will shape society in this century. Working with these great levers permitted Kennedy to name the factors that distinguish winning societies from losing societies and, hence, to predict which the winners would be, and which the losers. We'll get to those great levers shortly. I would first like to point out that Professor Kennedy has no known connection to journalism.

He was followed by the Harvard political scientist Samuel P Huntington, whose only career embarrassment known to me was his failed venture to advise the P W Botha government on reform strategy. Huntington redeemed himself with one of the most important works of political analysis our time, *The Clash of Civilizations and the Remaking of World Order*[10] — the sort of title, one must concede, only a theoretician of unassailable stature would dare. Huntington went for the patterns underlying the global politics of our era, and said they followed — and would follow

---

[8] Paul Kennedy, *The Rise and Fall of the Great Powers: Economic Change & Military Conflict from 1500–2000*, Harper Collins, London, 1987.
[9] Paul Kennedy, *Preparing for the Twenty-First Century*, Harper Collins, London, 1993.
[10] Samuel P Huntigton, *The Clash of Civilisations and the Remaking of World Order*, Touchstone Books, London, 1998.

ever more intensively — the fracture lines between cultural and religious value systems.

In the closing years of the 1990s there was a pervasive recognition that the principles by which the world was put together ... or was coming apart ... differed fundamentally from what had applied before. The need to explain the new rules was a pressing one.

A provocative contribution came from another Washington intellectual, Francis Fukuyama, with an uncompromising title — *The End of History*.[11] Looking back on the collapse of the Soviet Union and the symbolic fall of the Berlin Wall, Professor Fukuyama concluded that the ideological storms that had buffeted the second half of the 20th Century were over. Furthermore, there was a clear winner: the free market system had demonstrated beyond argument its superiority as a means to prosperity. From here on success among nations would be graded simply by who conformed to the market how soon and how well.

Writing at roughly the same time was the Spanish-born Berkeley sociologist Manuel Castells. In a dense text spread over three volumes under the overall title of *The Information Age: Economy, Society and Culture*[12] Castells described the world's developed societies as networked by technology, trading in technology, innovating technology and modifying lifestyles through technology. Toffler's earlier vision was thus given a comprehensive validation by one of the world's most luminous thinkers.

The foregoing is my view of the main flag posts along the route of understanding the political organisation of the world's communities in recent time. Of course, there is much else along that road. Many others, thoughtful and far-seeing, have added volition — the economists Galbraith and Thurow, the historians Toynbee, Hobsbawm, Fernández-Armesto of Oxford and Ponting in his thematic analysis of the 20th Century.[13] There is a growing number of institutes and groups dedicated to understanding the future and how it is created. Futurism is emerging as a critical discipline in the corporate world. The oil company Shell has put enormous resources into pioneering futures studies under luminaries of the new discipline like Pierre Wack, and Arie de Geus.

---

[11] Francis Fukuyama, *The End of History and the Last Man*, Avon Books, 1993.

[12] Manuel Castells, *The Rise of the Network Society (Vol 1, The Information Age: Economy Society & Culture)* Blackwell, Massachusetts, 1999.

[13] Clive Ponting, *The 20th Century: A World History*, Henry Holt & Co, New York, 1999.

What cracks the world up

Okay, back to the great levers. In the descriptions of Kennedy and the others the great levers thrust the world into disruptive rushes of change such as had never occurred before.

The two great transformations of the past, the Agricultural Revolution and the Industrial Revolution (Toffler's first two waves of change), altered the course of social evolution — but they did so at a modest pace, taking thousands of years in the first case, and hundreds in the second, to reach the majority of people on earth. In some respects even, their effects remain unfelt today in numerous places. Not so with the third wave. It is unmatched in human experience in its charge, its immediacy and its global sweep. One measure of it suffices: it took radio 38 years to build an audience of 50 million; it took television 13; and the Internet four.

The great levers of this change process join in an amalgam of forces that span the globe. These forces push aside all that would impede their reach — not merely the heroic individuals who were the masters of history in time before, but the will of nations.

The impact of such accelerated change would have been great even if it were evenly distributed. But it isn't. It's grossly uneven in both is benefits and its costs. Worse, it's getting more uneven, at a faster pace, all the time. Therein lies its drama.

Across the world populations are growing well beyond the capacity of their often-rudimentary economies to support them. In real terms, economies and national resources are in precipitous decline and entire cities are crumbling. This is happening at a time when wealth in advanced nations is reaching peaks only dreamed of by visionaries of the past. In the opening years of the new century the United States posted the longest ever unbroken run of growth in its gross domestic product. At the same time the gap between the rich and the poor of the world reached its greatest extent, too — swelling into the fundamental dynamic of global conflict.

Poverty is growing pitiably even as we celebrate the great advances we are making in other fields. In the knowledge-intensive economies jobs are an ever-receding prospect for the people who need them most. So unemployment increases and poverty deepens.

With poverty a characteristic of entire nations, the health of millions of people at a time is attacked by epidemics of frightening diseases, and the energy of nations is sapped even further.

Enticed by unrealistic dreams and impelled from places of origin that cannot sustain them, the poor flock to cities — in search of lifestyles they cannot ever attain.

From this doubling of desperation new levels of social disorder are bred. Crime and inter-personal violence become the scourge of the urban landscapes.

Many of the present schisms in humanity are, of course, as old as history. The difference, most simplistically put, is that now there are more people involved and the stakes are higher — dangerously so. The difference is multiplied by global media saturation. Now the daily agonies of the world are replayed in the nightly news in every home where anyone cares to flick a TV remote.

The media, especially the electronic media, has recreated the conditions under which democracy was practised in its golden age. In Athens under Pericles every enfranchised citizen was able to attend the business of the governing assembly — and every voice, from the statesman, the poet and the fisherman, was heard and weighed. Population growth, among other things, in time put a stop to the idealistic exercise of democratic government. Now we're back there. The media has created an electronic community where every voice is once again heard. It's just that those voices are much angrier now.

The components of world society, demarcated by the schisms, derive their individual cohesion from value systems. As each of the components differ, so their supporting value systems differ. As the priorities within each component differ, so the goals of each value system differ, and so does the fervour with which they are pursued. Along with these vexatious trends, the fulcrum of political power is shifting, within nations and among them. It is slipping from the hands of elites, despite their economic power, into the hands of masses. The strident voice of the poor is swelling through the sheer power of their growing numbers. And it is amplified by their anger. Moreover, it is abetted by a growing realisation among the privileged that their perch is threatened unless they make space for those not as blessed as they. Offering itself as a partner to this growing realisation is a growing sensitivity to the unfairness of the way we have structured life on our planet. The media sates society with images of the latter-day John Bull gorging himself on the fattened calf while the loin-clothed ones who pampered it for his gluttony cry weakly in hunger at his door.

None of us knows what to do about it. So we swim with the tide, craning our heads above water, hoping it might be revealed to us where we are being taken.

It took me longer than, doubtlessly, it has taken you to make the critical breakthrough: *all of the above is as much a description of South Africa as it is a description of the world*. It's a fit: the yawning gap between the rich and the poor and the politics of conflict arising therefrom, the exclusion of the un-skilled from the knowledge economy, the consequent spread of unemployment and poverty, the rise of crime, the abrasion of contesting value systems ... and the lurching shift of power from elites to masses. South Africa, in brief, is a microcosm of the main dynamics that are shaping the world.

The reason, naturally, is that South Africa is two worlds in one. Within a single set of borders it contains both a developed world component and a developing world component ... and they occur in a size relationship comparable to that in which they exist in the greater world.

Further tantalizing ramifications present themselves. In as much as South Africa and the world as a whole are reflections of one another in the given sense, the fate of the one will likely reflect the fate of the other. The way the relevant dynamics unfold in the world will probably reflect the way they unfold in South Africa, and *vice versa*. This means there is much that can be learned about the one by observing the other. It means South Africa can, in important respects, be seen as a socio-political laboratory for global developments.

A note of caution: comparisons and analogies such as the one I am suggesting between world affairs and South African realities are an aid to comprehension. They are a valuable aid, but if they are applied too inflexibly, pushed too far, or used to the exclusion of other tools, they break down. So don't.

All I am trying to extract from it is the bedrock idea for *When Mandela Goes*. The proposition was simple and appealing: apply the conceptual template created by the big thinkers to the specific case of South Africa. Then let the great forces continue their onward march in the laboratory of the mind ... and try to imagine what sort of society would arise.

It would be a venture without guarantees, I realised straight away, and it would be strewn with pitfalls. The basic idea — South Africa as the microcosm of the global macrocosm — was sound. But that's all it was — a basic idea. There would be too many variables in the application to make it acceptable in a formal, academic sense. This was a relief. I would be free to establish the factual base and then raise a speculative construct on it. I have heard it said that if you start with an acorn you can predict that you will end up with a tree, although you won't be able to predict precisely the shape of it. Accordingly, I had no specific idea of what the exercise would produce.

All but a fool, however, could see the result would not be comforting and palatable. The great levers that would drive the operation were harsh and unforgiving. It was clear, and it remains clear, that the future was going to present us with great problems. Saying so would undoubtedly raise the ire of the politicians, who see it as their business to peddle social saccharine. Those quarters of the media that formed part of the social contract with the politicians would echo the displeasure. In spite of this, the call of the exercise was too challenging to ignore and too deserving to abandon for fear of the unpopularity it would bring.

In the end, it turned out that I misjudged the tolerance among academics for an acknowledgedly faulty, but worthwhile, thought experiment. It turned out I figured the politicians perfectly. As for particular ranks in the media … well, we'll get to that.

The smartest place in town

The question I then confronted is the one I left unattended when we opened this discussion: to fast-forward to the future to gain an advantage on the present is an attractive idea — but how?

Fortunately, a great deal of work was starting up on supplying an answer. Future studies have taken hold, and have become established as an emerging discipline over the last two decades. Their strategic value appeared first in a military context and, soon thereafter, in business.

In both cases, the accelerating advance of technology was shifting the advantage from where it traditionally resided — with those who commanded sheer size, dominating numbers and superior capital reserves. Technology was placing in the hands of the quick, the smart, and the often-unseen, instruments of power not imagined before. It became vital for war rooms and boardrooms to be able to anticipate both probable and improbable developments. It is sometimes said that what is most worrying to Microsoft, the giant that dominates the software industry, is not another of its visible competitors in the field, but the thought of some kid in his bedroom coming up with a better operating system than the vexatious Windows.

The accelerating pace of change was doing something else to foster the discipline of futurism. It was eroding the luxury of easy, incremental adjustments to change in the operating environment. In politics, in the behaviour of economies and in the market place, developments came speeding over the time horizon and crashed into the present. The future was no longer posting timely announcements of its imminent arrival. It was just turning up without warning. For those with strategic responsibility a new dictum was presenting itself: he who waits until tomorrow to discover what it holds is doomed; tomorrow must be understood today, so that preparations can be made.

Naturally, the desire to anticipate future events and the probable actions of adversaries and competitors is as old as human scheming. What is different now are the levels of formality, the intensity of need, and the costs of failure.

As a result, scenario building became an important strategic tool in the closing decades of last century.

Many techniques are employed. This is no place to go into them in detail and, anyway, they rest on shared rudiments. My own working distillation, extracted from many sources, became the following: (Any resemblance to Peter Schwartz's advice is entirely due to the seminal influence on futurism of his work *The Art of the Long View.*[14])

- *Isolate the fundamentals.* You need to decide what really matters in the subject you are going to project. You may want to ask yourself: "What can be taken away without really affecting the nature of the subject?" This you want to disregard. The correlating question is: "What, if taken away, will meaningfully alter the nature of the subject?" these are the fundamentals you want to work with.
- *Determine the inevitables.* There are certain things that just have to happen, because they always do in the applicable conditions. Add them to the fundamentals.
- *Roll out.* You have to have some expertise, at least, in your subject. From its history and the trends within it, you can extend the fundamentals and the inevitables into the future. If you can't, skip this bit — I'll be doing it for you shortly. Remember, too, that the further forward you roll the more diminished your accuracy.

[14] Peter Schwartz, *The Art of the Long view: Planning for the Future in an Uncertain World,* Doubleday, New York, 1996.

- *Weigh up the variables.* There are always random events and influences that you can't anticipate. Anticipate them anyway. Do the best you can. Decide on their probability and factor them into your roll out ... or leave them parked in a lay-by so you can pull them out later and claim you *did* think about that.
- *Draw your picture.* Don't be afraid to use your imagination. This is what it's made for. But make sure your imaginings are tempered and guided by the discipline of the preceding steps.

Practitioners who are timid or who have to justify a salary doing this sort of thing usually produce more than one scenario by the above method, or some variation of it. The convention is to produce four. The practitioners then present them to their chief executives and say: "These represent the range of probabilities." That's future-speak for "this is how I minimise the chances of ending up with my breakfast on my face". It doesn't help an awful lot because the chief executive still has to decide which of the scenarios to act on. That's what I like to call forecasting — knowing the scope of possibilities, then choosing one as opposed to a number. It's also what I decided to do with *When Mandela Goes.* Far better to lash yourself to the mast you have rigged, have a definite forecast, then monitor it and measure it as you go along, and adjust it as you need to. That's what we're doing here.

There's another criticism you'll come across of this process of unfolding the evolution of events. You'll be told that the future is largely unpredictable — that there are any number of examples to bear this out, which is true — and therefore any method based on linear extrapolation from the present is useless. To be sure, there is a degree of face-value truth to this assertion. However, the method recommended above is not based on linear extrapolation. It is extrapolation modulated by variables. Additionally, you might remember the conclusion of the great Hobsbawm:[15]

> The structures of human societies, their processes and mechanisms of reproduction, change and transformation, are such as to restrict the number of things that can happen, determine some of the things that will happen, and make it possible to assign greater or lesser probabilities to much of the rest.

Before we leave the five-step process above, though, I would like to confirm what you feel about it: it's short on science and long on "feel". This means the technique matters less than what you bring to it. And one of the main things to bring is a willingness to think boldly.

[15] Eric Hobsbawm, *On History,* Abacus, London, 1998.

Here's something that happened around *When Mandela Goes,* that shows the need for, and the difficulty of, bold thought. Somewhere in the *When Mandela Goes* argument I had mentioned the Carlton Centre in Johannesburg's now decayed city centre. It had been built 30 years before, and at the time of writing, it was put on sale for roughly half of what it had cost to erect ... and found an eventual buyer for roughly half again of the asking. My old pal, Rob Davies, and I decided to include this in the video we set out to make of *When Mandela Goes* — especially when Rob heard that the Carlton Hotel, for long Johannesburg's prime hotel, was to be closed and abandoned. Rob set off with his camera and I, far away in my coastal retreat, mused over the fate of The Carlton. As I did so, I remembered a day about 10 years before. It was a day in which some event of high political drama, characteristic of the time, was taking place. Like so many of these events, it was happening at The Carlton. This was especially the case when persons of elevated and foreign extraction were involved and they preferred not to meet in South African government buildings. The instance I began to recall may have been one of the many that involved the USA's redoubtable Assistant Secretary of State for Africa, Chester Crocker. Whoever. You get the idea. A familiar brood of journalists and diplomats was encamped round a table in the *Koffiehuis,* the ground floor coffee lounge that was in its day the most desirable Johannesburg rendezvous. They were talking the kind of talk you would expect.

As Rob trained his camera on the workmen sealing up the doors and windows of the stripped hotel and I recalled the past event, I wondered what might have been the reaction of my high-minded friends in the *Koffiehuis* that day if I had broken into the conversation and said: "Listen, people, I want to tell you that, in contrast to all your grand opinion-spinning, in 10 years' time the socio-political landscape will have changed so dramatically that not only will this ... " and at this I would have made a sweeping gesture that took in the coffee room, it's fashionable and important clientele and the luxury hotel itself " ... no longer be the smartest hotel in Johannesburg, it will be an empty, desolate wreck that nobody will want as a gift?"

My companions would have looked at me with a mixture of irritation and disbelief. Then they would have dismissed me as "unduly negative". Yet, a decade later, that imaginary prophecy had become a reality we had embraced and to which we had adjusted; then moved on.

So, when it comes to contemplating the Carlton Hotel factors that face us now, we must be prepared to think the unthinkable.

So, don't prevaricate. Say something. If you don't you may run into a guileless smartaleck, as did a well-meaning professor in Namibia many years ago. The professor was a charmingly dotty and bookish man. He approached the branch office of an international oil company, the name of which shouldn't be mentioned but has a marine connotation. The professor requested a grant to study the rainfall patterns of Namibia. Namibia is a dry country, and rainfall is a national preoccupation. The matter was agreed. Time went by and so did the money. Then, one day, the professor announced he was ready to announce his findings. A cocktail party was arranged by the eager sponsors and the professor was ushered to the lectern provided for the occasion.

The professor said he had studied the rainfall pattern of Namibia and had discovered that, indeed, it occurred in cycles — but that the rainfall records did not go back far enough to allow him to determine the duration of the cycles.

The professor let his arms fall to his sides, indicating the close of his presentation. There was a silence in the room. The professor stared at the gathered businessmen. They gazed back. The ice melted in their drinks. Then, after a tense and uncomfortable silence, a voice spoke from the group. With dismay, I recognised it as my own. The voice said: "In other words, professor, you have determined that sometimes it rains, and sometimes it doesn't — but you can't say which it will do, when." The voice, to my further dismay, then laughed abrasively at its own attempted wit. None other joined. As an exercise in forecasting, it was better left unsaid, not to mention unfunded.

Boarding now for the future

The conceptual tracks for the *When Mandela Goes* exercise were now laid. The journey would be guided by three principles, the first of which — that South Africa is two worlds in one, a world of the *haves* and a world of the *have-nots* — has been noted above.

The second of the principles was that in 1994, when South Africa changed from a racial oligarchy to a democracy, it underwent little more than a political decapitation. The mainly white political head of the society was cut off and discarded, and a mainly black head was put in its place. The body of society remained largely unchanged. In a most important sense, South Africa had not really experienced a revolution. An accommodation between politicians had bean reached. This meant that the watershed 1994 election was not change itself, but a signal for the start of a process that would, by one means or another, eventually bring deep changes to South African society. This was the meaning of the sub-title of *When Mandela Goes — The Coming of South Africa's Second Revolution.*

The third principle was to recognise that the agenda for change would be determined by society's deepest and most-felt needs. These needs would arise from the fundamentals that determine the quality of people's lives. They would present themselves as escalating demands in the political arena. Everything would flow from this agenda. Everything would be a consequence of, a response to, a compliance with, an attempt to resist, or a fatal blindness to these fundamental drivers. The kind of change we are talking about here is the kind of change that happens whether politicians or policies recognise it, miss it, help it, or resist it.

I referred to the fundamental drivers as the "silent dynamics" because the most interesting thing about them was that they were frequently the issues that received the least attention in the public debate and in the thrust of government action. In themselves, the silent dynamics are not astonishing. Here they are: unchecked population growth, failure of economic growth to match population growth effectively, growing unemployment, growing poverty, growing homelessness, declining public health ... and growing social destabilisation, manifested as crime and inter-personal violence.

The foregoing is a simple and uncluttered statement. It is, nevertheless, profoundly sobering and depressing in its ramifications. It also collided head-on with the feelings of hope and celebration that accompanied the initial experience of what everyone called "the new South Africa".

One would not need a very big heart, nor a great imagination, to empathise with the people — leaders and followers, activists and fellow-travellers — who had sacrificed so much to achieve a better moral order ... only to be told, once they had it, that their lot was doomed.

One would not need special powers, either, to imagine the antipathy that would be trained on such a message and its messenger.[16]

For these reasons, *When Mandela Goes* had to substantiate carefully each of the dynamics. The dynamics served a dual purpose. They were the

---

[16] I must register right away that my argument was not that the world's conflict dynamic, and its manifestation in South Africa, spelled doom. That would be simplistic and pointless. It would also, probably, be wrong because societies have powerful self-correcting mechanisms. Still, it is not hard to see how such a view could be extracted from the argument. I would also be disingenuous if I didn't admit I consciously left room for such an interpretation in order to endow the argument with shock value.

principles the argument of *When Mandela Goes* was built on and, because of their nature, were in themselves predictions. In 1977 it was uncommon to talk of certain of the dynamics in the context of the new society. Since then some have become familiar issues. Here is a brief overview. Where details or substantiations are lacking, they will be found in later chapters.

- *Population growth. When Mandela Goes* highlighted the imbalance between population growth and economic growth as one of the fundamental problems that would impede prosperity for the foreseeable future. Although the population growth rate has slowed from 2.3% to 1.4% since *When Mandela Goes* was published — mainly as a result of HIV/Aids and partly because of a world trend to slower growth — the population continues to grow at a pace far greater than the economy can sustain. By way of perspective, South Africa has an economic growth rate similar to that of a developed country — but a population growth rate typical of a developing nation. The population growth rate of a developed country would typically be under 0.5%.

- *Economic growth. When Mandela Goes* stated: "South Africa's growth pattern is locked in the 2% to 3.5% bracket." The elapsed period has borne this out, and economists' predictions at time of writing (2001) hold to the bracket. There is consensus that South Africa needs a growth rate of above 5% — with 6% to 8% being desirable — in order to solve its socio-economic problems.

- *Unemployment.* The truly frightening spectre of two out of every five workers without jobs looms portentously. It is not far off. Prospects for reversal are slashed by a double cross cut: population growth is creating growing numbers of job seekers (making the problem worst among the young) while the economy continues to prune away jobs. The statistics of job losses have themselves, predictably, become subject of a political tussle with claims and counter-claims — but you are safe reckoning that the economy is shedding about 100 000 jobs a year, and that the rate of losses is growing at about 3%. *When Mandela Goes* predicted that unemployment would grow unchecked in the years that followed. This has been and remains the case.

- *Poverty.* If you put together a swelling population, a lagging economy and galloping unemployment you don't need to be a political scientist to figure you've got poverty, and that it's growing. For the record, government statistics say that about 30% of South African households live below the poverty line of R800 (US$100) income per month per household. Because of the large variation in size of households among different socio-economic groups, this is a measure that embraces more than half the population. The gap between the rich and the poor, too, is getting bigger. While about a quarter of the rich in South Africa are a post-1994 black elite, the lowest 40% bracket on the socio-economic scale has taken about a 20% drop in income over the period. Taken together these sad realities mean that more than 70% of the country's children have insufficient resources for proper development. *When Mandela Goes* argued that this factor, which has showed continued deterioration, would add to the swelling impetus for political change.

- *Homelessness.* South Africa's new government set out in 1994 with the emblematic promise to build one million houses in five years. It came within a whisker of the target, flouting the more dismal expectations of *When Mandela Goes.* The aim was noble and its near-achievement an act worthy of celebration. It is therefore all the more painful to point out that the aim, while laudable, was inadequate. It fell short of the pace at which the need for housing escalated in the period. The reality, then, is that there were more unhoused South Africans at the end of the building campaign than there were when it started. The spurt of house-building has not been maintained. Yet the need inflates. Land invasions by desperate home seekers have swept the sub-continent, becoming alarmingly commonplace in South Africa.

- *Public Health.* At the time of researching *When Mandela Goes* — 1996, the year before publication — society was in the early stages of comprehending the HIV/Aids pandemic. (When you read on, you may conclude it still is — but let's wait till we get there.) The book therefore treated HIV/Aids as a health issue only. Nothing was done about measuring its economic and political impact, nor its effect on the mind and psychology of the nation. This was a serious failure to practice the foresight the work preached. The work focused instead on the bid to extend health services laterally to people who had lacked even rudimentary care until then ... but sounded an alarm on the catastrophic decline in resources, integrity of policy and levels of quality at the high end of health services. The course predicted has turned out to be the one followed and, even though a modest campaign was embarked on to establish clinics mainly in rural areas, even the low end has ailed. Infant mortality, a measure of national health standards, climbed steadily through the 1990s. In HIV/Aids alone, South Africa now faces the biggest natural disaster that has confronted any country, ever.

● *Crime and violence.* These phenomena are a necessary and unavoidable outcome of all of the foregoing. South Africa would have had a crime problem, anyway, because of the damage wrought by apartheid. The social dominance of the dynamics described above has simply made it impossible for the country to escape this outcome. As the effects of the above dynamics have cut deeper, so crime and other forms of instability have intensified. Some of us hope crime will go away of its own accord, some of us hope our society will undergo a rebirth of attitude and purpose, some of us hope the government will "do something", some of us hope the police will transform into an effective preventative force. Alas, none of these hopes is realistic. While the main causes intensify, so will the result escalate.

Building dark castles

The principles, or dynamics, enumerated above were measurable. All were, and remain, hard issues that could be established statistically — and their continued evolution could likewise be measured. The tracks that the forecasting exercise was to run on were, therefore, empirically verifiable.

The work would stand or fall by these measures. However, it had to go further. It had to leave the world of facts for the less reliable realm of speculation. It was necessary to imagine the sort of society and events that would arise from the base of the evolving dynamics.

It was clear that the silent dynamics would produce a nation in which there would be an escalation of social needs. Inevitably, these needs would express themselves in the political arena. No government, particularly not one dependent on votes, could forever ignore or fail to satisfy needs without paying a price. Sooner or later the unemployed, the un-housed, the un-fed, the un-well … just call them the un-satisfied … would demand effective alleviation of their plight.

That's not all. The needs of the *have-nots* differ in principle from those of the *haves.* Underdeveloped societies have an appetite for government that is big, benevolent, parental and pervasive.

Developed constituencies want the opposite. Government must be small, compliant, service-oriented and a rules monitor that stays out of the game. In other words, governing a dualistic society like South Africa is a form of political hell. Often, it's impossible. Usually, governments in such situations try to play to both constituencies. They end up satisfying neither, and get torn apart. Frequently, the catalyst for break-up is the appearance of a new party that defines itself as the voice of only one constituency

— the biggest. If there isn't a party that the majority believes speaks adequately for its needs, it's worth remembering that the political market place is much like the commercial market: where there is a demand, there will soon be a supply.

The South African government is a tripartite alliance between the political movement that spearheaded liberation, the African National Congress (ANC), the Congress of South African Trade Unions (Cosatu), and the South African Communist Party (SACP). Despite the left-leaning face value of this alliance, the government is fiscally conservative, middle of the road in broad policy, and bourgeois in character. It is a sitting duck. It is currently compelled to serve two competing constituencies. In as much as they are moving further apart, driven by the dynamics, so must government move in two diverging directions simultaneously. Plain logic says it can't do so indefinitely without splitting.

There is no significant political grouping to the government's left.

I believed (and still do) that these fundamentals allowed for four possible options in South Africa.

- *The political option.* The social shifts created by the factors described above remain within the formal political arena. The rising tide of needs causes the government to move to the left, or a new party arises there — and challenges the government.

- *The strongman option.* Fearing a challenge from its left, the leadership of the incumbent party moves to quell the swell of voices and activism emanating from that quarter. The soft elements of democracy start taking pressure. The status of the media is recast from public watchdog to "enemy of nation-building". Political opposition is demonised. The ranks of elites close and become less permeable.

- *Chaos power.* Politics goes to the streets and social instability becomes the main medium of change. Urban terrorism appears. (South Africa knows this option only too well.)

- *Inertia.* According to the journalist's dictum: suddenly, nothing happens. Societies, especially African societies, have surprising tolerance of suffering. We thus stick with what we've got, and muddle through much as we are doing now.

As you've already figured, South Africa has elements of all four within its body politic. Nevertheless, one must predominate. I chose the political option.

The strongman option is where bets are placed by the most cogent of those who regard a break-up of the governing alliance, or the rise of a new party strong enough to challenge it, or both, too implausible.

Social chaos cannot be eliminated from future scenarios in a society as precariously poised as South Africa's. But *When Mandela Goes* was predicated on the belief that alternatives are available. So is this book. The chaos option falls away on this basis.

The inertia option I discounted on the grounds that (a) there would be no point in writing a book about it and (b) that where it applies in Africa it does so in peasant-based societies. South Africa has a proletariat-based society — more than half of South Africans live in cities and are therefore dependent on urban culture for a living. South Africans, in the main, do not have the option of stoically enduring denial of their political, economic and social aspirations — because they do not, as peasant societies do, have access to a land-based subsistence economy and lifestyle. The survival of the majority is dependent on an adequate industrial economy.

The sequence of future events that *When Mandela Goes* thus suggested was: tensions within the governing alliance intensify as it is pulled in opposite directions by the diverging need-sets of the developed and the developing sectors of society. These opposing forces cause the alliance to split as it is already perforated along accommodating fissures — the moderate, bourgeois elements on one side and the radical, populist elements of the unionists and communists on the other. The split is facilitated by the perception that there are sufficient need-driven votes and enough disillusioned voters to the government's left to make a serious bid for electoral victory feasible by a new party.

I then had to assign a time frame to these events. The choice was to locate the events within the first term of Nelson Mandela's successor, Thabo Mbeki, or in his second. The second would clearly have been the safer bet, but I decided the forces were mounting sufficiently to give the first a running chance. Besides, it made better reading. Additionally, I was mindful of the lesson of a predecessor. I had modelled *When Mandela Goes* on the political classic *When Smuts Goes*,[17] published a neat 50 years before by the historian Arthur Keppel-Jones. Writing in 1946, Keppel-Jones had forecast the National Party victory and the start of apartheid for the second election hence; that is, the election of 1952. He under-read the very

---

[17] Arthur Keppel-Jones, *When Smuts Goes, A History of South Africa from 1952–2010 First Published in 2015*, Shuter & Shooter, Pietermaritzburg, 1950.

forces he recognised. The Afrikaner nationalists won in 1948. They won by focusing on the *have-not* constituency of the day — the economically dis-empowered Afrikaners, while the United Party government (its very name a clue to its weakness) tried to play to both constituencies, satisfying also the "foreign money powers" of the day. Was it Yogi Berra who said: "It's like *déjà vu* all over again"?

At the time of this writing (early 2001) events had not borne out the prediction of a split in the governing alliance. However, the reasons forwarded for such a split burst into the public arena. The outrage that greeted the publication of the ideas above died down when it become apparent that the strains in the alliance were far greater than anyone outside alliance ranks realised. Even the disenchantment with the alliance's bourgeois drift engendered deeper animosity than many in the leadership ranks realised. Soon the cracks were one of the main topics of political news reporting. The idea of an alternative, labour-leaning party became the subject of subdued but open debate in African nationalist and left wing circles. Conditions within the alliance became so precarious that Mbeki had to make several public appearances to admonish the rebellious cadres. In one notable case, the party leaders levered the great symbolic weight of the retired president, Mandela, to hold things together.

In as much as there have been no material changes in the applicable political dynamics and relationships, it is reasonable to assume that the patch-up job that followed has been just that — a papering over the cracks. The issue took a down-stage, holding position while other dramas gripped the political audience's attention.

In sum, then, the time frame for the predicted split has been faulty — but the machinating forces have not dissolved and I am not yet persuaded to withdraw the bet.

On the matter of time — *When Mandela Goes* contained a prediction that Mandela would formally hand over the sceptre of power to Mbeki before his full term had run its course. This would entail the calling of an early election. The motivation was the fact that transfer of the day-to-day exercise of power was an evolving reality in the presidency. Mandela was doing an artful segue into his purely symbolic role. The early election prediction was a calculated gamble. If it paid off, I could claim a victory for foresight. If it didn't I could dismiss it as a detail irrelevant to the main thrust of the argument, which I hereby do. See how easy futurology is?

Where I missed not just the target but the barn it was painted on was in regard to the evolution of opposition on the government's right flank.

Like Keppel-Jones before me, I under-read the signs — this time the forces of decay in the National Party, the party that lost the family farm in the political settlement. I described the rot in the party but failed to see that it was terminal.

I predicted that the party's then-leader, F W de Klerk, would lead the creation of a united opposition with the Democratic Party. As it happened, De Klerk withdrew from politics while the book was at the printers. This gave those critics unschooled in publishing lead times a handy cudgel to beat me with.

My inability to appreciate the full effects of the National Party's moral and spiritual implosion misled me into predicting it would lead the merged opposition. What I did get right was that there would be a merged opposition between the Democratic Party and National Party, that the Inkatha Freedom Party would stay out of the merger mainly because of the prickly personality and ambitions of its leader, and that De Klerk would before long (like a fellow reformer in another part of the world, Gorbachev) become alienated from active politics.

My projections led me to the belief that the existing opposition's support ceiling was fixed at 30%. Nothing has happened that gives reason to alter that.

Intimations of policy and economy

The escalation of social need in South Africa provided a platform for a prediction easy to make: a post-Mandela government would have little alternative but to follow the Mandela government's theme of reconciliation with a policy theme of delivery into the social need. Public dissatisfaction with the political decapitation and head transplant that had constituted the quasi-revolution would leave a new government little room for dither or choice.

The mood of the transformation, when it came, was accordingly one of a South Africa of miracles led by a secular saint converting into a more practical "South Africa Inc." led by a businesslike chief executive. That was the mood, but it went little further than that. *When Mandela Goes* predicted that the kind of transformation that would match the pent-up need of the society would require enormous resources. It would require more resources than the government of the time, or a government to come, had access to. Furthermore, the view was put forward that resources would decline.

The reasoning was this. South Africa was a low-skilled and dependency-oriented society. It would not transform into an educated and productive working nation overnight. That meant first-phase economic revival could not be generated from within. It would have to come from without — foreign investment. This is where the problem lay. For a variety of reasons that are themselves interesting but not relevant here, foreign investors adopted a wait-and-see attitude to the new South Africa. Mandela's secular sainthood was not sufficient, on its own, to entice billions of dollars, marks, yen, krona, pounds, francs into the South African market. It was an easy bet that the wait-and-see reluctance would be even more exaggerated with Mandela's lesser-known successor.

In the event, that has been the case. Foreign investment in South Africa has declined sharply in the period of the Mbeki administration. Mr Mbeki failed to appreciate his challenge. He cast himself as a Don Quixote tilting at windmills in his blundering on HIV/Aids. History will yet weigh the cost. He failed to rescue South Africa's fiscal image from the Zimbabwe land-grab imbroglio. These missteps have burdened the task of reassuring overly cautious investors with a probably insurmountable handicap.

Government's intention to elevate the disadvantaged and create a successful state has been, and remains, to a large extent, sincere. It therefore experiences great frustration at not being able to deliver according to its promises and ambitions. Being an agglomeration of human foibles, *When Mandela Goes* predicted that government would soon begin looking round for surrogates — who can pick up the delivery slack — and scapegoats, who can be blamed for government's under-performance.

Business and the media were the logical candidates for the roles. Acting as if according to prescription, the Mbeki government has berated business for "not doing enough" and the media for being its enemy in "national transformation".

We must now leave the broad thrust of the forecasts of *When Mandela Goes* and their aftermath. Before we do, however, we might note one view the book put forward regarding the nation's state of mind.

The moral tenor of the Mandela era was such as to give South Africa its best shot at going straight. Up to then the national psyche had been profoundly scarred by apartheid. Apart from the official brutality needed to govern against the will of the governed, the white nationalist government had to foster a miasma of deceptions, delusions and outright lies to armour itself in a world that reviled its existence. It infused South African society with moral corrosion.

Mandela signified the opposite pole on the longitude of morality. Drawing inspiration from the values he embodied, South Africa had the opportunity of his leadership to undertake a healing process that might close its internal divisions, and to begin to repair the moral fabric of society so that respect and honesty would become the character of social intercourse.

A post-Mandela government, however, would have to move on to other business. Ideally, it would be able to devote no more than maintenance time to the process of reconciliation and moral healing begun under Mandela. The practical needs of a new society would have moved to the top of the political agenda.

Each of us must entertain our own opinions of how successfully South Africans embraced the opportunity Mandela's stewardship afforded them. My own view will have made itself apparent by the time our discussion has run its course.

Sticks and stones

Many readers saw in *When Mandela Goes* an honest, if multiply flawed, attempt to figure out where one of the world's most interesting developing societies was heading. These were the readers who were themselves honest, were erudite, insightful, brave, quick-witted, far-sighted, good-looking, likeable and warm-hearted, dressed with restrained flair, cared about people and the environment, helped little old ladies across the street and loved furry animals. The rest didn't like it, but I'll get to them in a minute.

Readers who were honest, erudite, insightful … you know the ones I mean … understood the book was an illustration of a future nobody wanted. By illustrating that future, it thus contributed to the ability to avoid it. They understood that the new South Africa could be many things. Robust debate and vigilant self-examination was an indispensable part of ensuring the right choice of the available alternatives — and was thus to be welcomed, not condemned. They understood, too, that the man who stops you on a stormy night along a dark country road, and warns you that the bridge has washed out ahead, is your friend not your enemy, despite his tidings. Among these readers were those who easily saw the connection between the South African experience and the global reality. The book was consequently prescribed, read, or discussed at a handful of institutions in South Africa and abroad.

Readers who were not as happily endowed as those above saw the work as an attack on the new society and its new and unsteady elite. They fell into a common thought trap found in transforming societies: those who are not proponents of the new deal are, *ipso facto,* adherents of the old. They failed to see that there are many possible forms of the new. One of their number invited another to review *When Mandela Goes* in a Johannesburg Sunday paper that yearns to emulate its distant, quality relatives in other world cities. The reviewer obligingly pitched in with accusations of racism, ignorance and, possibly … I don't remember very well … worse. The reviewer, it turned out, was a capped fellow who had thrown in his lot with the working class in the SA Communist Party — as a full-time activist. No problem with that, of course. It would have been most interesting to read an aggressively reasoned critique of the ideas from a communist point of view. The problem was the editor passed through an ethical blind spot — momentary, I am sure — and failed to declare to her readers the reviewer's ideological standpoint.

In a subsequent development — unconnected, assuredly — the hapless reviewer was expelled from the communist party … for being ideologically too rigid. Bless me, the ways of politics!

Floating above this squalling, apparently unseen, has been the irony that, in effect, warning the incumbent elites of the perils of not heeding the legitimate aspirations of the masses might have earned *When Mandela Goes* an A grade in Marxism One-oh-One.

Light the Shadow

We are now across the bridge that separates *When Mandela Goes* from the questions that we must tackle next. We agreed when we started out that this bridge would, paradoxically, return us to the present. That is where we are now; and one of the first sights that confronts our reopened eyes is a very curious one.

We see our South African compatriots, and our fellows in the shadow of the world's great divide, sleep walking through a nightmare. It is a nightmare in which we are threatened by monsters of society. It is within our power to act, to vanquish the monsters — but for a reason that the dream does not reveal, we do nothing to save ourselves.

It is not that we, who take the time to consider and involve ourselves in the social problems of our time are the only ones who know that poverty cannot be allowed to grow unchecked, that unemployment cannot be permitted to rise indefinitely, that the envy gap between the rich and the poor cannot widen for ever, that righteous anger cannot for ever be contained. Our compatriots and fellows know it too. Together we know, whether we articulate it or not, that these social evils cannot be left to burgeon without a terrible social pressure burst occurring — somewhere, sometime, but certainly.

Some of us deny there will be such a cataclysm. We can't really say why, it just won't be, that's all. It can't be. Some of us think things will "sort themselves out". Some of us trust that the government "has a plan". Some of us don't believe any of this. But none of us acts.

Why is this?

Why, for that matter, have some countries succeeded and others failed? The world's developing countries started off on more or less the same footing at the start of the post-colonial era half a century ago. Why are some today as much as 10 times better off than others? What are the attitudes that presage success, or failure? And what are the triggers that cause societies to adopt or not adopt them?

Why, in South Africa, specifically, do we have a society of an acknowledged miracle — Archbishop Tutu's rainbow people — that seems little happier than it was before? Why is our criminal profile becoming the thing we are most known by? Beyond the crime, why the appalling inter-personal violence? Why the wanton killing of our aged and the vulnerable? Why the sexual torture of women and children on such a scale?

And why, above all, do we not have satisfactory answers to these questions?

Whatever the quest for answers may reveal to us, it is likely to reveal it in the domain of the underlying patterns. This is the undertaking we must now turn to. Let us turn at a signpost illuminated by one of our era's most important scientists, Stephen Jay Gould. Writing in the *New York Times*[18] on the findings contained in the decoding of the human genome, Gould tied this great step in understanding the underlying patterns of life itself with a great turning in the evolution of knowledge. Gould commented on the surprise that the human genome contained only about 30 000 active genes — far fewer than the 140 000 expected. The reduction in number was so great, in fact, as to raise an entirely new principle in the structuring of life, and the understanding of it.

Since science took its present course in the 17th Century, Gould argued, it has been based on reductionist thought. We have venerated the analytical approach above all others. As we set out to understand the mechanistic universe we found analysis a convenient way of reaching

---

[18] Stephen Jay Gould, "Humbled by the genome's mysteries", *New York Times*, February 19, 2001.

understanding where the whole was too large to comprehend at one sweep. We accordingly set about taking it apart, on the basis that, if we understood the pieces, then put them together again, we would understand the working of the whole. Gould says this worked fine for systems like the movement of the planets, but it won't work for complex systems like life.

The reason is that life cannot have its clearly observable complexity if it is based on only 30 000 genes — each with one message and one outcome. The properties of life have to be a consequence of interactions among the genes, and those properties are more than, and different to, a mere sum of the interacting parts. This idea, that complex systems — societies are such systems — have properties that are not found in their parts is one that has been appearing in other fields on the frontiers of knowledge: systems theory, complexity theory and chaos theory.

Gould's summation is that a turning point in knowledge has been reached. The analytical approach must now make way for a synthesising approach. We can no longer hope to understand complex systems only by understanding their parts.

There is today a great drawing together of strands in human understanding. Carl Jung, in one of his characteristic insights into the spirit of our time, said:

> If we stick to one field of experience only, it is not really possible to see clearly what is happening. It is not a matter of a single thrust aimed at one definite spot, but of an almost universal 'restratification' of modern man, who is in the process of shaking off a world that has become obsolete.[19]

I believe that the drive to understand the whole rather than the parts of the mystery of living is the emerging *leitmotif* of the journey of our minds from here onwards.

For our present purposes, I don't mean to suggest that I can accompany you to the forefronts of knowledge, but I am suggesting that we have exhausted the search for understanding of politics by looking within politics only; and by talking to politicians and political scientists only. Likewise with economics. To understand our society and where we are going in it — a process of which our political and economic lives are a consequence and not a cause — we need to range more widely than we have before. We need to go to where light conventionally does not fall.

We must enter the shadow.

[19] C G Jung, *The Spirit in Man, Art and Literature*, Ark Paperbacks, London, 1984.

CHAPTER ONE

The Space Trip Postulate

If the world isn't getting better, what's going on?

Are things getting better, or worse? This is the question we most want answered. We've lived through the promise of post-War gadget-driven entrepreneurial capitalism and we've accepted that a bank account, a car and a secured mortgage, while desirable, can't be what it's about. This is how we experience the dilemma on a personal level; and we've accepted that a satisfying answer is not apparent. Not yet, anyway. So we shift our attention to the bigger picture, and we ask a bigger question: are we, at least, part of something greater than ourselves that is meaningful?

Rats. No sooner is the question off our lips than we realise the answer is as murky as the dilemma that led us to it.

The frantic St Vitus's dance of humanity is speeding up. We're moving as fast as we can, just to keep up. He who hesitates to ask the question risks being left behind, or being trampled by others in their mindless jig. Yet we need an answer like never before. Already we are in a world without God, without moral authority, without heroes and without decency in government. So we need the answer soon, really soon.

Commensurate with our urgency, the answer is being hunted with a yearning that grows ever stronger. Sure, the search for meaning is as old as thought itself, but the yearning has never been as widespread as it is now. Never before has it infused as much of society as it does today, and never before have we been as persistently nagged by the suspicion that our lives and all we do in them doesn't amount to a hill of beans.

Alas, we're not going to solve the riddle of existence for the price of this book. So let's knock down the task to something more manageable. How about this one: Is the world becoming a more, or less, happy place? It's not as grand a question, but it's more accessible. We stand a better chance of coming out the other side with an answer, and that answer will help us locate the first step in the journey towards the bigger answer.

What's more, I have an idea of how we can tackle it. It will be a device of our own invention; and we can make up for the loss in grandiosity in our pared down question by giving the device a suitably inflated title. Let's call it the Space Trip Postulate.

It works like this. We will imagine that we are silently and invisibly in the company of beings from another world, who have paid to take a tour of earth. The tour guide has been on this trip before. Back where the group comes from, there has long been an interest in this planet, our earth — about as long as space tours have been a commercial reality. There has been great fascination with an eco-system that is based on a principle of everything eats everything else. There was particular curiosity about the rise of a dominant life form, especially when its consciousness evolved to the inclusion of reason and it began to separate itself from the natural order of which it was part. From that moment, in fact, its fate had become a helter-skelter affair and things were now building to a crescendo. There was, accordingly, great interest in the choices Earthers would make in their current generation, and the one following — for these choices would almost certainly lock in the fate of their planet. The less reverent, of course, gleefully seized on earth life as a subject of lampoons. Much mirth was extracted, in particular, from how the roiling mass blundered blindly past the answers to its dilemmas, frequently even irritated by those who articulated them. Instead the mass extruded individuals who did no more than embody the ignorance and callousness of the mass, then designated those as "leaders", to whom the mass then gratefully suborned itself.

Come to think of it, it is pretty funny, isn't it?

It's a trip not without its amusements. What we most want to know, though, is what will strike us first as we approach the tragic-comic planet. What will be most obvious and what will we see first? What will the guide need to explain first? Will it make us laugh or … wait — shoosh, now. The tour guide is adjusting his mike. He's clearing his throat. Ah, bummer. He's telling us we have to divide our exploration of earth happiness into two sections. Because humanity, he says, is divided into two distinct sections. Different circumstances — even conflicting circumstances — apply to each. The most noticeable distinction between people on earth, he says, is that some — a few, actually — have an abundance of possessions and resources and most struggle for even the basics they need to sustain themselves. They are the rich and the poor, he says, and the glaring difference between them is the first distinction we will register. Oh, right, okay — he says we'll focus most of our attention on the sector that has charged furthest into its future. That's the rich. It's the group that's closest to its decisive moment and if there is to be a smash, this is where the biggest mess will be.

Well, doctor, you see, it's like this ...

The tour guide says one of the many Earthers who have grappled with the happiness topic has come up with a novel and revealing approach. They call him Oliver James and he's a psychologist — that's an Earther who ... no, never mind. He undertook a study of a leading nation and published it in 1998 as *Britain on the Couch*.[1] Most revealing, however, was a subtitle in which he captured the quandary of the age: *Why we're unhappier than we were in the 1950s — despite being richer.*

In his book James reviews the evidence that charts the manifold rise of depression, inter-personal violence, crime, angst and suicide in advanced societies in the second half of the 20th Century. According to the studies he cites, a person born between 1945 and 1955 has a three-to-ten times greater chance of suffering from severe, that is, life threatening, depression before the age of 34 than a person born between 1905 and 1914. Rates of suicide among young men trebled in Britain in the last three decades of the century. Violence against the person increased fivefold in the USA. Roughly three-quarters of men convicted of violence in Western societies suffered from depression. Anecdotally, the rise in what James called "incivility" — like road rage and outbursts against teachers, police, bureaucrats and medical practitioners — along with an increase in drug abuse and alcoholism, all point to elevated levels of angst.

Then James demonstrates how the presence of these phenomena is linked with low levels of serotonin, the brain chemical that is associated with feelings of well-being — or their absence. He works through the various studies that show low levels of serotonin are implicated in depression, aggression and compulsion. In effect, he casts low serotonin as both a cause and an effect of the social maladies in question. James arrives at the conclusion that mean levels of serotonin in the population of a country like Britain — and, by implication, other Western societies — are lower than they used to be ... and they are dropping further.

James's work becomes really interesting, however, when he shifts his attention from the dominant societies to emerging nations and communities. He presents a key term: "relative deprivation". It is a concept critical to understanding the psyche of nations and the core of conflict in the world this century.

---

[1] Oliver James, *Britain on the Couch — Treating a Low Serotonin Society*, Arrow Books, London, 1988.

Here is a précis of his argument. Once people have surmounted the struggle for survival — that is, once elementary needs such as those for food, shelter and clothing can be taken, by and large, for granted — people then find themselves on a runged ladder whereon prosperity is pursued for its own sake, or for the sake of social status.

It is at this point that the individual starts to look around ... and realises that he is doing poorly by the standards he can see enjoyed by others around him. He is not deprived in an absolute sense. His survival is assured. But he is deprived by new measures through which he relates his status to that of others, others above him. He now sees himself as deprived by comparison.

This comparison is thrown in his face if he lives in a society where there are wide differentials in living standards — if he trudges to work alongside a rode on which others cruise in luxurious vehicles; if, in the unforgettable lament of a nameless Palestinian, he does not have water for his family to drink while his neighbour's children splash about in a swimming pool. To the extent the comparison is drawn negatively, to that degree is the resulting dissatisfaction intensified.

There is much evidence to support this view. Social scientists have for long known that material prosperity is no guarantor, nor measure, of social contentment (hey, even my mom said that — she just didn't use the smart words). For this reason, relatively impoverished societies — but where the poverty is pervasive and general — have sometimes registered surprising levels of contentment on social studies. I would venture, though, that this is a declining phenomenon as the media intrudes in all social strata and becomes the agent of comparison. From the favelas of Rio de Janeiro to the shanties of Johannesburg, *Sex and the City, The Bold and the Beautiful* and *Ally McBeal* provide a common social denominator.

The machinations of relative deprivation are illustrated most graphically in James's citation of psychological studies tracking African American soldiers who were fast-tracked upwards through the promotional ranks. The studies found that the higher the officers were promoted in the ranks, the lower their levels of self-esteem and satisfaction became. There are, of course, many negative psychological effects that can arise from the "artificiality" of affirmative action — primarily the feeling that the rise in status is not a result of inner qualities and is thus not genuinely deserved.

Follow up work to the studies, however, revealed the main reason: as candidates rose in the ranks, they began comparing themselves negatively to others who had earned their promotions, and to yet others in higher ranks.

The comparison to others in higher ranks is especially important. The critical point is this: when an individual's circumstances begin to change, a set of expectations is unleashed within the individual; and these expectations usually out-run the improving circumstances. Further, this dynamic is particularly sharp and psychologically poisonous in environments where negative comparisons impinge readily and easily on the individual's perception range — for example, when he is in regular proximity to those who enjoy a status that he aspires to. James decodes the socio-speak in the headings of two chapters in which these arguments are set out: *"Death By A Thousand Social Comparisons"* and *"Why We May Feel Like Losers Even If We Are Winners"*. The headings say it all.

One cannot get far into James's reasoning without being overwhelmed by the ramifications for a society like South Africa's. South Africa's Gini Co-efficient, the standard measure of the gap between the lowest and highest incomes in a country, is the highest in the world. South Africa's score was nudging 0.7 in early 2001 on the scale that spans from 0 (most equal) to 1 (most unequal). In 2000 South Africa had moved ahead of Brazil, the country that had for long been the most unequal in the world. Tellingly, South Africa moved ahead not because of growing disparities in incomes between blacks and whites (where the gap is actually closing) but in the increasing chasm among black South Africans.

This creates a double bind for South Africa in terms of relative deprivation. It works like this: the disparities are great and growing. That's bad enough. It means comparisons produce more dramatically negative results here than elsewhere. More unhappily, though, in the counter-intuitive way the dynamic works, the comparisons that take place among black South Africans are more damaging than those between whites and blacks. The reason is that the comparison by black persons with other black persons is a more accessible comparison because of ethnic, social, cultural and economic affinities. The comparison with whites is more remote, and thus less abrasive, because there is a greater degree of inevitability in the disparity.

As reprehensible as the racial divide may be, most South Africans have grown up with it. It has acquired a sense of "that's the way things are" in peoples' minds. There is, consequently, less expectation of the gap closing between blacks and whites than there is chagrin, envy and anger at the gap opening between blacks and blacks. This uncomfortable conclusion is backed up by other studies cited by James — which show that in the years following World War ll African Americans in the northern states were less satisfied with their lot — although, materially, they were better off — than their compatriots in southern states. The dynamic is clear once more: the southern African Americans had less *expectation* that their lot would improve. So they were happier.

South Africans have recently, in the liberation from apartheid, experienced a great leap forward and upward in their expectations. Not unreasonably, everyday people anticipated a tangible and visible improvement in their lives. It is in the nature of South Africa's partial revolution that the improvements that have occurred in post-apartheid society have been mainly in the realm of intangibles — great intangibles, to be sure, like democratic norms, but intangibles nevertheless. Material improvement has come only to an elevated elite. For the majority of people the harsh realities of day-to-day living are, if anything, harsher. As a result, the implications of frustrated expectations, seen through the lens of relative deprivation, are far more serious than is ordinarily thought in South Africa and similar societies.

These are ideas that we need to suspend, now. We'll want to call on them when our examination comes round to a closer focus on South Africa, and we look at rising social instability, manifested in crime and violence, and the effects of the national experience on the national psyche.

For the present, we're imagining more of the preparatory remarks that the space guide might make, the better to aid the visitors' understanding of the world they are calling on.

Travel narrows the mind

The guide might decide not to dwell on some of the better-known curiosities concerning this world. After all, these would have been the things that motivated the travellers, in the first place, to come on the tour. Things like: this was a world that produced enough food for all, yet millions starved; like the fact that just 500 of the richest people possessed more than the poorest half of humanity did; like one sixth being obsessed with ways of losing weight, while one third was preoccupied with ways of putting some on; like one million of the young of humankind dying each month from, effectively, neglect — because no more than one twentieth of the wealth of those 500 richest could end the paucities of clean water, basic hygiene and sewerage that would save those children; like the fact that the Earthers had used their technology as much for intra-species slaughter as for any other purpose; that the science that had penetrated the peripheries of the knowledge of matter, learning to use its energy stores, had been employed for the greatest acts of destruction; that the threat of more such acts had been the main countervailance of their politics ... while the employment of the energy for peaceful ends aroused such fears and passions that it remained largely unused.

These things, as unbelievable as they seem, were common knowledge about earth. It was well understood that the planet was home to a species that had evolved to a certain level of reason, on the one hand, while on the other it remained ensnared and retarded by primitive impulses and fears.

The opportunity to see a reasoning species on this evolutionary cusp gave these tours their special interest and fascination. Travellers got the opportunity — quite rare, really — to observe a decisive evolutionary juncture. Earth's dominant life form would either make the right choices for itself, or it would fail to do so. The species called humanity had come to the stage where choice had become a component of its evolution. This is what added the exquisite spice to the experience and made the seats on these tours sell at a premium. Particularly now. If humanity made the right choices it would adjust the path it was on accordingly. If it didn't it would remain on its present course, further mounting the stresses on itself and its environment — and risk severe setbacks, or even disintegration.

It was a poignant moment in the unfolding of time, pregnant with both promise and danger. The Earthers had come a long way on their path. To see them lose it now would be a pity — good box office, but a pity. They had reached a stage in which they were exerting more control over those among them they called "leaders". The dimensions of their ability to educate themselves were extending both vertically and horizontally, hence their mean level of reasoning ability was notching upwards. Commensurately, their need to be "led" was declining. Especially when it meant, as it so often so clearly did, being led to ruin. In turn, this meant they were developing better abilities to create global institutions that recognised their commonality of interest — and to adapt and improve the institutions that existed. One outstanding example was the emergence of a notion of "crimes against humanity". This was a direct outcome of their ability to start to think wholly rather than segmentally — or, to use their own terminology, globally instead of nationally. Within decades this critical development produced a desire to apply and enforce the emerging sense of global justice, and an international criminal court was established. Its intention was to create a means of prosecuting — for the first time in earth history — those who abused power to harm others, and those who betrayed public trust. It was a novel idea at its inception. Few, however, grasped its true significance and it worked only falteringly at first.

The tour guide would almost certainly skip detailed comment on the technology Earthers had evolved. It was important to note that know-how on earth had advanced to the ability to escape the planet's gravitation — but that's as far as it went. The Earthers left their eco system and atmosphere only rarely and when they did it was by combusting gases and liquids in crude incendiary eruptions, barely controlled, in vehicles that consisted 90% of fuel. All their efforts had got them no further than their solitary and barren satellite, the moon. This usually provoked laughter among certain of the travellers. But, then, you always got those who came on these trips for dubious reasons — more for derision and amusement than genuine interest. The tour guide disapproved. He was a qualified cosmobiologist and those who mocked with such glee merely displayed their own insensitivity to a life group that stood — in all probability — on the edge of a new, great step forward in evolving consciousness. Even though, at times, it was hard to believe.

One humanity, one mind

So, we have a first-sweep view of a world whose pace of evolution is both speeding up and becoming more complex; in which its people, despite remarkable achievements, are, right now, making themselves less rather than more happy; yet a world, nevertheless, that is tantalisingly close to making a better set of choices, and re-directing its fate.

We need, now, another conceptual tool. It will help us transcend the commonplace knowledge of earth, such as the tour guide skipped over. This tool is one of a small number we shall assemble, which will help us, instead, to apprehend the underlying patterns that determine the nature of life on earth and the changes it is undergoing.

This tool will be of particular use to us when we come to focus on South African society later in this discussion.

For now, however, we are faced with a teensy difficulty. The tool fits more easily into the comprehension of the tour guide than it does into ours. For it is the ability to see humankind, and the societies it is gathered in, as an integrated system. The reason that it is easier for the tour guide, and his visitors, to work with this view is that they get to look at us from the outside, while we have to look at ourselves from the inside. They see the forest; we see the trees, to use the handy expression once more.

This is not to say that systemic thought is not practised here, among us. It is, to a degree. Sociology and anthropology seek to understand systems within the larger human system, and religion and philosophy try to understand the system itself. But religion and philosophy are constrained by the limitations of the insider's view.

The conceptual tool we need is neither of these. It is an aspect of these. It is, simply and sweepingly, the recognition that society possesses a collective mind.

It's not an orthodox view. Psychology understands pretty well the nature, functions and responses of the individual mind. Surprisingly little, though, is said about collective psychology. That which is referred to as group psychology usually refers to the behaviour of crowds — at sports matches, for example — and is just as usually dismissed as a lower order of the overall discipline. Yet it seems axiomatic that a group of individuals, particularly if subjected to the same environment and stimuli, can, and do, share psychological traits. Naturally, in any given group one individual is going to be sadder, madder, gladder or badder than another. But this by no means excludes the existence of a mean for the group. And what is true for a group can be true for a class, for a nation, for a race, and, by extension, for humanity. One might want to argue that by the time the metaphor is extended so far, it has been reduced to so broad a set of common denominators that it is of little effective use. This is not so. By the time we have used the tool to understand some of the reactions of society around us I hope you will agree.

It is, nevertheless, uncommon to talk of society's collective mind. So let's reconnoitre the terrain to ensure we are on good ground when we use the term.

Carl Gustav Jung's monumental notion of a collective unconscious presents itself as the strongest reason for believing in a collective mind. If a collective unconscious, why not a collective conscious arising from it? This simple argument strengthens when it embraces schools of contemporary cognitive science. Almost without exception, cognitive scientists now accept that the greater part of brain activity takes place below the level of awareness. As I understand them, even thinkers on thought as prominent as Steven Pinker,[2] who advance the computational model (the brain computes in a binary pattern with synapses and neurons acting as switches), accept the preponderance of brain activity below the consciousness line. These theorists appear ambivalent on the degree of commonality there is in the unconscious between individuals, groups, and humanity itself. No matter.

[2] Steven Pinker, *How the Mind Works*, Penguin Books, London, 1988.

Either way, the chain of ideas tells us that most thought is unconscious, and at least some of it is shared by many or all people. If one accepts, now, that consciousness is a capacity rooted in, and rising from, the unconscious then we already have sufficient reason to accept the existence of collective awareness.

Nevertheless, let's stay with the idea a little longer. There is enough reason in physiology to embrace the notion of deep memories being lodged in the unconscious and cascading down the generations. We are quite happy, for example, with the genetic inheritance of information in the many species of animals that know from birth how to migrate over great distances. By any definition, the knowledge of sparrows concerning when to fly south is a collective, inherited memory.

The controversial biochemist Rupert Sheldrake[3] explores consciousness in animals and notes both familiar and unfamiliar phenomena. Familiar, and seldom questioned by science, is the ability many dogs appear to have to know when their owners are about to come home; some cats seem to know when the telephone is about to ring, especially if the animal's owner is calling. The phenomena are adequately documented. The simple yet resounding question that hangs over them is: How do the animals know? By what process or mechanism do they receive the information?

Sheldrake also cites less familiar mysteries. He notes for example that when schools of fish scatter — as when they are frightened by an intrusion — one thing, strangely, never happens: the fish never collide. If the scattering were random, it would be mathematically impossible for there not to be collisions among the fish. Therefore, the scattering cannot be random. Thus, there must be a cohesive intelligence that is a property of the school — as opposed to the individual fish.

One would hesitate to use the expression collective consciousness in connection with fish, naturally. Sheldrake speaks of "morphic fields". The very term outraged the scientific establishment. Yet the establishment has not been able to offer a better explanation than Sheldrake's for the phenomena he documents.

The literature documents numerous manifestations of the phenomena. One of the most intriguing is a change of behaviour in colonies of macaque monkeys in the Pacific, described by Lyall Watson in his study of the

---

[3] Rupert Sheldrake, *Dogs that Know When Their Owners are Coming Home and Other Unexplained Powers of Animals*, Arrow Books, London, 2000.

natural history of evil.[4] While under observation by scientists in the 1950s, a female monkey departed from the norm — and washed her food in sea water before eating it. Presumably, this obviated the unpleasantness of crunching sand and other detritus clinging to the food — something that the female macaque's ancestors had put up with for millennia. For some while she was the only one to indulge in the new practice. Then a few others around her adopted her innovation. The progress in macaque table manners advanced, but slowly. Then, one fateful day, a critical level was reached. A monkey, nameless and unseen, but who has since been immortalised as "the hundredth monkey", washed its food. From then on the behaviour spread, literally within a day or two, to all other monkeys, reaching even distant colonies with whom there was no known physical contact. The hundredth monkey syndrome — as it has since become known — has been observed in the decades since then, but never explained. For our purposes, though, it clearly implies a decisive point in emerging collective consciousness. Moreover, it tells us that consciousness *does* evolve, and that it progresses not only along a gradual incline; sometimes it can take a great lurch forward within an observable time span.

Let's make a giddy leap from the animal kingdom to the human realm. It has been frequently remarked that human tribes, communities and societies have common basic values. This is something that has happened despite the groups having evolved independently. Almost without exception, human collectives proscribe murder, theft, incest, adultery, covetousness, public sex — and extol valour, virtue, fidelity and honour. This is a collective consciousness; it is not part of the physiology of existence; it's a matter of mind; and it's common to humankind as a whole.

The Cape Town psychiatrist Anthony Teggin documented two episodes of what he termed collective depression in the city in the 1980s. This was a time of intense political turmoil and uncertainty in Cape Town, to which the focus of social unrest had moved, from Soweto, where it had begun. In the nature of things, political activity and its accompanying sense of instability and uncertainty surged and waned to peaks and into troughs. When I read Teggin's work I felt there was a *prima facie* case for aligning the mood depressions with these political surges.

At this time the idea was forming strongly in my mind: there was a link between the socio-political circumstances of a society and the reigning

---

[4] Lyall Watson, *Dark Nature,* Hodder & Stoughton, London, 1995. Watson cites Kwai, M, "Newly acquired precultural behaviour", in *Primates* 6:1, 1965.

mood of that society, and that the mood itself became the wellspring of action or inaction in that society. Thus, understanding the mood was a big step to understanding the society and what was likely to happen, or not to happen, within it.

An even better, and more contemporary example, exists for the notion of collective consciousness, and the dominant mood that forms a sub-set of that consciousness, the combination of which influences life and behaviour. It is present-day Russia. Post-glasnost Russia is described as being in the grip of a "psycho-social depression".[5] Releases from the state statistics committee show that two-thirds of men dying between 20 and 55 expire drunk — a function of rocketing abuse of alcohol. The disintegration of the social psyche is revealed in an average of 146 suicides and 108 murders a day. The depressing picture is even more awesome, however, when it points to deep behavioural changes right down at the level of evolutionary patterns. In the years since the fall of communism, and the acceleration of Russia's socio-economic woes, the birth rate has fallen by half. Mortality rates are climbing and the World Health Organisation puts male life expectancy at 59, 14 years lower than in Western Europe. This is an underlying pattern of collective behaviour with a perceptible design and purpose. The society is reducing itself to a proportion more in keeping with its available economic resources, and curtailing the duration of its suffering. The behaviour is being governed by an intelligence that is a property of the society, rather than the individuals within it.

To return, then, from the reconnaissance we have undertaken in the evidence, I would say we can be comfortable with the idea that societies have a collective consciousness, that mental and emotional states are a function of that consciousness, and that people's attitudes and moods are vital determinants of how they behave. The usefulness of this for us is that it will aid us greatly when we come to probe South Africa and try to understand what makes it the society it is now.

We can leave this point now with one venturesome forecast. We have noted in the prologue to this chapter that systems theory, chaos theory and complexity theory share a broad characteristic of saying something about the distinct properties of a whole rather than the summation of properties of its parts. I, for one, do not know the extent to which these essentially scientific and mathematical theorems have penetrated social science — it usually takes a while. It cannot be long, however, before

[5] Ian Traynor, "Russia dying of drink and despair", *Mail & Guardian*, July 7–13, 2000.

these thought models are applied much more extensively to the understanding of society. Furthermore, there must in the same process be a wider acceptance of the fact that we can very usefully apply to the study of the collective social mind the knowledge we have of how various stimuli affect the individual mind.

The clock ticks while we sleep

Here is another peculiarity of life on earth that the tour guide is sure to mention. It is that our understanding of ourselves, and our collective behaviour, is still so underdeveloped that we seldom know what we are about to do next. This condemns us to live permanently suspended in the one-minute-to-midnight syndrome.

To understand this we need to place ourselves in the collective mind of Western society a hundred years ago. The last decade of the 19th Century and the first of the 20th Century were almost certainly the golden age of Western civilisation, certainly the greatest since classical Athens. The post-Victorian mind was bold and buoyant. It had a sense of grandeur and a sense that humankind had a noble purpose. After centuries of darkness and a fitful awakening, great empires once again spanned the globe. The British Empire bestrode a third of the world's landmass. Mass transport was being created — rail, the car, the *Titanic*, even flight. The telephone had transcended the impediment of distance. The human mind was revealing the invisible world — the atom, bacteria, viruses, and Freud uncovered the existence of an unconscious mind. First sights of the hidden processes of life came in the understanding of cell division. The basis of genetics was laid. Pure thought was at an apogee. The counter-intuitive truths of relativity suggested man might grasp the laws of creation. New insights into the structure of reality unfolded in quantum physics. As ever, the artists had led the way: the impressionists of Paris had started the redefinition of reality, the surrealists had inflated it, the cubists had deconstructed it and re-arranged it, and the expressionists brandished it as a rough tool of social statement. Over all this rose the symbol of man's brash, mechanistic hubris — the Eiffel Tower. And Nietzsche irritably dispensed with God.

There was just one problem. As Western man strutted his proudest moment he was, actually, on the brink of a vertiginous and shameful plunge into a dark orgy of brutality and destruction such as had never been seen on earth. The clock of civilisation stood at one minute to midnight.

This strange and portentous period of the human story is depicted in what Anthony Burgess described as the best book of the 20th Century — Barbara Tuchman's *The Proud Tower.*[6]

Another writer, one of last century's most thoughtful persons, Isaiah Berlin, captured the grandeur of the time and man's peculiar blindness to what awaited:

> There are, in my view, two factors that, above all others, have shaped human history in this century. One is the development of the natural sciences and technology, certainly the greatest success story of our time — to this, great and mounting attention has been paid from all quarters. The other, without doubt, consists in the great ideological storms that have altered the lives of virtually all mankind: the Russian revolution and its aftermath — totalitarian tyrannies of both right and left and the explosions of nationalism, racism, and, in places, of religious bigotry, which, interestingly enough, not one among the most perceptive social thinkers of the nineteenth century had ever predicted.[7]

What we are extracting from the mood of the opening years of the 20th Century is of great relevance to us, here, at the beginning of the 21st. There is a pervasive anxiety abroad in the world today that we stand poised on just such a brink of something terrible. The feeling is not articulated now, as it was not then. Our age does not have a sense of grandeur and we have lost the belief that we are charged with a noble purpose. But the feeling is unmistakable.

In January 2000 I stood on the slopes of the Simonsberg, on the Cape Peninsula, watching several of the roughly 400 unexplained fires that broke out in the Western Cape over a few days. I had observed two, beginning without a cause I could see, or reasonably deduce. With me, looking out over Simon's Town was Charles Marais, a scientist and colleague in the now-defunct think tank, Deep Tech. Shortly before, we had, with our computer processor units under our arms, fled our offices in a finely restored 19th Century hotel which, along with the rest of the village below us, was then threatened by a broad front of flames. Unreality pervaded the air. Charles said: "People feel there is something strange in the world."

Charles was right. People do.

Only days before, the millennium had passed. It had been preceded by a build up of apocalyptic sentiment. It would have been strange, indeed, if any of the inflated expectations surrounding the turn of the millennium

---

[6] Barbara W. Tuchman, *The Proud Tower, A Portrait of the World Before the War 1890–1914.* Ballantine Books, New York, 1996.

[7] Isaiah Berlin, *The Crooked Timber of Humanity,* Fontana Press, London, 1991.

had manifested. In truth, the strangest thing of all was that expectations existed at the level they did in the first place. For one thing the world, by and large, had got the millennium wrong on at least two counts: two thousand years had not elapsed since the start of the Christian calendar, and the calendar had Christ's birth wrong by six years. For another thing, if there were some pattern to the psychic evolution of man, it would be more than passingly strange if it worked according to a calendar. Yet there was no mistaking the millenarian sentiment.

A curious outbreak of the millenarian mood took up residence in the collective mind of society. It was Y2K, technology's Antichrist. It was as if humanity fully expected to be punished for its blaspheming technology. Catastrophes in air travel were envisaged. Large corporations forbade their top executives air travel at the fateful crossing of time. Electricity would fail and cities would slip into darkness. Stock exchanges would convulse. Your fridge would die. Afterwards, when nothing mentionable had happened, there was an overwhelming question to ask. Did nothing happen because of the brilliant completeness of our preparations, or because nothing was going to happen anyway? What made the question doubly interesting was that no one wanted to ask it. The entire global fiasco was swept nonchalantly, as if it had never really been there, into obscurity.

There is only one conclusion a sensible mind can come to: for that time, we needed to feel that way; we needed a big reason to feel that Yeats was right, that the centre couldn't hold, and that the rough beast that had been slouching towards Bethlehem had arrived; we needed to vent our belief that all we have could fall into shards at the next tick of the clock.

When it didn't, we felt much better and carried on.

Nevertheless, the background chords of anxiety that produced the strange passing dance of Y2K have not gone away. On the contrary, they become increasingly insistent.

In the dream-like suspension of the Cold War we lived a febrile existence, with the knowledge that in the bi-polar world our security rested on a shaky paradox. Each of the two superpowers was constrained by the realisation that the victim's response to an act of overt aggression would lead to the annihilation of the aggressor. We called this a balance of power and knew it, straight-facedly, by the term "mutually assured destruction" and its acronym, MAD. This is a self-revealing irony that will yet give much relief and amusement to future readers of the history of our time.

Since the collapse of one of the superpowers we have come to live in a multi-polar world. Anxiety has partly migrated to a more invisible — but no less real — threat dissipated among a loose array of rogue states whose logic and values the developed world does not understand and cannot anticipate. There is nothing mutually assured about the threat of destruction any longer. At the time of writing, the well source of the developed world's economic wealth and values, the United States, was asking its second-rank relatives to endorse its plan to build a protective anti-nuclear shield around North America — against a threat it could not specifically identify.

The greater part of the migration of the nameless dread, however, has been into the economic life of the globe. This is a development of singular gravity, because it is a globe that has accepted economic performance as the only measure of success.

The period that followed World War ll was a time of dependable solidity in the world's financial system, despite the wartime disruptions that Europe experienced and the post-war debts challenges many countries faced. At Bretton Woods,[8] soon after the war, the World Bank and the International Monetary Fund were created to ensure the stability of the financial system. Exchange rates were fixed. South Africans, for example, gazed with re-assurance — and just a little perplexity — on the legend printed on currency notes. Above his signature, the governor of the Reserve Bank made the following undertaking: "I promise to pay the bearer on demand at Pretoria R20" (or whatever the designated value of the note was).[9] The sense that the money took its value from something absolute that transcended the money itself was a sense shared by all.

However, the certainty was not long-lived. Looking back, the abandonment by the British of the gold standard in the 1930s was ominous. In its wake, the amount of control exercised by the IMF, after its creation, over liquidity in world currencies waned progressively. Fixed exchange rates had to be artificially maintained by devaluations and revaluations in major currencies such as the US dollar and the German mark. Eventually, the USA ended the dollar's convertibility to gold. Fixed exchange rates crumbled and currencies were allowed to float. By the mid-1970s the post-war world monetary system had dissolved. The institutions created to

---

[8] The New Hampshire, USA, town where the World Bank and the IMF were agreed on in 1944.

[9] There was good cause for perplexity. When South Africa, as part of the British Empire, moved off the gold standard in the 1930s, its currency ceased having its denominated equivalence in gold. The increasingly meaningless promise was dropped, finally, in 1992 — possibly to forestall mischief makers who, like me, yearned to go to Pretoria and ask the governor to make good on his promise.

perpetuate it, however, remain today, but that's something we must return to later.

Looking back, it is easy to see that the fate of the international monetary system reflected the macro trends in society and changing consciousness. Early in the 20th Century Einstein's theories of relativity confronted humanity with a monumental revelation: the two most rudimentary constituents of reality, space and time, did not exist independently and as absolutes. They existed only in so far as they did so relative to each other. For a while, this seemed to be little more than an intriguing intellectual abstraction. Then a series of experiments, starting with the measuring of light bent by gravity, showed that relativity was, after all, a correct description of reality. The revolutionary impact of this on physics is well known. What is less frequently commented on is its impact on the evolution of consciousness. For it is so that before long the notion of relativity found its way into other spheres of the life of society. In politics it manifested as the belief that any act or policy that could be justified in terms of the national interest was morally defensible. This no matter how grossly it contravened standards in any other ethical framework, e.g. the lying of governments to "protect" their population. In popular morality, relativism surfaced as the creed "Do whatever you want to do — as long as you don't hurt anybody." That is, the justification of behaviour was arrived at not by a pre-existing value set, but by its effect or absence of effect on others. In cultural values, relativism, known as multiculturalism, held that human cultures were not better or worse than one another, they merely differed. In art, external standards were jettisoned in favour of authentication by the artist's subjective impulse.

So it is not difficult, in hindsight, to see that the monetary system was likely to evolve along the same lines. While the gold standard, or convertibility to gold, were in force currencies had an external, objective value. They had an absolute worth that, because it was true on one day, could reasonably be reckoned to be true the next. In the last twenty years this reasonable expectation has evaporated. Currencies now have values relative to one another. There is no longer an external standard.

Once money had broken from its mooring to objective value, many unforeseen things became possible. One of them, the most notable, has been the rise since 1990 of so-called derivative instruments, wherein monetary value — and its relationship to real-world objects, like stocks — has become so abstracted a concept that it is understood by only a priesthood of initiates.

The upshot of this, for our purposes, has been that the value of the currencies that we live by has become something beyond our reach. For those of us who live outside the dollar, especially, the value of our currency may rise or it may fall — but we don't know why. Earnest-sounding commentators speculate on what has pushed the rand, for example, up; or what is holding it down. Often their explanations sound quite plausible. Yet if they really knew, they should be able to tell us *when* the rand will go up and *when* it will come down. This they cannot do. *Ergo:* they, like us, don't really understand.

Without understanding there is no possibility of control, and it is axiomatic that governments today have no control over the value of their currencies. They can influence value, to a greater or lesser degree in different circumstances, but they cannot control it.

This is worth a pause for reflection. In the last two hundred years we have created material societies wherein money is the measure of all, even life and death. (If the latter sounds a trifle hyperbolic, just think of the fate of Aids sufferers, in their millions, who want for the price of life-prolonging drugs in countries of moderate wealth, like South Africa.)

We don't understand the source of value of the lifeblood of our economies, we cannot control it, and we cannot predict what it will do.

It means that crisis can fall upon us without notice; and this, indeed, has been our experience. The Black Monday Wall Street crash of 1987 came without warning. The markets had closed for the weekend on the preceding Friday with a long bull run at its peak. On Monday the markets fell nearly twice as steeply as they had in 1929 and about 15 000 people lost their jobs on Wall Street. Similar conditions accompanied the Asian currency crisis of 1997/98. The Thai baht collapsed and the contagion spread to many other economies associated either by regional affiliation or their status as fellow emerging countries. Again, this happened as the Eastern economies were basking in the shine of their fast track growth.

When the dot.com bubble burst in global markets in 2001, we all held our breath to see if the bust would trip the dollar and take us sprawling with it. Those of us who had breath to spare used it to speculate colourfully on whether we stood on the brink of recession, and if we did, whether it would be V-shaped, U-shaped or L-shaped. Once more, we didn't know what lay ahead.

Most of us have learned to live with the imminence of crisis. Some of us have even learned to profit from it. Neither case, however, detracts from the blanket of anxiety and stress that forms the backdrop of our lives. It is felt all the more intensely in a place like South Africa. This country, like others in the emerging world, trails in the whiplash of value fluctuation, and the governing class frequently fails to appreciate how forms of behaviour affect the perception of value — especially on terrains that do not have a direct and apparent connection with the value of money.

Let us move now from examining economic fear to understanding an intriguing aspect of our broader, nameless angst. It is a matter of fascination and interest that one of the greatest symbols of the West's sense of its own grandeur in the pre-World War 1 era, the *Titanic*, should be resurrected in our time. The Institute for Psychohistory — based in New York and led by the innovative thinker, Lloyd deMause — does what its name suggests: it applies a psychological template to history. The institute has published articles on the grip the *Titanic* story has on our society's collective imagination, what it meant in the mind of society then, and why it should surge so markedly now. There must be a reason that interest did not peak, say, in the 1960s, or at any other time in the nine decades that have passed since the unthinkable happened when the "unsinkable" sank in 1912. As a measure of our fascination with the *Titanic,* James Cameron's 1997 film of the *Titanic's* fate has become one of the most-seen films in cinema — no mean feat, as more than one commentator has pointed out, for a story in which everyone knows the outcome: the ship sinks.

Writing in the institute's journal, William K Joseph explains the significance of the *Titanic's* symbolic value, and the timing of its revival. "(1) Because extraordinarily popular cultural events give us a window on the psychology of the group, a glimpse of its collective unconscious fantasies, (2) Because group-fantasies always precede group behaviour ... "[10] Moreover, Joseph points out, the film coincides with a glut of disaster epics — *Independence Day, Twister, Deep Impact, Armageddon, Godzilla* — in which everything from extra-terrestrial invaders, tornadoes, asteroids and monsters dredged from the murky deeps of the unconscious bring havoc to civilisation.

The conclusion is all but unavoidable: we are living with a background anxiety that disaster is imminent, and the *Titanic* and all the other manifestations of disaster that fascinate us are a projection of that anxiety.

Another psychohistorian has no doubt. Adam J Green links the *Titanic* with the symbolism of the Old Testament Ark and says the *Titanic* carries a new message of a second deluge. "Deep down we know that we're still

---

[10] William K Joseph, "Titanic America", *The Journal of Psychohistory,* 26:2, 1998.

on that Ark. Still on board the *Titanic*. We know the world we have created. In our own arrogance, we may have once again ignored the warnings of icebergs and death up ahead. In our own impertinence, consumed in our own sense of greatness and vanity, we have damned ourselves."[11]

It is not only from obscure commentators, on the peripheries of the mainstream, from whom the sense of impending catastrophe emanates. The world's best-known physicist, Stephen Hawking, has stated his belief that humanity will destroy itself in this millennium either through a great technological blunder or by fatally disrupting the eco system.

The world as a moving target

The space tour guide and his visitors would be looking down on a world where the dominant life form — us — is engaged in various forms of movement. There is our frenetic, on-the-spot jiggery. There is the mushrooming of our numbers. There are tidal drifts in the concentrations of where the greatest number of us lives, and there are intermittent surges as groups move from place to place. These movements are well documented and much commented on (they are also much ignored, but that, too, is another story). So the guide will gloss over these observations. As we see, the visitors are more interested in detecting the underlying patterns of life on earth. Their purpose in this is sensible and clear. With the underlying patterns in clear sight, it becomes easier to track changes and to anticipate developments. It makes these tours more interesting and more rewarding.

The movements the guide will accordingly skim across concern, firstly, the awesome recent growth in numbers: it took from the beginning of human time — the emergence of the first homo sapiens about 220 000 years ago — until 1950 for the human population to mount to 2.5 billion. Then it took only an astonishing 37 years for the same growth to occur again — reaching 5 billion humans in 1987. Since then the growth rate has slowed, mercifully. But those young humans starting their schooling in the present will still confront a world with the added equivalent of another China before they leave school. The guide will almost certainly mention the second most worrying thing about this ominous trend — that 95 % of the growth is happening in the world's least developed nations.

Among the most developed nations population growth rates had declined in recent time so markedly that steady population levels were maintained more through longer life spans than by the birth rate. The prob-

[11] Adam J Green, "Titanic Fever: Why then? Why now?", ibid.

lem with the growth front in the under-developed regions of the world was precisely that these were areas that offered people fewest opportunities for education and employment, thus multiplying their potential for becoming a destabilising element in an already fractious world.

The second movement the guide would briefly touch on would be the migration to the world's cities. So extensive is this migration that in the next decade and a half more than half of the world's people will have become urban dwellers. This is a fundamental shift in the character of the larger portion of humanity — from a rural peasantry to an urban proletariat. Almost. The problem is that the migrating peasants do not effectively convert to a proletariat — that is, a class without property but employed in an industrial economy. The migrating peasants of the present day cannot, generally speaking, evolve the skills required for a successful urban lifestyle in modern and postmodern economies. So they become, in effect, an urban peasantry. They become consumers of urban services without having the opportunity to contribute meaningfully to a more extended tax base to support those services. The services decline and fail; those deprived of the services become restive and, once more, the potential for instability is multiplied.

The third movement the guide might register briefly in the visitor's minds is the number of humans displaced by international and, increasingly, intra-national, conflict. Drifting, helpless, hungry and desperate in 2001, were about 22 million refugees. These people were not, in all cases, displaced by conflict. Many of them were on the move to escape poverty, persecution or both in their home countries, and to get into nearby countries that offered their citizens prosperity and freedom.

Altogether the number of displaced persons in 2001 made up a total equivalent to the combined populations of Switzerland and the Netherlands. Their number was growing alarmingly as the mounting forces of inequality around the globe intensified the horror of some places and added lustre to the allure of others.

Much of wealthy Western Europe was facing a deepening problem in policing its borders. Italian police struggled to contain the floods of Balkan refugees. French and British police arrested up to 200 desperados a night trying to smuggle themselves through the Channel Tunnel.[12]

In South Africa, conservative estimates endorsed by the government claim that the number of refugees and illegal migrants crossing the coun-

[12] *New York Times*, March 15, 2001.

try's borders from impoverished states to the north at least equal the country's own birth rate — meaning that the natural growth rate of the country is doubled by illegal migrations.

The means employed by the desperate ones in their flight and their determination to penetrate the rich countries became increasingly fervent and bizarre. Boats and aircraft were commandeered. In early 2000 an Afghani Boeing 727 was hijacked — and when it landed in England the hijackers surrendered and members of the crew and 60 passengers promptly asked for asylum.[13]

In August of the same year 11 members of a soccer team from Sierra Leone that had been touring Norway fled and hid when it was time to return home, and five more pleaded for asylum.[14] The migrations were changing the social profiles of many wealthy countries. In California, Americans of non-Hispanic European extraction have already become a minority — and in the lifetime of today's 20-year-olds that will become true for the United States as a whole.[15]

The political ramifications, for one thing, are considerable.

One German study estimated that Germany will have to accommodate an influx of economic migrants equal to the population of Israel, once European Union membership is extended to the less developed states that were knocking on the EU membership committee's door in 2001.

These were the most readily visible population trends. Most people on earth could do no more than shrug and hope vaguely that "something would happen" to change the clear course to disaster that these trends were tracking along. Certainly, governments did no more than host conferences on the trends and try to contain border violations. Their activities went no further doubtlessly because the problem in its full scope exceeded their grasp. As we shall soon discuss, the time horizons of government today are shrinking ever closer to the immediate. Ever more, governments of today's societies are concerned with tonight's sound byte on the news, and the next round of voting. The idea of creating a legacy for future generations has become an archaic curiosity.

So the guide and his visitors would simply have to register humanity's disinterest in one of its most ominous developments, and move their focus

---

[13] The Aviation Safety Network's database at http://aviation-safety.net/database/hijackings.

[14] *Cape Times*, August 9, 2000.

[15] I have taken the global and USA population projections in this section from the database of the US Census Bureau at http://www.census.gov/ipc/www/world.html

instead to more interesting patterns of movement, of equal or even greater portent. The most significant of these is the shift of the fulcrum of power across the political landscape of the globe.

The great power shift — one of the primary characteristics of global politics over the last four decades — can be viewed and defined from different perspectives. Here are three straight off: political and economic power has shifted from right to left; from west to east; and from elites to masses. In large measure these perspectives overlap, interlock and are expressions of one another. It helps, though, to disentangle them to enhance their visibility.

To say that political power has shifted from right to left is easy to misunderstand. This is because it implies, at first apprehension, a shift from liberal government to socialist government — and so much of political development in the last 20 years contradicts this. One has only to think of the fall of the soviet socialist regimes and the move-to-centre of the nominally left-of-centre political parties and governments of Germany, France, Britain and the United States to recognise the contradiction. However, this contradiction arises only if the focal distance of the observation is too short. In longer view (such as inter-planetary visitors might enjoy) it is quite apparent that the political mood of the post-World War ll world has shifted from authoritarian modes of political control to more participative systems. Democracy, while admittedly a broad notion, has established itself as the only acceptable mode and measure of social management. This is revealed both in the societies that practise it successfully, and those that claim it with a fervour that is usually proportionate to how short they fall of it. Whichever way, it is a standard they measure themselves by, or against which others find them wanting. It's democracy or nothing.

Democracy, in its broadest meaning, is synonymous with a striving for high levels of popular inclusion in social management decisions. In this meaning, evidence for its spread is everywhere: there is a measurable trend to more inclusive national regimes, and the number of outright dictatorships is shrinking.

The character of global institutions is displaying the same tendency — to be seen in the UN ensemble of agencies and the Bretton Woods organs which began their lives, effectively, as clubs for the rich and their consciences ... and have become platforms for the articulation of developing world values and demands.

As regards the West-East drift, up until 1970 a history of money would have said that the world's financial capital had decamped from Paris, to

London, to New York. No mention would have been found of Tokyo, Taipei, Hong Kong, or Singapore. Today there would be little — or, at least, less — to choose between London and Tokyo. And if one should broaden the ambit to financial-industrial hubs, one could not exclude Beijing and Delhi. The latter are the only countries with populations in excess of one billion and from that enormous resource has risen growth rates around an average of 8% for the last 10 years. On this trajectory, the production power of these two countries will outstrip that of Europe by the start of the next decade. As ever, political leverage grows with economic muscle. So the power of political economy previously retained in the West is now substantially diluted in the East, and the trend continues.

Embracing both the movement from right to left, and from west to east, is the shift from elites to masses. It is the essence of the story of politics — from theocracy to aristocracy to democracy. It is also the dominant theme of politics over the last half century. Midway through the 20th Century an elite assembly of developed nations held dominion over most of the globe. Great empires, such as the British, the Spanish, the French and the Portuguese, saw themselves in possession of pantry nations, from whom they drew food and commodity supplies. The British empire, alone, had one quarter of humanity as its subjects in 1900. In addition, the empires used their possessions (that is the word they used) to fortify their standing in diplomatic intrigues among themselves.

After the brutal catharsis of World War ll a great shift in the political consciousness of the West began to show itself. The scarred and exhausted combatant nations staggered from the war chastened, contrite, reflective ... and stripped of the view that they owned the right to possess other peoples. A ripple of independent nations emerged — India, Israel, and a portentous change to white nationalist government in South Africa. The ripple became a wave and independence cascaded through Africa, in particular.

For the duration of the Cold War, which followed, the yearning of global powers for human and geographic possessions lingered in the competition for client states. This was even more short-lived than colonialism.

The world today is one in which power is diffused among many possessors. It is, concomitantly, a more chaotic world. The order of the powerful and the few, who divided global influence quite visibly and clearly among themselves, is gone. The holders of power are now many, and the balance of power is less easy to detect. It is also less easy to understand and to manage. For among its many wielders some are responsible and some are reckless, some are noble and some are malicious, some comprehend consequences and some seek only ready gains. At this juncture of its political evolution, the world is without a formal and effective arbiter to adjudicate among the contenders.

The great shift in power in the last half century was transmitted through diverse processes. In some cases power transferred from the hands of rulers, foreign and domestic, to subjects in an orderly manner, as in the case of Hong Kong in 1997. In most cases, however, it was messy and even violent, as in the cases of Malaysia in the 1950s, Algeria in the 1960s, the Philippines and the Soviet Union in the 1980s, and Indonesia in the 1990s. In rare instances it was less messy and violent than it was expected to be — as in South Africa in the 1990s.

When all is said about the shift of power that can be said at present, one lingering curiosity is sure to bring a wry smile to a distant observer. It is that most Earthers believe, or act as if, the shift is over.

Why do they think that?

The tyranny of the masses

The diffusion of power from elites to masses, both within and among nations, and the rise of democracy are simply two facets of the same thing. And it's a noble thing. The emergence of democracy reflects a maturing of humanity. It recognises the individual as a sentient being, not only capable of deciding how society should be managed, but inalienably entitled to do so. Accordingly, democracy has become a universal standard. The greatest struggles of modern history have been waged in its name. It is a cause, embraced without qualification or question, that justifies any sacrifice. Quite literally millions of lives have been offered in its pursuit or defence. It is the crowning arbitration of any argument about the method or purpose of social action. It is a secular blasphemy to question democracy. Which is a pity.

Winston Churchill's parliamentary witticism is well known: "It has been said that democracy is the worst form of government except all those other forms that have been tried from time to time." Sir Winston's point is twofold: democracy remains the best way to go about society's affairs, but it is shot through with problems and failings.

Now that we have more democracy than ever before, we have more of the problems and failings that come along with it. The point I am gingerly coming round to is that if we understand these problems and failings we stand a better chance of limiting their damage. So we should explore the failings of democracy. We might thereby eliminate the damage brought on by the accumulating shortcomings, which are threatening a degree of harm nearly as great as the good democracy brings. Moreover, understanding, the limitations of democracy takes us a long way to understanding the underlying patterns of the political ills of our time.

After all, it is these patterns that would interest visitors to our world, should there ever be any. They would learn more about who we are and where we are going by understanding the pattern of Western politics than by knowing the swaying vicissitudes, the gains and losses, of democratic contests. If I may use a sporting analogy, their interest would be in the fact that organised fist fighting is a popular entertainment, where our interest in boxing is ordinarily limited to who wins or loses any particular match.

The wickedest blasphemer against the holy tenets of democracy I know is a three-times prime minister of the nation that has served democracy most honourably of all. The last of Lord Salisbury's terms at the head of government in Britain was during the South African War at the beginning of the 20th Century. It was a time in which South Africans struggled — not for the first time and not for the last — to shrug themselves free of ties with the Old World.

More to the point of our argument here, however, is the fact that Lord Salisbury was a prominent Tory at a time when there was mounting pressure to extend the vote in Britain. It was an important time in the advance towards the universal franchise that is familiar to us today. Salisbury didn't like the idea. In *The Proud Tower* Barbara Tuchman[16] portrays him as among the last of the aristocracy to govern Britain.

If we gird our pro-democracy prejudices against the irascible Salisbury's intellectual guerrilla attacks, however, there is helpful perspective to gain on our world's current political drift by weighing up his objections.

An extended franchise would give the working classes a decisive majority in parliament. This is what Salisbury balked at. It adds to our perspective if we recall that the extension of franchise being proposed at the time was not universal. It was limited to males who owned property worth a certain minimum value and male tenants who paid a certain minimum in rents. (The minimum standards were low and, effectively, only the very poor were excluded.)

We would argue from today's standards that the poor and the very poor have every much as vested an interest in how society's resources are man-

[16] Barbara Tuchman, op. cit.

aged as do the rich. Furthermore, if Salisbury were making his argument in South Africa today he would not merely have to worry about the working classes. He would have to add to his calculation the non-working classes — the nearly 40% of the adult population without employment.

Salisbury's objection went beyond social snobbery. His deepest concern was that the extended franchise would shift the balance of power to mere numbers. There was nothing inherently superior about numbers, he argued; there was nothing to say the beliefs held by most people were correct simply because they were held by most people.

The problem magnified, in Salisbury's mind, when he looked more closely at the body of greatest numbers in English society, and assayed the difference between the mass and the aristocracy. The main difference, for the purpose of political argument, Salisbury believed, was that the working classes had less education and less property. This increased the danger in Salisbury's view that government would become stained "with the taint of sordid greed".[17] Government was best left to men of leisure and fortune (at the time members of parliament were not paid, as they are today — government being regarded a calling to those of noble spirit). The paucity of education among the lower classes also worried Salisbury. Tuchman says he held it was "perfectly impossible" to commend a farsighted passionless policy to "men whose minds are unused to thought and undisciplined to study".

Salisbury perceived, in addition, a dangerous emotive dimension to democracy that was not driven by high reason; invariably, he claimed, "passion is not the exception but the rule".

In the patriarchal view of the third Marquess of Salisbury this amounted to an assault on the very freedoms that democracy purported to protect. It was a danger that grew as power precipitated down the social wealth scales: for "in proportion as the property is small the danger of misusing the franchise is great". The net result, in Tuchman's summation of his views, would be a complete divorce of power from responsibility. The "rich would pay all the taxes and the poor make all the laws".

In its essence Salisbury's argument was that people who did not have wealth would have different needs and priorities to those who had wealth. They would, by the dictates of human nature, be focused on acquiring more wealth more rapidly. The aristocracy, by contrast, was liberated from

---

[17] In the absence of my own study of Salisbury's writings, I rely entirely on selections made by Tuchman in *The Proud Tower*, op. cit.

material need and could look at the interests of society dispassionately, and on the broad canvass of history.

If this is a fair distillation of Salisbury's view then it is easy to see what's wrong with it. Firstly, it makes the assumption that greed is a characteristic of the lower classes and is absent among the higher. Secondly, the vesting of power permanently in the hands of one class of society entails permanently excluding it from other classes — a notion that doesn't even go into the starting blocks. Thirdly, the view is unworkably narrow. It sets only one standard — pecuniary wealth — for an individual's worth. The final objection arises from the foregoing three. There is no acceptable alternative, and Salisbury doesn't offer one.

Let's not, however, dismiss the heresy of Salisbury out of hand. For he does no more than embody Churchill's paradox. The fact that there is nothing better at hand does not mean that what exists is perfect. So let's see what has happened to Lord Salisbury's fears nearly a century and a half after he expressed them.

The problem of sheer numbers now exists in a proportion that the anxious Salisbury could not have imagined. Whether one looks at a global level or at the national level, sheer numbers have overwhelmed the state of political play. The United Nations, for example, had only 60 members in 1950. Fifty years later the UN had 189 members, the greater majority of them populous, less-developed nations. The dynamic is reflected within the world's population, too. In 1950 humanity numbered 2.5 billion. Fifty years later the number had more than doubled to 6 billion. Almost all of that growth took place in the poor nations that harboured the poorest and least literate of the world. Among nations and within nations the educated and wealthy have become an ever-shrinking minority.

Again, this does not mean that the poor and their views are not entitled to the same dignity and consideration as those of the rich. Of course not. The contrary may be true. The views of the poor may be more important because they are the humans in greatest need.

The rich can, and generally do, take care of themselves. Politics is often an impediment and an irritation to them.

Politics, on the face of it, means or should mean more to the poor person than the rich. Our concern here, though, is with something different. Our concern is with the fact that the fulcrum of humanity has shifty dramatically over the last half century. It is still moving, today. And it will continue its direction of movement for the foreseeable future — even though the pace is not as accelerated as it has been up to now, because the rate of population growth is coming off peak.

Along with the shifting fulcrum of population numbers, a rapidly democratising world has shifted the centre weight of politics. And it will continue to shift. This is something the rich must know, and reckon with.

The underlying pattern we are observing is the changing nature of politics. It is a change brought on in great part by the evolving role that sheer numbers play. Having said that, though, one must reckon in that politics is usually not the product of just one force, but is the result of opposing forces seeking equilibrium. The chief opposing force to the role of numbers in democracy is the power held by the rich and privileged. It is a hold that once was absolute — but since the death of feudalism it has been slackening. It remains powerful, certainly; a good example being the election of George Bush junior to the presidency of the United States largely through the support and machinations of the nation's oil-rich aristocracy. Try to imagine Bush winning the vote on brains and personality alone and you get the idea. Yet it is a power that is increasingly being pried out of the hands of those who jealously clutch it.

One of the most powerful instruments in the hands of the challengers of power is the media. The media is cheap and everywhere, and it broadcasts universal values. These values, generally, work against the sectarian interests of the rich.

Thus, retarded by the grip of elites, but accelerated by the perpetuation of common values, the fulcrum of power moves into the hands of the numerous, who grow more so every day.

The media is eroding, additionally, a secondary force that has kept the balance of power between the rich and the poor: inertia. The bitter self-reflexive irony of poverty is its ability to enchain itself. The poor have low-quality education; therefore, their ability to escape their malaise is limited. Sophisticated levels of social organisation are not characteristics of their lives, so the mechanisms whereby they might change their lot are limited. The struggle for survival pervades their class, and so the luxury of social activism is limited. But all this is changing, and changing quickly. The universality of values propagated by the media is making sure of this. Oliver James's *relative deprivation* is spread by every soap opera and sitcom. Global awareness is growing, just as poverty itself is. The great democratic shift is working in the favour of the underprivileged. CNN, BBC World, Coca-Cola advertising and rap music disseminate the politics of envy whether they mean to or not. With each tick of the clock, the world's poor become less weak, less silent and less unorganised. The politics of our time are the politics of declining acquiescence. In the ringing phrase of Manuel Castells, we are facing "the exclusion of the excluders by the excluded".

The consequence of the drift to numbers is much as Salisbury feared. The more power devolves to the masses the shorter its focal distance becomes. Because of the urgency of the needs of the poor, political power concentrates on satisfying present material demands. It is right that it does so. A hungry man would rather have a meal than a course in haute cuisine, and so he should. But the cost to society is that immediate gains are preferred over long-term goals; and the repositories of excellence are attacked.

There are many examples where this cost wreaks long-term damage on a society's interests. In South Africa, for example, the voice of the masses expressed in the trades unions has checked the privatisation of state industries and utilities. The unions' purpose has been to prevent the loss of jobs that will result from streamlining and greater efficiency, and in this short-term analysis they are correct. However, the lesson of privatisation all over the world has been the stimulation of a more vigorous economy that, ultimately, creates more jobs and more sustainable jobs.

Enough of this. Let's leave the movement of power and its consequences here. The space guide's purpose would not be to delay the serving of snacks with a dreary lecture. His task would simply be to see that his visitors had the tools to understand the shifting patterns of life by the time they got to their destination, South Africa.

The fall of the father

In the over-arching story of the rise of civilisations the biggest role is played by religion. Not so, anymore, in ours. This alone makes present-day Western civilisation interesting, and distinct from those that have preceded it. So great has been the role of religion in society, in fact, that now our society is no longer defined by it, it is characterised by what has replaced religion. Politics has supplanted the rule of the church, reason has surpassed faith, and massification phenomena like mass sport, abetted by mass media, have usurped the need for congregation.

The long unfolding of the religious story, nevertheless, has left deep imprints on our minds, and these imprints continue to shape more of what we are and what we do than we realise.

At religion's fundamental level lies a simple but resounding division. It is the division between god the mother, and god the father.

By the greatest measure, humanity's worship has always been directed at a pantheon dominated either by mother gods or father gods. A sweep over the entire story, seen through a Western perspective, shows a progression from mother gods to father gods.

For the longest era of human religious experience, from the stone age to the iron age, the mind of man was dominated by mother gods. Then, in ancient Egypt, Ra and Isis came to rule the sky and the underworld in unison; later in Greece the pantheon became filled by male and female gods who embodied the spectrum of human qualities — but who were dominated by the patriarchal Zeus. From Greece the pantheon was transplanted to Rome. In this way Egypt, Greece and Rome, where deities of both genders were venerated, can be seen as a transition between mother gods and father gods.

A transition must have a destination, and, during this time of transition, the destination was being composed in the Middle East in a process of immense portent for Westerners. The notion of a single, all-powerful father god was being assembled from a variety of geographic localities and ethnic origins.

The principle character of God came from Yahweh, who revealed himself to Moses in Egypt. Subsidiary inputs came from El, whose name survives in the word *Isra-El* and who was the original god of Abraham the Canaanite, founding father of the Israelites. Abraham's birthplace of Mesopotamia contributed much to the image of the new Hebrew God — his rule from the sky and mountain tops, the accompaniment of thunder and lighting, and traits that seem surprising by contemporary standards, like jealousy and anger.[18]

The decline of Rome was accompanied by the consolidating grip of the father God of the Judaic-Christian ethos, to be joined within two centuries of Rome's fall by the Muslim deity, known by another name but in the same father-guise, Allah.

From that time, the reign of the father was fixed in the spiritual faculties of the societies of the West and the Middle East. However, as far as the West was concerned, this was not entirely the end of the story. The imprint

---

[18] The best accounts of the evolution of God in the mind of man I know are Anne Baring & Jules Cashford, *The Myth of the Goddess — Evolution of an Image*, Penguin Books, London, 1993 and the definitive *A History of God*, by the former nun and now prominent theologian, Karen Armstrong, Ballantine Books, New York, 1994.

of the mother god lingered, as imprints on our psyche like to do. It is seen most prominently in the way the Catholic Church, the ecumenical womb of all Christian churches, elevated Mary to near-deity status in order to satisfy the lingering yearning for a mother god.

By the same mechanism of the psyche, various epochs of Western history have vacillated between inclinations to matriarchy and leanings to patriarchy, all under the inflexible aegis of the father God.

This is a matter of the most crucial importance for a discussion we will soon plunge into regarding one of the perplexing agonies of contemporary South African life — the sexual violation and torture of children, women and aged women. Because of this importance of the idea and the topic, we must leave further examination of this issue until we get to the discussion itself, where we can approach it with the care and detail it calls for.

For now, we must train our focus on the thought that the decline of religion in our present-day society amounts to the disintegration of the father image in the psyche of Western humanity.

The ramifications of this are the underlying patterns that account for seismic shifts in our lives today. It is these patterns that first-time visitors from afar would want to be acquainted with, so that they might understand what we so often don't here in the rush on earth — why what is happening to us is happening. For these ramifications are implicated in the decline of the nation state, the devaluation of politics, lasting changes to the structure of the family and the workplace, as well as the rise of crime, social conflict and interpersonal violence. They even inform the clothing fashions we choose to follow, but that is a diverting frivolity that unfortunately lies outside this discussion of our political and economic lives.

It would be an oversimplification to claim that the decaying of the father image is solely responsible for the changes we currently witness. Equally, it would open a tiresome controversy to try to measure the degree of responsibility. It is enough to accept that none of the foregoing tidal swells in society could have risen without the fall of the father, nor, if these changes had flowed from other causes, would they have happened in the way that they are happening now. Let us then look at them.

The nation state is a political construction that everyone reading this book was born into. It is understandable, then, that our tendency is to think of the nation state as an immutable *status quo* — that the sovereign nation wherein all power is vested in a self-contained government is simply something that has always been and always will be. Well, it won't. Not only that, the nation state is already subject to forces that are altering it, and us, in far-reaching ways. Some of those ways carry great promise for a much-enhanced future for at least a sector of humanity ... but we're getting ahead of ourselves.

The second and third quarters of the 20th Century were the heydays of the national state. In the two centuries before, the state as a politically discreet entity, defined by its location and inhabitants, was in formation. The United States was under construction with a revolt against British imperial suzerainty and a civil war as the instruments of the work. In Europe national borders continued to be a movable fight as the age-old struggle for territory and power persisted between fiefdoms and duchies, the malleable Holy Roman Empire, the grand houses of Hohenzollern and Hapsburg, Napoleon and Bourbon and others too numerous to recall or to matter. At the same time, in the Third World the empires set about demarcating self-contained states so they might count them among their possessions.

The absurdity of the race for colonial possessions lives on to the present day. In Namibia, it is not infrequent for rivers (or what pass for rivers in the parched land) to bear the local word for "river" as their name. This came about when the first European travellers would point and ask: "What is the name?" The bemused inhabitants would reply: "River".

The breakdown of understanding went further than rivers called "River", however, and reaches into the present day. I stood one day at the till counter of a modest general store in the Caprivi Strip of Namibia. The strip is a tongue of land that laps implausibly, as a glance at the map will reveal to you, from the northeast corner of Namibia into south central Africa. It is the creation of the Count Von Caprivi, the German *Reichskanzler* who wanted his territory to reach the Zambesi River in order to give him access to present-day Botswana, Zimbabwe and Zambia.

The store I stood in was on the Namibian bank of the Zambezi. In front of me, waiting patiently to pay for a few items at the till, was on old man who carried the air of timeless Africa with quiet nobility about him, despite his well-worn and equally timeless clothes. When his turn came to pay, the old man placed a number of crumpled kwatchas, the Zambian currency, on the counter. The shopkeeper looked at me helplessly. I shrugged. The old man was a member of an ethnic community that had lived for generations on either side of the Zambezi, using the river as the community's common resource. He was from the Zambian side.

He had poled his dugout across the brown water to come shopping. That, by doing so, he had crossed a border made in the white man's mind, which now rendered him an illegal alien in his ancestral land, was something the old man could not, nor would ever, accept. And I felt there was no reason he should.

In Europe, which, in the first half of the 20th Century, remained the crucible of the Western spirit, the nation state served as the platform for its unlovely by-products — nationalism and patriotism. It was necessary to accelerate both to a fervour in order to sustain the two great wars. The wars, in turn, produced a reactionary generation of peaceniks, appalled by the degradation and violence of their parents' era. Patriotism and nationalism slipped from veneration to scorn.

The flower power movement visible in the parks and on the campuses, however, was only the lifestyle manifestation of a serious movement in formal society to create practices, institutions and foster attitudes that would prevent the world from sliding back into the darkness of its collective psyche. These broad innovations sought to reassure humanity that it would not again fall prey to evil demagoguery that would awaken the perversions of patriotism and nationalism to spawn chaos and bloodletting. From this sprang the global institutions we are familiar with today — the UN and the Bretton Woods group.

More important than the institutions themselves, which are now ailing, was the growth of a human rights culture that informed them, and flowed from them.

Increasingly, the rights of man were perceived for what they in truth were — universal. It was not a big step from there to a political ethos wherein individual states were judged by the degree to which they enforced, or denied, these universal rights. It was a good thing, to be sure. It was a great step in the evolution of global consciousness — but it was also the start of the erosion of the nation state. In the human rights culture that dominated the post-war West the nation state was placed in a subordinate position to the rights of its citizens.

In the emerging global mind, the function of the nation state was that of an agent enforcing those rights — and the state would be judged from then on, in a degree that did not exist before, by how well it did or did not enforce those rights. Individual states would be ranked in status by this measure in the eyes of the global community.

By way of illustration, the economic successes of Chile in the 1980s did little to elevate the country's status in the view of a world repelled by its abrogation of citizens' rights.

Once, therefore, the view took hold that there was a value set that supplanted the interests of the state, the start of the decline of the state was in motion. Like all downward motion, it accelerates. A perception of human rights begins with first order rights — like the rights to life and liberty — and rapidly devolves to second order rights like the rights to shelter, food, basic good health, medical treatment, and freedom from economic restriction and persecution.

The history of the institutions that rise to embody these perceptions of rights generally follow the same course, from principles to practicalities.

At first, high-minded, almost ephemeral institutions give form and voice to the rights. This was the nature of the United Nations in its early years. It was an elevated body, a desirable entity, but significantly removed from the *realpolitik* of the day. Individual states, by and large, resisted its attempts to acquire any influence over their affairs.

Then, as second order rights rise above the perception horizon, the institutions are found wanting because of their inability to implement the rights they propagate. The rapid decline in the status of the UN from the 1970s onward tells this story.

At this juncture, two things happen: a need is spoken for the reform of the institutions; and tentative signs begin to emerge of the future positions and forms the re-invigorated bodies might take. An illustration of this, in turn, is the recent creation of an International Court of Criminal Justice.

This is the stage we are at now. The shape and the challenge of our future lie in the creation of renewed global instruments of social, political and economic justice so that the progression of rights may be suitably accommodated. It's not a challenge we can avoid. The rising anger of those without the rights they seek will not acquiesce in the world's failure indefinitely.

The power that once resided in the nation state has not evaporated. It has migrated. It has migrated downwards to local level, people generally preferring to have decisions taken close to where they can influence them. More importantly, though, it has devolved downwards as far the individual. Davidson and Rees-Mogg documented this migration of power in their work *The Sovereign Individual*.[19] In it they depict the postmodern citizen who is no longer dependent on the state for education or information, who has little or no need for welfare, can create his or her own job, who is apt

---

[19] James Davidson & William Rees-Mogg, *The Sovereign Individual*, Pan Books, London, 1998.

to choose his or her domicile on criteria that have ever-less to do with nationality, who is liberated more by technology than by politics, and who can transact financially outside the state's tax reach via the networked computer power he or she has.

Power has also migrated upwards, to regional levels. Despite — or, because of — the rise and decline of global institutions, one of the important developments in world politics has been the creation of regional institutions. The European Union is the best example. There, some of the world's most advanced nations have handed many of the prerogatives of national government upward to a regional body.

The European exercise has spawned many emulators, Africa being the last to embrace the idea. The continent of sadness is hoping that one generic house of rules, supported by economic unions in the south, west and eastern reaches of the continent, will help it rise above the ethnic conflicts and social catastrophes that have torn its human fabric.

On the face of it, the ballooning number of states in the world in the last half-century is difficult to reconcile with the decline of the nation state, and some people feel it points, rather, to the growth of the nation state concept and attendant nationalism. Not really.

The multiplication of states, in fact, reveals what's wrong with nationalism and many of the half-century's attempts to create nation states — which proved to be inherently unsustainable. This growth occurred mainly in Africa, the Balkans and through the collapse of the Soviet Union.

Here's the problem with nationalism: once a group of people embarks on a process of manufacturing an identity by defining those who do not belong to the group, and cannot be part of it and share its resources, then that group has adopted a principle of exclusion. Once the principle is adopted, it becomes progressively applicable; so that once the *Alphalucians*, say, have excluded the *Betalucians* the *southern Alphalucians* will discover they are distinct from the *northern Alphalucians*. They will then soon want some structural recognition for the difference. Then among the *southern Alphalucians* the *Polly*-speakers will feel a necessity to separate from the *Glot*-speakers, and so on, until the term *Alphalucian*, meant to denote a cohesive group, becomes absurd.

If, however, the *Alphalucians* had adopted a principle of inclusion in making an identity — that is, aspiring to commonalities with others — their story would have been different. This aspiration to commonality is the spirit that has created the European Union (in this case it is an aspiration to commonalities of economic aspirations) and others like it, and is leaving behind the *Alphalucian* anxieties embedded in the nation state.

There is something else, however. Not all parts of the world are on the same track of aspirations and development. Many societies in the developing world are aspiring to a notion of statehood and nationalism that is being outgrown by more advanced societies. Walter Truett Anderson observes in his study of postmodern identity, *The Future of the Self*: "The appeal of having a good, clear identity — national, racial, whatever — is strongest for those who don't have much of anything else."[20]

And so the gap continues to grow.

The erosion of the meaning and authority of the nation state has left some states with very difficult problems and challenges. Like South Africa. Without evolving an aspiration to an inclusive identity, one that looks beyond itself to a global measure of existence, what is the post-apartheid state going to base nationhood on? Ethnic likeness? Shared history? Cultural unity? Common values? None of these, obviously. A shared geography, south of the Limpopo River? Yes, well … not much to go on, you might say.

To the degree that the rest of the world resembles South Africa, it leaves no wonder that nationalism nowadays is something that can be detected only at sporting events, like the Olympics or the soccer world cup. Even then, nationalist emotions require some heavy pumping. More often than not, the pumping is done by government, which has a vested interest, naturally, in nationalism; or it is pumped by commercial advertisers who are keen to lever the event for gain. Between them they hype it to levels of falsity that induce the rest of us to cringe.

Even speedier and more ignominious than the decline of old-style politics has been the decline of politicians. There is no objective way of measuring the quality of politicians but you would have to go a long way to find a significant number of sensible people who would tell you that the quality of politicians has increased in recent time.

It would have been unthinkable in Lord Salisbury's time, for example, that a president would be a man, such as Bill Clinton was, of so little honour that he would not hesitate to tell a pack of lies to get himself out of a tight spot. This is not to say, mind you, that in Lord Salisbury's time there

[20] Walter Truett Anderson, *The Future of the Self: Inventing the Post-Modern Person*, Tarcher/Putnam, New York, 1997.

were not politicians who were possessed of so juvenile a sexuality as Clinton was.

I have little doubt on this point. There is no doubt, however, that the timbre of public thought held the stature of the politician in a higher register. It has since fallen.

The very notion of a "statesman" is something of an anachronism in today's world. A measure of this loss is the pent up veneration that has been directed at Nelson Mandela. His old-fashioned sense of propriety and honour stands in vivid contrast to the shabby heads of state who were, at the turn of this century, in France, the USA, Germany and elsewhere, trying to extricate themselves from financial, sexual and electoral scandals.

A further measure of the latent desire for a sense of honour in public life, driven by an acute perception of its absence, is a curiosity that is little remarked on: Nelson Mandela's image as a secular saint was already established when he emerged from prison in 1990, where he had not been heard from for 27 years, nor, indeed, even glimpsed.

His image had been created by others. His contribution during the 27 years of his incarceration was minimal; not through any failing of his, naturally.

If ever there was a case of a living human being embodying a projection of the collective, unconscious, desires of society, this was it.

Of course, Mandela disappointed no one. As it turned out, he had a stature equal to what was ordained for him in the global mind. But it was not his stature that created his image in the first place. His stature rather maintained and enhanced the image that pre-existed.

Mandela aside, there is evidence that people, particularly in developed societies, are turning away from politics and politicians in a broad disillusionment. It is an ominous development. It is a pattern that is initiating pervasive changes in the lives we lead — not all of them pleasant. We'll be getting down to the specifics in the chapters that lie ahead. Before we get there, let's briefly weigh the evidence.

In Britain in 2001 the lowest number of voters since World War 1 elected a government. In the USA there has been a steady disaffection evident in congressional and presidential elections, it not being uncommon, since 1980, for less than half the entitled voters to turn out to the polls.

In Europe today fringe parties parody elections and politics. The best known, of course, is Britain's Monster Raving Loony Party. This party was led into the election by a cat and centred its 2001 campaign on the question: *Why is there only one monopolies commission?* Italy has had a porn actress, Illona Staller, *aka* Cicciolina, stand for parliament … and win. Her party's platform? Honesty in government. German now has a word, a long one of course, for political disaffection — *Politikverdrossenheit.*

Beyond the welcome levity and deserved lampooning lies a serious development. We are living through nothing less than a collapse of authority.

If authority is drifting from the hands of politicians, even from politics as we know it, where is it going to come to rest?

Part of the answer we know already. The power and authority until recently held by politicians and the state is dissipating in civil society — to business, for example. Of the 100 largest economic entities in the world in 2001, 49 were countries and 51 were corporations.[21] The pull of commercial brands, in many parts of the world, is a greater attractor of the mind than government decrees.

The fall of the father and the erosion of authority have brought big changes in other important areas of our lives — the home and the office. The customary notion of the family — mom, dad, kids — called the nuclear family in a term specially invented for it soon after World War ll, is fading away. According to an actuarial study by the British government the majority of British adults by the end of this decade will be single. The US census has found that no one particular family structure dominates American society today — the nuclear family is no longer the norm. Similar trends are reported in France, Canada, Italy and Germany.

In this discussion we are not saying that the fall of the father is a good or a bad thing. Nor are we saying it is the only cause of the changes being wrought on the family. We are observing, only, that the family unit has over the last 200 hundred years narrowed, from the extended family to the nuclear family, ending with the father at its apex until he began to fade again in the last half century.

The family is our core social unit. It is our first and primary experience of the structure of living. We cannot change it without changing ourselves. China, for example, has found that its one-child policy has created a generation of individuals that differ meaningfully from their predecessors. The young one-child-per-family adults that are now taking their places in society are more self-centred, demanding and intolerant than those before.

---

[21] It's a trend — the 200 largest corporations are growing faster than global economic activity generally. See the Institute for Policy Studies http://www.ips-dc.org/reports/top200text.htm.

They are also more confident. Together they will make up a society that is more self-centred, more demanding, less tolerant and has more self-confidence. What it will demand, and what it will be disinclined to tolerate remains to be seen. If, however, the emerging Chinese generation demands more personal freedom and is less tolerant of the authoritarian patriarchs of Chinese society — and is more confident of its ability to change what it doesn't like — then China's future may be heavily influenced by a factor that so far has been left out of the reckoning.

The fall of the father has changed the work place, too. Today's firm, and the view we have of it, is markedly different to the view that propelled the great engines of prosperity in the post-World War II West. For decades the firm has been authoritarian and patriarchal. To wit, it was unusual in the extreme to find a woman at the head of a large business. True, it is not yet that common — but the extent to which it is changing is a measure of the fall of the father image in business.

The disintegration of patriarchy and the decline of authority in the post-modern firm has been changing the firm's structure for some time now. Previously, the firm was regarded as an impersonal, mechanistic organisation dedicated to the self-affirming good of making profit. Employees of the firm adapted to the firm and left their personal lives at the front door, like hats that they would pick up again when they left. The fate of their desires and ambitions relevant to the life of the firm were left to the authority of the firm to decide on. Promotion, demotion and even dismissal were powers the firm exercised over the individual, without the individual having any say in the matter.

None of this applies in the postmodern firm.

Power has left the executive suite and has migrated to the ranks of the work force. "Empowerment" of the operational workers is the mantra of business today. Empowerment has taken on the additional meaning of elevating genders, races and the physically impaired to executive levels, altering the profile of the power domain of the white male manager. All of this is part of the process of diluting the image of authority that existed up to now in society.

The machine metaphor for corporate organisation has been replaced by the conceit of "a community of work". As implied, in this community the individual is treated as a whole. The proposition is: to be productive the worker must be happy at work; and the worker is unlikely to be happy at work if he or she is burdened by unhappiness outside of the workplace. Ineluctably, the manager's role changes from giver-of-orders to guide and counsellor. Russ Ackoff, the sage eminent of new business, has captured the changing pattern and structure of the work environment in a phrase: "from hierarchies to lowerarchies".

Once again, the decline of authoritarianism is not the only thing happening in business now. It will also be sometime before the results of present changes can be measured for sure. But what is for sure is that the ultimate and underlying goal of business cannot change: productivity. In America, the litmus environment for anything to do with business, production figures climbed phenomenally through the 1990s. The infusion of information and communications technology to the productivity formula is taken to be the primary cause. At the time of writing, 2001, new statistics were showing a fall-off in productivity. Will this fall-off be sustained? Was the technology-driven productivity gain a burst energised by novelty? Will the more people-oriented, authority-diminished business prove to be more, or less, productive? Is productivity the only measure that matters? Is the workplace more than a place of production? Should it be?

It won't be long before we know.

The final dimension of the fall of the father that we need to register before moving on is at once the most serious, the most vexing and needs the most delicate approach. It is the rise of crime and social conflict in our world.

Let's deal with the delicacy first. I don't want to suggest that receding authoritarianism is *responsible* for the crime wave — and thereby, by implication, advocate a return to authoritarianism. Further, I don't want to imply that a more humane world, and a society that is more nurturing of its members, necessarily also has to be a less disciplined and a more threatening one. That would be a gross misapprehension. Yet we cannot escape the fact that crime, which springs from many causes, as we shall see when we examine it in the South African context, has burgeoned in tandem with the decline of a strong father image.

The truth is that a strong father image and rigid authoritarianism are not the same thing; likewise, authority and authoritarianism are not the same thing. Thus the decline of the one does not necessitate the decline of the other. The fact that this is largely what has happened does not mean it has to, or it had to, be so.

The view we must take before we can proceed usefully is that the rise of crime and social conflict are phenomena that have capitalised on the decline of authority; that the fall of the father was a pre-condition without which they could not have happened, but that this is not the same as saying that the fall of the father *caused* the rise in crime and the social conflict we see today.

Phew.

The examples tell the story. Societies that are presently losing the war against crime — Colombia, South Africa, Albania and Russia — have in the past dozen years experienced dramatic shifts away from authoritarianism. On a lesser level, societies that are currently losing battles in the war against crime, such as the struggle against drugs in America and Britain, are primary indicator nations in the West's collective experience of the fall of the father. On the other hand, the last redoubt of patriarchy *in extremis*, the Taliban's Afghanistan, has been achieving the only undisputed success against drug trafficking.

Rising crime is one of the great challenges of the future world, and how we deal with it will go a long way to deciding what kind of lives we will lead.

Organised crime today has been pegged by research groups as one of the ten biggest economic entities in the world. At least one study has estimated the turnover of organised crime to be equal to the GDP of Britain.

Sheer size, though, is not the worst of it. The very nature of crime in society is changing. Where it once was an aberration of the social system, an anomaly on the fringes of the social order, it is now insinuating itself to the point of becoming a feature of the system. More and more, the formal economy becomes interlinked with the sub-formal, criminal economy. This happens in many ways. Many criminal organisations are only partly criminal; aspects of their operations may be quite conventional. For example, it is common practice for a criminal ring that wants to export or import goods illegally to acquire or develop a legitimate import-export business and feed the contraband in along with the legitimate movement of regular goods. Even more often, a mirrored form applies — legitimate companies indulge in illegitimate practices selectively. For example, a company bearing a world quality brand became implicated in allegations of improper transactions relating to large-scale armaments tenders in South Africa. Similarly, oil giant Elf Acquitaine has been accused of entering into illegal deals with French politicians.

Is a criminal organisation only one that commits crime *all* the time, not just *some* of the time? The citizen subliminally taking a bearing from the institutions of society can be understandably confused.

The formal economy interacts with the sub-formal criminal economy in other ways, too. In South Africa, for example, one of the fastest growing industries — 30% a year since 1970 — has been the security industry. By 2001 there were nearly twice as many private security guards in the country as regular police, which must make the industry one of the land's largest employers. This industry, an important source of national prosperity, is entirely dependent on the existence of crime. No crime, no security industry.

I have been unable to find, or calculate, an accurate figure — but I estimate that about 25% of car purchases in South Africa take place as a result of the purchaser's previous car being stolen. Car sales figures are a popular barometer of national economic performance ... a performance, it turns out, then, that is significantly dependent on crime!

It is, however, the breakdown of the moral compass in society that provides the essential matrix for crime in society. It begins with the fall of the good father, who embodied this moral compass in our first experiences in the family, and then it moves through business and into politics. Eventually, the disintegrated and dysfunctional matrix is the amoral underblanket of our lives.

Just as the British police are fond of referring to the rain as "the silent police officer" (crime activity drops when it rains)[22] so an intact moral fabric of society is a prime insurer against that society becoming dishonest, corrupt and criminal. It seems that it is merely because this fabric is invisible that we have neglected its maintenance, to such great cost.

Regrettably, all we can do here is recognise the fall of the father image. This is not the place to go into the likely ramifications for Western society, as fascinating as such an exercise would be. We will, however, according to my alert above, need this tool of understanding when we attempt to explain vital parts of South Africa's present-day experience.

The Decency Revolution

Society is not a river whose currents all flow in the same direction. Society is more chaotic than that. It is a constant coming together of competing forces, and the churn they create is our experience of living. Therefore, while many of the forces, patterns and directions of flow discussed up to now are, shall we say, anxiety inducing, there is relief. Here is a force, an

---

[22] When I was a younger news reporter in the time of political upheaval in South Africa I extracted a casual principle about the quirkiness of human nature and politics: there never was a riot in the rain. Stone-throwing groups would brave police teargas and bullets — but everyone would run for shelter at the first drops of rain.

evolving pattern in society, which radiates promise for the future. I call it the decency revolution.

We have only recently turned our backs on the close of a century crammed with experiment and argument. In it, we experimented with science and society at levels of intensity unknown before, and we argued over these experiments and just about everything else. It has been a time of great disputes. Often they became violent. The violence, though, was of a type that differed from what went before.

From the earliest time humans fought aggressively — as opposed to defensively — mainly to acquire territory deemed necessary for optimising survival. The rest of the animal kingdom still does so. This territorial instinct, infused with good doses of that distinctly human trait, greed, lasted well into the Middle Ages when it, like the rest of life, became commandeered by the church.

The cause of religious dogma then became the prime motivation and character of organised aggression. At the very least, religion channelled aggression in the guise of service to dogma. With territorialism as an underlay, humans thus fought over what they believed, rather than what they merely wanted, as before.

Only in the 20th Century, after the two great wars, when capitalism, socialism and communism became the demarcations of social orders, did humankind begin to fight over what it thought. The aggression storms that buffeted the half-century squalled in the name of ideology. And when the century was over, the argument was more or less settled.

Looking back to the end of the 20th Century, we can see that Fukuyama was right in an important sense in *The End of History:* a great clash of ideas had delivered an outcome.

From where we stand now we can see that the right won the economic argument. There is no way of gainsaying it: where markets are the most free, they are also the most prosperous.

The left, however, won the moral argument. There is no way of gainsaying it: we cannot pursue profit without taking into account the human cost of the pursuit, lest we bring calumny upon our heads.

Out of this conjunction, the victory of the right and the victory of the left, the new ethos of a global economy is being made. In the emerging view, *how* profits are made is being ranked in equal importance with the fact *that* they are being made.

Progressive oil companies are re-casting themselves as energy companies. It is not only an outcome of business strategy; it is a nomenclature with a softer feel. The new energy companies are careful to promote an image of being aware of the need to conserve resources.

Manufacturers of all stripe are having to give account of their employment practices, no matter that they may be located in far-off developing countries ... indeed, especially when they are located in far-off developing countries.

Green lobbyists and consumer activists of all kinds are active as never before.

The Internet is both a tool and a platform that has given activists a greater reach, penetration and influence than they ever had.

The overall result is a rising level of awareness among consumers. The ethical provenance and pedigree of products matters increasingly to them. It is not likely to be long before products will bear ethical guarantees in the same way they now bear assurances about their ingredients. So, a guarantee that a foodstuff does not contain tartrazine, for example, may soon see added to the same label the assurance that no exploited labour was involved in the manufacture.

Yet another manifestation of the pattern of emerging decency is the recent appearance on the global agenda of compensation for collective crimes. The victims of Nazi concentration camps were the first focus of this public debut of conscience. The agenda then shifted to forced labour in wartime Germany. Predictably, slavery and racism in the USA and South Africa soon joined the list. In 2001 a tense stand-off brewed between developed and developing countries over compensation for excesses under colonialism.

Some of the appearances of the phenomenon have a quirkiness about them. In 2000, a Nigerian court ordered the Shell oil company to pay $40 million in compensation for an oil spill that happened 30 years ago. In the USA, the descendants of the Salem women who were hanged for witchcraft petitioned for their exoneration — 309 years after the event.

The merits, and otherwise, of these issues are complex — but less interesting than the question: Why now? Most of the true victims are dead. One commentator has observed: those who did not perpetrate the crimes are being asked to recompense those who were not the victims. It would, of course, have been more appropriate, effective and logical to make the claims for compensation closer to the misdeeds, to benefit more of those who had suffered the wrongs. Instead, there is an unavoidable sense of strangeness about the appearance of the effect so long after the cause.

Only one thing can explain it: this is first time the world's collective conscience has been ready to produce the issue, and grapple with it. Our consciousness, with conscience as a part of it, has evolved and brought us to a stage of that evolution where — just as if we were talking about psychotherapy for an individual — we are only now ready, collectively, to return to the past and deal with unresolved hurt.

The rise of the feminine archetype in society and a more marked inclination to matriarchy — both related and both inevitable shifts resulting from declining patriarchy — are leading to a more humane world. It is also a more troubled world, as we have seen, but it may prove to have more compassion to deal with those troubles.

Globalisation is all over the place

So much hot air has been expelled over globalisation that I am loathe to add to the gasses misting up a clear view of the issue. So let's rely instead on what the wise have had to say about globalisation:

> The inhabitant of London could order ... , sipping his morning tea in bed, the various products of the whole earth and reasonably expect their delivery on his doorstep; he could at the same moment and by the same means adventure his wealth in the natural resources and new enterprises of any quarter of the world, and share, without exertion or even trouble, in their prospective fruits and advantages.

No, on second thoughts, that won't do. It's John Maynard Keynes commenting at the end of the 19th Century on the use of the telephone. Let's try another sage on the benefits of internationalism, whose view is that a world community of trading nations ensures a more peaceful globe. He writes that "two trading nations who traffic with each other become reciprocally dependent; for if one has an interest in buying, the other has an interest in selling; and thus their union is founded on their mutual necessities".

Oh dear, no. That won't do either. It's Montesquieu[23] writing in the 18th Century.

The point is made, though. Globalisation is as old as the human desire to trade and to prosper, and to seek opportunities ever further afield to do so. The best that can be said for the injection of the world "globalisation" into the vocabulary of world politics in recent time is that the age old move

---

[23] Montesquieu is quoted by Thomas Friedman in his account of globalisation, *The Lexus and the Olive Tree*, Harper Collins, London, 1999.

towards a trading global community has been energised into a surge as part of the information revolution.

The best description of the evolution of globalisation I know of is that of *New York Times* feature writer, Thomas Friedman, who depicts the international trading scene as a great plain. Until recently various national fiefdoms existed on this plain, all walled off to demarcate their domains. Over time, fissures had appeared, or had been made, in the walls and means had been developed of leapfrogging those walls. The purpose was to facilitate the flow of communications and goods. Then came the latter-day surge. The Internet, e-mail, and other advances in communication and transport effectively destroyed the walls and swept them from the plain. What is left, now, on the great open space is what Friedman graphically terms an "electronic herd". The herd is the international trading fraternity, particularly the financial and currency traders. The herd roams the plain largely unhindered, seeking out the greenest and most succulent grass. Like any other herd,.it can be spooked, often by something inconsequential. Then the herd will stampede, harmlessly, or doing various degrees of damage, before things return to equilibrium.

From these views alone it is clear to see that trying to stop globalisation is pointless. It is also a bad thing. It is contrary to the best interests of the advance of humanity.

Stepping up vigilance, however, to ensure that globalisation proceeds in the best and fairest manner possible, is something entirely different. That is a good thing.

This is the balance that has been lost in the fury of the debate. Globalisation needs better management, not resistance.

The benefits of international intercourse are easily taken for granted — a foible that is tellingly satirised in Monty Python's film, *Life of Brian*. Brian is a timid and hapless individual living in Jerusalem at the start of the Christian era, who becomes mistaken for the messiah. John Cleese plays Reg, a ragged and intemperate revolutionary who leads a group of scrappy, bumbling insurgents against the Roman occupation. Addressing a secret meeting of the Peoples' Front of Judea, Reg rants about what the Romans have "stolen from our fathers and their fathers".

"What have they ever given us in return?" Reg cries rhetorically, and unwisely ...

1st Bumbling Insurgent:	... the aqueduct?
Reg:	What?? ... oh, yeah — the aqueduct.
2nd Bumbling Insurgent:	... and sanitation ...

Reg (exasperated):	Oh, alright, I'll grant you — the aqueduct and sanitation are two things the Romans have given us.
3rd Bumbling Insurgent:	And the roads!
Reg:	Yes, well, obviously the roads. The roads go without saying, don't they? But *apart* from the aqueduct and sanitation and the roads ...
Another Bumbling Insurgent:	Irrigation.
Yet another Bumbling Insurgent:	Medicine.
Still another Bumbling Insurgent:	Education.
Reg:	Yeah, alright, fair enough.
Another Bumbling Insurgent:	And the wine!
Another Bumbling Insurgent:	Public baths!
1st Bumbling Insurgent:	And it's safe to walk in the streets at night, now, Reg.
Reg:	Alright! But apart from sanitation, medicine, education, wine, public order, irrigation, roads, the fresh water system and public health — what have the Romans ever done for us?
Bumbling Insurgent:	... brought peace?
Reg:	Argh, peace! Shuddup!

In the 1960s and 1970s I partook in a value set that dreamed of a global family of man, free of impediments to movement, communication and enterprise, where individuals and voluntary associations of individuals would be at liberty to transact and contract with one another, producer and consumer, artist and audience, entrepreneur and worker, entirely on the basis of the willingness of all parties.

Globalisation, both of trade and of the mind of humanity, is the means by which that dream is becoming reality.

That in it's implementation it is not perfect, and may fairly be said to be riddled with problems, goes, as Reg might have it, without saying. But that's no reason to trash the system. In fact, to resist it is mule-headed folly, and reduces the chances of the victims of the rich-poor gap of doing something about their predicament. Cutting them off from the global economy and its activities is no way to help the poor. The way to help the poor is to clear the obstacles preventing them from more and freer participation in globalisation.

This is not to say the protests against globalisation at the now epony-mous localities of Seattle, Prague and Stockholm have been without effect. On the contrary, they have served notice on the mandarins of economic power that they cannot wield their advantage to the detriment of others. But the singular and glaring failure of the protest movement to put work-able alternatives on the agenda means that that's as far as protest goes. And it's done. From here on, anti-globalisation protest can only remain what it has become — a vehicle of social anger only incidentally attached to globalisation.

Because globalisation is an irresistible tide in social evolution, protest is doomed unless and until it shifts focus to where it can be effective: those nations that can be deemed to be on "the receiving end" of globalisation. That is, countries where corporations locate their manufacturing opera-tions to take advantage of amenable labour supplies. Activism should be aimed at assisting such countries to ensure that the transaction between the foreign entity and their local labour — or other resources — is reason-able and fair.

It is unlikely in the extreme that the putative victims of globalisation — the third world employees of the first world factories — would praise the street mobs of Seattle, Prague and Stockholm for forcing actions that would result in the closure of the factories. Those employees may be cycling or walking to work. But their children will almost certainly, in the main, drive. This is the already-mapped path to the future. Those who embark on it will reap the greatest reward.

One last thing about globalisation. It's not an isolated thing, restricted to the economy of the world. Economic globalisation is a reflection of glo-balisation in many other respects. It is part of a whole. I have a (only partly playful) *theory of general consistency*. Through it I try to convey the idea that phenomena in one field of human endeavour — say, politics — will be reflected and have equivalents in other fields — like painting, or psycho-logy, or economics, or music, or culture ... or, most probably, all of these. This idea has weaved as a theme through our discussion up to now, and it will continue to do so as we try to understand the societies we live in — South Africa in particular, as it is our chosen socio-political laboratory.

In this sense, the globalisation that gives rise to the controversies that rage across the headlines is, in reality, a phenomenon found in virtually everything else we do.

Culture and attitudes are globalising. Like economic globalisation, cultural globalisation may not be happening in the most desirable way. The shallow Coca-Cola culture of America perpetuated by Hollywood is more of a subject for lament and dismay than celebration. But it's happening.

Music is globalising. This week's "top ten" differ little between Minneapolis, Manila and Moscow.

Speech is globalising. English is rising as a *lingua franca* for the world, spurred by the Internet. The French rail vainly against the incursion of English, and so do the Germans and the Spanish and just about everyone else who isn't English. But they need to register their protest in English, if they want it heard and noticed. Across the world, the number of spoken languages is declining.

Politics is globalising.

Communication is globalising. Cyber space is governed by no authority, no government, no nation.

Information is globalising. Excuse me for a minute while I click into the Internet Public Library from my laptop, in Rangoon.

Transport and travel are globalising. Tourism has become the world's biggest industry.

Identity is globalising. I care less about my nationality than my place in the world. I would rather be a good person than a good South African. I am not alone.

The mind of humanity is globalising. Let's get with it.

Realising awareness

It's a curious statement, but indulge me: there is, in the world today, a growing awareness of consciousness. Descartes — the one who said "I think therefore I am" — started us thinking about thinking. For most of the time since then, this esoteric activity was the preserve of philosophers.

These days, however, there is growing realisation that consciousness is a fundamental part of the experience of living. There is a recognition, too, that it has specific functions. It determines our perception of reality. It governs the way we live. It steers us in certain directions, and closes others that might otherwise be open to us. It makes us capable of some actions, and not of others. It reveals parts of the truth of existence to us, and it hides other parts of that truth from us. What it is is who we are. What's more, it isn't always the same. Yours might differ from mine. In fact, it does.

There's something else. It's a bigger pattern and to understand it we need to borrow an idea from the Polish-American mathematician Benoit

Mandelbrot who, through his work on the mathematics of patterns,[24] has uncovered a significant corner of the underlying structure of reality. In 1975 he coined the term "fractals". These are mathematical entities that demonstrate patterns can remain consistent over very large variations in scale — a process also known as *self-similarity.*

Now, let's join the lamplighters, mavericks, adventurers, and pioneers who are striving for Gould's synthesis of knowledge by tying theories of mathematics, physics, psychology, history, biology and sociology together. Let's apply Mandelbrot's self-similarity ideas of fractals to society. If we do, this is what we get: the same patterns of input stimulus and output behaviour that occur in the psychology of the individual — something that we understand quite well — apply equally up the scale at the social level — something that we don't understand very well.

Just as individuals have thoughts and particular ways of thinking, so do whole societies. And these mental patterns pre-determine what can and what can't happen — even what is likely or unlikely to happen.

This basic idea has underpinned much of our discussion up to now — the collective consciousness, the disintegration of the father image, the decency revolution and globalisation. All we're doing right now is adding sails to our ship, and checking the rigging, because we'll shortly be heading deeper into the shadow. The water is dark and the winds are not yet fully calibrated and charted.

Many assumptions we hold in familiarity seem odd and even comically archaic once we have abandoned them. Our assumptions about consciousness are an example. So, as curious as the notion seems once we abandon it, we have traditionally thought of consciousness as something that either exists, or does not. Either I am conscious or I am not.

It is not so. Consciousness comes in various quantities and qualities. My Airedale, admittedly asleep right now at my feet, has consciousness. Believe me, she has. But it is not the same as mine. Once the difference is realised, we could easily fit ranges of living things between Jessie and me on a scale of consciousness; also below Jessie and above me — a dolphin and a chimpanzee between us, a fish below her, and a swami above me. Therefore, if consciousness *per se* can exist on an evolving scale, surely it is not a great leap to accept that it can evolve *within* a species. Like us. Our minds have been changing and evolving for thousands of years. They

[24] Don't ask.

are changing and evolving right now; they will continue to do so, and the rate of change and evolution is probably exponential.

This is a leap I have taken, and ever-more people are doing the same. A number of American universities now teach macro-history. Macro-history is nothing less than an intellectual perch from which the evolution of the mind of humankind and its consciousness can be observed. The history of consciousness, although it comes in many guises, from the physiological to the social, is a subject that is emerging from the apocrypha of enquiry into the mainstream.

Okay, here's the really exciting part. If consciousness is evolving, what's it doing right now? Where is it at, and where might it be going? The psychologist C G Jung, originator of the notion of the collective unconscious, believed that humankind was preparing for an important step forward in consciousness. Jung was right about everything else, so he is probably right about his too.

The course of our discussion to this point, I sincerely hope, has awakened some thoughts within you about where our evolving consciousness might be going. My own view is that we are moving out of an age of exaggerated materialism into what Arie de Geus has called "humanistic capitalism". Our slavish adherence to the rational is also making room for the irrational. In short, we are moving towards an attitudinal terrain that the developing world has long claimed precedence on. The essence of the developing world's critique of the first world is that, in its rush for efficiency and wealth, the developed world has forgotten how to stop along the way and consider the lilies, how they grow.

Now a great middle path beckons, and the immensely intriguing possibility presents itself — that, if it can get its act right on the basics of successful social life, a place like South Africa, microcosm of the world today, could find itself in the forefront of the consciousness of tomorrow, and its new possibilities. So let's go there.

CHAPTER TWO

The Theory of Everything

Politics, economics and other crimes: why we can't solve them

Have I got a deal for you. It's a humdinger. In the next six minutes of reading time I will reveal to you everything there is to know about politics and economics, and then we can get down to some really interesting stuff. That's right, in just six minutes from now you will never again have to wonder what's going on, and the politics of nations will become a transparent process to you. There's no trick, honest. You can trust me; I'm a journalist.

The Theory of Everything is also sometimes referred to (by me, no-one else has heard of it) as the Six-Minute Street Theory of Politics and Economics. It works like this: imagine the street where you live. If you don't live in a regular house in a suburban street, imagine it anyway. The street is getting along just fine and everything is ticking over nicely. You may not dwell on this, but the reason the street is getting on nicely is that it is adequately supplied with the resources it needs to get on nicely. When you need electricity it is there at the flick of a switch; when you want clean water all you have to do is turn the tap.

Now imagine the street without an adequate supply of resources. Imagine the supplying authority announces there will only be a limited amount of electricity supplied to the street and a quantity of water that falls far short of present consumption.

What will happen in this situation?

The first move, of course, will be for the residents to get together to decide how the reduced resources will be divided among them.

There will probably be a suggestion that the available resources should be distributed equally among the homes. That would be communism, in its undiluted form.

There will be a counter-suggestion that will point out that not all homes have the same level of need. One home might house a baby and a toddler, for example, and a grandmother; while another might have only a childless couple. In as much as their needs are different, then, the resources should be apportioned to each according to their needs. This would be communism in its applied form.

Doubtlessly some would argue that the foregoing is all sentimental nonsense and that, seeing as the resources are for sale, those who are able to buy the most would have demonstrated through their ability that they are entitled to as much as they are able to afford. First come, first served; the market will decide. That would be naked capitalism.

Naturally, there will be those who will argue that all of the above positions are unnecessary and unacceptable extremes, and that a middle way is possible ... and the most desirable. These people would argue that neither needs nor means alone should determine the apportionment of resources. They would say that the individual initiative, freedom and integrity of the "means" argument should be preserved — but that there should be a mechanism to ensure that means were reasonably evenly distributed among the potential purchasers of the resources. In other words, no-one's genuine needs should be compromised by shortage of means. These views would be those of the social democrats.

Easy, huh?

The meta-question is who will decide which of the systems of apportioning the resources you will use. One level of abstraction up is how you will decide who will decide.

There you have it. Politics and economics are systems of apportioning resources, and methods of arriving at those systems. Everything you read and see in the news is a sub-set of these great social struggles.

We can go further. There is one thing we know for sure about the process in the imaginary street: there will be disagreement. There will probably even be conflict. We know something more: the intensity of the conflict will increase in proportion to the decrease in the resources. The fewer resources, the more intense the conflict. Should the resources dwindle to the point that they are insufficient to sustain everyone, no matter how they are divided, violence and even some form of war is likely to result.

If we understand that by resources, in this argument, we are employing the widest definition of the word, then we understand much about how conflict and violence arise within a society, and between societies. Resources, as the term functions here, include not the water and electricity of our somewhat simplistic example, but, in the real world, money, jobs, education, recreational facilities, good health, and peace and personal safety. When there are shortages of any or all of these, singly or in various combinations, the social edifice begins to crack.

There is one last near-certain lesson we can extract from our lengthy metaphor. It is that we can predict with a high degree of accuracy *how* the edifice will crack. It's no more complicated than that the cracks will follow already-existing fault lines in the social body. Those fault lines can be class, economic status, gender, culture or religion; but most usually and increasingly in the trend to cultural patchquilt societies, they are ethnic.

So, in our imaginary street, we will find that the opinions on the methods of dividing the resources will probably, and, sadly, follow ethnic patterns in the street. The whites against the blacks, the Chinese against the Greeks, the Portuguese against the Jews, the Hondurans against the Iroquois ... you can make it as absurd as you like, you won't be wrong. If the street lends itself to it, it will happen.

Let's be clear: that resource-deprived multi-ethnic societies will crack along ethnic lines is not *necessarily* the case. But if you used this surmise as a first analytical tool, you would be well served in most cases.

Now let us move from metaphors to reality. In South Africa's Western Cape province many people wishing for a stable and decent society have been perplexed at how vigilantes, who ostensibly have the same enemies as the rest of us, have ended up on the wrong side of the law.

The primary example is Pagad, a group whose acronym stands for People Against Gangsterism & Drugs. Pagad arose on the Cape Flats, a mainly working class (that means high unemployment!) area. The flat, sandy landscape was used primarily as a dumping ground for victims of the apartheid government's attempts to create segregated residential areas — meaning that people of colour were forcibly moved, in the main, from so-called white areas. On the Cape Flats these rebuffed people, dislocated and traumatised, struggled against the deprivation of almost any civic resource you care to name — housing, jobs, adequate schooling, familiar networks, a sense of continuum ... all the things that make people feel settled, cohesive and content. Gangs, which existed before, now proliferated. Pagad appeared. It was a uni-ethnic body: Muslim.

At first Pagad was what it appeared to be — working class and middle class family men who had burnt their fuse waiting for the police to suppress the gangs. Soon, however, it became clear that Pagad was as much a factor in the anxiety of life on the Flats as any of the gangs. The police seemed to be as much a Pagad target as the gangs themselves. Many suspected that it might be the other way round — that the police targeted Pagad as much as they did the gangs. The question wasn't relevant for long; it submerged in the pandemic violence that spread from the Flats to more sedate areas of Cape Town: Restaurants, malls and mall parking lots became bombing targets. The state and the body politic had become the enemy. Many of the bombings remain unexplained, but Pagad's name was linked to them — by the government, among others. At the time of writing, a trial of Pagad members who had allegedly placed a bomb near a restaurant terrace had to be abandoned because key witnesses were murdered.

How did this happen? How did the good guys go bad? How did they transform from gangster hunters to the most vicious gangsters themselves? How did the society they set out to protect become their enemy? The last of these questions contains the clue to the answer. Pagad has become substantively alienated from the social order and value system it set out, in its conscious purpose, to propagate and protect. It soon became driven by hatred and anger, directed at the society and its instruments — government and police ... to the point that the American government officially branded Pagad as a terrorist group.

The anger that so soon surfaced as Pagad's sustaining energy was not something of recent manufacture. It had been coagulating, slumbering in the unconscious of its carriers. It was woken by circumstances.

So the answer to the full set of questions we asked about Pagad's birth and transformation lies in a logic that is outside the conventional rationales we use for the struggle between the good and the bad in society. Pagad is, rather, reflective of a society cracking under burdens of stress it can no longer bear successfully. The stress produces levels of anger and aggression that must find expression. These symptomatic passions attach themselves to ready and convenient objects; then, once unleashed, erupt in a torrent that far passes the ostensible target.

Thus, formerly decent and law-abiding people suddenly and inexplicably behaving in ways that seem to betray and attack the foundations of their existence up to then, is the collective response to social stress. It is the logic that explains phenomena like Pagad.

This is not all there is to Pagad and the gangs of the Western Cape, of course. Humans are complex, and their behaviour is the product of a coming together of a range of forces. So we will be returning to Pagad and the gangs later in this chapter. Remind yourself that we are looking for the underlying patterns that will render explicable that which has been inexplicable.

Crime preys

From our first-sweep look at vigilantes and gangs in the Western Cape, above, we have seen how societies react to the stress that rises out of depleting resources. The stress morphs into a common, shared anger and predisposition towards aggression. Then, like a build-up of molten lava deep in the earth's crust, the red hot, fluid passions find the cracks and fissures in society to erupt in an outburst of blind destruction.

Crime, violence in association with crime, interpersonal violence (they're different), gangsterism and criminal sexual behaviour are inter-woven: and together they make up a portmanteau of symptoms typical of a society in stress overload. The crime matrix is the primary social space in which the stress eruption plays itself out. It is especially so in societies like South Africa where the wide disparities in wealth and values add to the likelihood of stress disruption. There is an emerging class war between the *haves* and the *have-nots*. The crime matrix, and on the global level this includes terrorism, is the chief terrain of battle.

This is not a view endorsed by convention. Right now many critics and defenders of orthodoxy will be reaching for their pencils. Therefore, I will allow this point to weave in and out of our discussion through the rest of this section, so that the case may build itself.

Let's clear up something right away about the nature of the discussion we are pursuing. This is not a book of facts. This is an exploration of ideas that may help us understand why a society such as South Africa is evolving the way it is — so that, in turn, we may alter its course if we have the will, or at least anticipate its future course.

We pre-occupy ourselves with the collection of data. We obsessively measure social phenomena, such as crime. We seldom range beyond our empirical endeavours to search for the explanations of why the phenome-non should be the way it is. Actually, I go further: I believe that we spend the greater portion of our time — and I have done so myself — in quanti-fication and measurement because we know, in the shadow of our minds, that when it will come time for explanations we're not going to have any. In times and places where we have explanations, we know that these explanations are, mostly, shallow and useless. There's an easy way to tell: the ills we explain do not react in any way to our attempts to understand them — they just keep on growing. We have summits to explain the neces-sity for reversing unemployment and to make sincere pledges to do so — but unemployment simply carries on getting worse, regardless. We analyse corruption and make speeches about the necessity of eliminating it and we undertake to do so; but it gets worse. We track the growth of crime and write endless articles about it and call for more police and make new crime-fighting plans and re-commitments; and it gets worse.

So when it comes to explaining just how bad crime is, I intend to bypass, largely, statistical arguments. It is enough to register that South Africa is one of the leading places in the world where you can expect to get robbed, mugged, ripped off, cheated, defrauded, raped, assaulted, hijacked or murdered.

In any event I do not imagine I can top the farce over statistics already perpetrated by the government. In 2000 the Mbeki administration became so alarmed at the bad image that was being created by crime statistics that it leapt into action and put a stop to it … no, not crime, the statistics. It stopped issuing them. The statistics were "unreliable", the government argued, and a new method needed to be devised for collecting and collating them. A year on and the public outcry had reached such a crescendo that the government had to relent. The depth of the farce was revealed: nothing had been done about improving the collection and collation system … and the Minister of Safety & Security unconcernedly argued on the basis of the statistics to hand that progress was being made in fighting particular crimes.

It was an inevitability that the statistics would, themselves, become part of the politicisation of the crime problem. The statistics were doomed to become instruments whereby the various political interests sought to gain advantage over one another. The result of this was, and remains, just as predictable: the credibility of the statistics will dissolve. For my part, I am inclined to the privately expressed view of a senior official in the Department of Safety & Security, who said that, at best, the statistics showed "fluctuations at high levels".

In truth, if one takes a longer perspective — the only way to genuinely understand where things are headed — then the nameless official is unduly optimistic. Martin Schönteich of the Institute for Strategic Studies[1] has shown that between 1949 and 1996 the proportion of prosecutions arising from reported crimes fell by half, and the proportion of convictions by two-thirds. By 1998 the proportion of convictions rising from reported crimes stood at under 20 % for serious assault and murder, and under 10 %

[1] Martin Schönteich, *Assessing the Crime Fighters: The Ability of the Criminal Justice System to Solve and Prosecute Crime.* Institute for Security Studies, Paper 40, September 1999.

for carjacking, car theft, robbery, housebreaking, rape and common assault. Only two crime categories enjoyed a conviction rate of above 50% — drunken driving and possession of drugs, both crimes in which offenders are apprehended "red-handed".

In fact, a practised carjacker, setting out to perpetrate his crime, stands a less than 2% chance of being punished. That's not bad odds for an ill-educated young man who would rather run that minimal risk than labour at some menial job — should he find himself in the increasingly rare position of having one.

There's something else that's wrong with these statistics, something that renders them close to pointless for our purpose of understanding crime. It is that they relate to the criminal justice system, a system that comes into the picture only once crime has occurred. The police, courts and jails, essentially, "catch" crime and criminals once they exist. Admittedly, in an important respect the justice system is designed to have the effect of dissuading crime and criminals from arising in the first place — but from what we have seen above, the deterrence effect is in decline.

If a claim earlier in this discussion — that South Africa was losing the battle against crime — seemed exaggerated, I trust the matter speaks for itself now.

What we want to understand is the very nature and origin of crime. That's where the profit lies; that's the route to any hope at all of doing something about it. We need a new way. Whatever it is we are doing now, is working against us.

I propose, then, instead of a statistical account, to do no more than tell you what I have known of crime in recent time. You can then judge to what extent it accords with your own experience and impressions, to what extent you think it is representative, and you can place it in the context of our discussion as you think fit.

Julia Sibara is our housekeeper. She has a deep, inborn personal dignity. She believes in the power of good and the redeeming value of honest work. She sets her own agenda and prides herself in her crackerjack efficiency and rock-solid reliability. She lives in a neat shanty on the Cape Flats. It is fenced, has a newly-painted front gate, and a brick-lined path from the gate to the front door, flanked by two patches of manicured lawn together the size of a blanket. She is, in my opinion, hanging on to her old-time values by a grip that must be slipping.

You see, Julia raised her son, Hayman, with those values instilled in him. After matriculating, despite help from my wife, Madeline, and others,

Hayman eventually despaired of ever finding a job. He then joined Julia's long-time partner, Eric Mhamhi, in Eric's car-wash business. In the pre-dawn hours of 2 January 2001, an unruly group, some of whom Julia and Eric recognised as security guards on strike, pulled Hayman from his bed and into the street, accusing him of stealing a cell phone. In front of his frantic, traumatised mother and stepfather, they beat him and stabbed him to death.

Shortly afterwards, his murder was reported to the police.

A month went by, and nothing was heard. I telephoned the police and followed up with a fax to make sure they were aware that Julia and Eric had information about the identity of Hayman's murderers ... and that the police knew there were interested parties aside from the victim's family. On a subsequent call I was told the detective on whose case load Hayman's death was listed was "off with stress". Julia was not eager for me to press the police too hard. I felt certain she and Eric had been in an agonising debate about whether to point the police in the direction of the killers (we had dissuaded Eric, at the height of his grief and rage, from going after the killers himself). Such acts would almost certainly result in nothing less than an added death toll for the family to bear. We did not talk about this; to do so would have roused anger, grief and shame all together.

Nearly four months later, on 24 May, the police telephoned to say they were ready to begin the investigation into Hayman's murder. They asked Julia and Eric to come to the police station a few days hence. Again, we did not discuss the merits, or fears, about being seen to be helping the police track down the killers.

Julia told me in due course, in her stoic manner that gave away nothing, that she and Eric had decided to respond to the police's call.

When they did, the detective asked them for the names and addresses of the killers. Julia and Eric said they did not have such detailed information but could tell the police the areas the killers frequented, who their relatives were and the community groups they were affiliated to.

Nothing more was heard.

In June we read in *Saturday Argus* that the Western Cape's commissioner of police had told the provincial government's standing committee on community safety that Western Cape police were staggering under a 47 % staff shortage, and that detectives carried case loads of 519 dockets each.

We do not expect to hear more.

Let us pause a minute and look into the heart and life of Julia Sibara. Julia's contract with society has been broken — by society, not by her. She has given her best, but society cannot respond in a like manner. Julia cannot expect the state to offer her instruments of justice. Out there on the Cape Flats, Julia Sibara lives within the laws of survival, not the laws of civilisation. And Julia Sibara, despite the fact that she does not appear so, and has never said so, is angry. How can she not be? Even if she herself is not conscious of her anger? Her child, her hope for the future, had his life savagely taken from him before her eyes. And she can do nothing, achieve no resolution or satisfaction. She has to be angry at someone, at something; hers is a dangerous anger. It will also prove to be an explosive anger should it ever be awoken by a voice of the collective suffering of her peers. Yet she is angry not in spite of being a decent person. She is angry because she is a decent person.

The punishment of the innocent

A holocaust of moral degradation has struck South Africa. It has come in the form of the sexual assault and torture of the vulnerable: women — aged women — and children of both genders. South Africa leads the world in the prevalence of these crimes. Why is this? What causes us to be set apart in this way? What unique turn did our society take in its evolution to acquire this grotesque distinction? Why has it appeared to get worse after the putative miracle of our transformation from an oppressed to a tolerant society? And if it hasn't got worse since then, and is something that has always been here, percolating malevolently, then why hasn't it gone away since our transformation?

Like everyone else, I find it painful to live with the knowledge of the suffering of children and the aged. So, these questions have torn at me for some uncomfortable time. Most disturbing, I found, was the numb acceptance of these appalling ills. I don't mean to suggest society, any society, nor this one in particular, endorses such aberrations. Yet it cannot be refuted that there is a dream-like acceptance of the existence of these phenomena. I cannot help but think of us as primitives, in this respect, who unthinkingly accept that the rain god sends, or withholds, the rain — without our making an attempt to understand the causes and nature of the rain cycle. In just such a way do we accept the phenomenon of these evils, without the requisite determination to understand why they should occur in the first place ... and give ourselves a real chance of intervening to some positive effect.

Stung into action by these thoughts, I set out to look for explanations, discarding impotent conventions along the way. In what follows I report to you the discoveries I have made so far.

As a preliminary observation, a clue is to be found in the oft-repeated assertion that rape is not, in its essence, a sex crime. There is substance to this. If rape were merely an expression of uncontrollable libido, an over-flow, as it were, of the male's evolutionary drive to procreate, then rape victims would be almost entirely restricted to the evolutionary object of the sex drive — the female of breeding age. Physical appearance would be part of the breeding attractor, too. Neither of these is the case. Rape, especially in the sense we are interested in it, blights also the very old and the very young.

The contemporary predilection for explaining rape as the imposition of the power of machismo on the female is wide of the target by a big miss. It might offer a rationale for the male using rape to dominate the competing female, but it fails to explain its exercise upon non-competing females like, again, the very old and the very young.

What, then, is the driving force behind rape? There must be a powerful force and it must come from somewhere deep to produce so horrific an aberration. Whatever the force is, it must be commanding, awful, and lurk beyond the light of our consciousness. It must be in the shadow. So, let us set off on our search of it.

Half a century ago an extraordinary mind spanned the thinking life of Britain. With a remarkably eclectic range and an encyclopaedic know-ledge, Gordon Rattray Taylor, chief science advisor to the British Broadcast-ing Corporation (BBC), surveyed the history and condition of humankind — and left a seminal, one-of-a-kind work, *Sex in History*.[2] In it he set forth a view of the role of sexuality in shaping the psyche of society. It is a view that has become obscured by time and forgotten, probably because it was ahead of its time. In fact, the evolution of the collective consciousness since then has turned into a resounding confirmation of Taylor's view.

Every person is born of a mother and a father, and these two poles of influence determine, in the largest measure, the formation of identity from there onwards, whether it be by their presence or their absence. The for-mation of identity will, also, be influenced more heavily by either the mother or the father. A perfect equilibrium of influence is desirable, of

[2] G Rattray Taylor, *Sex in History*, Thames & Hudson, London, 1959.

course, but rare. In this way, every individual will grow up with either a mother inclination, or a father inclination.

This inclination of the psyche of the individual can be aggregated through a collection of individuals. Just as we did in our earlier discussion of the collective consciousness, Taylor asserted that one could arrive at a unified mind of society; and that mind would be either mother-inclined, or father-inclined.

Taylor coined the terms *matrism* and *patrism* to describe the essential character and inclination of societies at different stages of their evolution. In *Sex in History,* he maps those stages out on the broad *tabula* of Western civilisation. Even more interesting, though, are his definitions of matrist and of patrist societies.

Patrist societies have restrictive attitudes to sex, limit the freedom of women, see women as inferior or even sinful, value chastity in society above welfare, are politically authoritarian, are conservative and suspicious of innovation, distrust research and enquiry, are inhibited and recoil from spontaneity, have a deep fear of homosexuality, produce maximised differences in dress for men and women, are ascetic and fear pleasure, and tend strongly to father-religion.

Matrist societies have permissive attitudes to sex, promote freedom of women, accord high status to women, value welfare more than chastity, are politically democratic, are progressive and even revolutionary, do not distrust research, are spontaneous and expressive, have a deep fear of incest, minimise dress differences between men and women, are hedonistic and welcome pleasure, and tend to mother-religion.

We're interested in what Taylor says about sex. Patrists, he tells us, fear homosexuality. It's not necessary for Taylor to take us further into the explication of this phobia, although he does. We know that obsessional fears indicate a pressing presence of the feared object, rather than its absence. We also know that the fear is accompanied by suppression of the feared object, and we know that when the feared object finally presses through the cracks and fissures it always finds, it most frequently erupts in a perverse and damaging way.

Let's review what we have in our readily accessed knowledge about this. The Victorian era was unquestionably patrist. The father dominated the family and society; the mother was a pale miasmic being who kept to the inner reaches of the home, weak and often despised. Afrikaner society has been, until this generation, intensely patrist in much the same way as the Victorians. Traditional African society is deeply patrist; the father is venerated and the mother is relegated.

Those of us who have experience of either of these societies know well what their attitudes to homosexuality are, or have been. Homosexuality is despised and recoiled from. Homosexuals are, or were, propelled to the fringes of society, where they form a distinctive and generally abhorred and persecuted minority.

Let's leave an examination of the role of incest in matrist societies temporarily in abeyance. We'll return to it.

Taylor's mapping of patrist and matrist societies in the West is deeply relevant to us, as we shall see. You will note that to Taylor, writing in the 1950s, Western civilisation and England are interchangeable concepts. It detracts but doesn't destroy his argument, and there is a sense in which it is largely true — so let's indulge him.

The Middle Ages, with the Dark Ages as its earliest component, were a time of moral anarchy. The character that would be lent to Western civilisation by the gentle and learned Greeks was eclipsed at this time. The human spirit was oppressed by ignorance, feudalism and the erratic social hegemony of the church. Perverse movements flared, such as the flagellants and the children's crusades. Institutions regulating sexual behaviour, such as marriage, had nothing of the form we know them in today. Even Satan, in the form and character we know him now, was assembled in the Middle Ages from various mythological sources, mainly by Clement I. Wantonness and wenching reigned in the Middle Ages, and not only among the laity. Taylor quotes the smirky farewell speech of Cardinal Hugo when the party of Pope Innocent IV left Lyon after a visit of eight years' duration: "Since we came here we have effected great improvements. When we came, we found but three or four brothels. We leave behind us but one. We must add, however, that it extends without interruption from the eastern to the western gate."[3]

The plague, near the end of the Middle Ages, provoked a "wave of frantic debauchery" and Taylor disclaims hyperbole when he tells us that, from the point of view of a historian of sexual mores, the Middle Ages resembled a "vast insane asylum". (In a striking parallel with beliefs that have accompanied the Aids pandemic in Africa in the present day, it was

---

[3] Taylor draws the quote from H C Lea, *A History of Sacerdotal Celibacy in the Christian Church,* Williams and Norgate, 1907.

believed during the plague that incestuous sex with a virgin would render one immune to infection.)

In as much as the character of Western civilisation has formed over time, Taylor's view is that the essential characteristics of matrist and patrist societies entrenched as epoch followed epoch. Early stages of Western society, like the Middle Ages, therefore display as much confusion in signals and traits as they do overt matrism or patrism. Neither of the inclinations is especially well developed — that is something that comes in time, as we shall see. Nevertheless, the overt traits of the Middle Ages tended strongly towards matrism.

The contrast is vividly shown once the church responds to the moral chaos of the time, and manages to consolidate its grip on society and its mores in the closing stages of the Middle Ages. This is the age of the crusades and the start of the Inquisition — both overt, aggressively domineering expressions of hyper-conservatism and intolerance.

The church consolidated, too, its hegemony over marriage. It had taken until roughly the 8th Century to establish the idea in society that the church was entitled to sanction and regulate personal relationships, and until the end of the Middle Ages to achieve complete social authority over sex and sexual practices. In order to achieve this, the church had had to launch itself on a crusade of a kind additional to the proselytising crusades aimed at capturing Jerusalem, one of the centres where learning had been kept alive by Islam. The extra crusade was against sex itself. The church became virulently anti-sex, and evolved a celibate priesthood. The avenues for sexual expression were narrow, rigidly defined and ferociously enforced by the church. We live today among the dying moral embers of this fevered crusade against elemental human nature.

Patrism had risen to a high tide.

Then came the Renaissance, and the pendulum swung back. So many things happened in the life of the individual and, by extension, the life of society in the Renaissances that resonate with us here in the present. For one thing, the Renaissance was humanity's final break with the natural order of which it had been an increasingly ill-fitting part up to then. The great (re)discoveries of the Renaissance were the mind and the self. The Greeks and, to a lesser degree, the Romans had revelled in the mind before it closed once more in darkness; but their sense of the self was indistinct, and too intractably vested in their many gods who were little more than externalisations of the self.

The combined bloom of the mind and the self, liberated Western society from the spiritual and intellectual tyranny of the church. Art broke free of iconography, philosophy escaped from dogma, and architecture was liberated from Catholicism. Most of all, men and women of the privileged classes realised they could be who and what they wanted to be. Their limitations lay within themselves, not in external authorities. The eponymous Renaissance Man was the master not only of art, science and thought, but of himself. Indulgent and urbane courts flourished and merchant dynasties were founded. The sophisticates and victors in reason set their own course and standards in sex, as much as life. Courtly life, not to put too fine a point on it, became usually libidinous and frequently debauched.

The Renaissance reawakened true matrism from the half sleep it had fallen into after the destruction of the goddess cults of Paganism.

The church fought back. From the 15th to the 17th centuries, the clergy and the newly emancipated laity maintained a polite front in daily intercourse, but behind the scenes fought pitched battles for the sceptre of authority over the mind and the soul. The church targeted the most dangerous of the flowerings of the mind: science. Galileo's telescope was banned for a hundred years on the grounds that it infringed on God's ordination of man's ability to see. Galileo himself was forced, in a humiliating trouncing of truth by dogma, to recant his astronomy before the Inquisition. Magellan circumnavigated the globe, but the church stubbornly taught the flatness of the earth for another two hundred years. The Inquisition ended, officially, only in 1908 and the Index of Forbidden Books was abolished in 1966.

Patrism held sway, with matrism a social undertow, until the Age of Reason in the late 17th and 18th centuries.

It is in this succeeding epoch of matrism that our interest begins to concentrate. This is not the first time that the emerging matrist society of present-day South Africa has been compared with newly industrialising, 18th Century England. The accelerated movement of people from the land to the cities, the rise of an industrial working class, the shift from an agricultural economy to a manufacturing economy, led by an elite rapidly expanding its possession of knowledge and capital … all these have powerful echoes in South Africa, and many other developing societies, today. Taylor's work gives us yet another, more profound, reason to strike parallels.

Matrist characteristics rose steeply to prominence. The period is also known as the Enlightenment — derived from the high-minded intellectual achievements of the age. It was the time of Newton and Milton, the ascendancy of parliament, the social contract and the rule of law. It was also a time when men dressed flamboyantly and enjoyed using cosmetics. So much more, then, one's surprise at learning of the mindless violence that was a feature of life in the streets. Taylor says: "By the eighteenth century this violence had become so widespread that men scarcely dared venture on the streets at night: in Kensington and Hampstead bells were rung when parties were about to set out for the city under armed guard, so that all who wished to make the hazardous journey might join them."

Taylor draws on histories of the time to relate how groups of drunken young men would "sally out" into the streets "to hunt the passers-by and subject them in mere wantonness to the most atrocious outrages".

There is an unmistakable quality to the acts in which malice and cruelty are extruded into the realm of pleasure. One of the favourite "amusements" was "tipping the lion" — whereby the tormentors would squash the victim's nose flat into his face, then bore out his eyes with their fingers. A group known and feared as "the sweaters" would encircle their prey and prick him with their swords until he dropped from fear, pain, mental exhaustion, and loss of blood. There were the "dancing masters" who would make men caper by thrusting their swords into their legs. Finally, Taylor tells us, there were the "tumblers" whose malicious delight it was to set women on their heads and "commit various indecencies and barbarities on the limbs that were exposed".

Violence brought to the very mixed party of 18th Century England its siblings of perversion: impotence and incest.

It is worth noting that impotence, experienced both in the lives of persons and in the psyche of society, is a phenomenon that occurs in times of ruling matrism.

The phenomenon has appeared before, most notably in the Middle Ages. One of the main crimes that witches were accused of and persecuted for in the Inquisition was that of rendering men impotent. Most often this was achieved, in the mind of the accusers — and, doubtlessly, in the minds of the victims, too — by the witch making the man's genitals disappear. This impotence hysteria has continued to make its appearance through time, and remains with us today in a pervasive and virulent form.

Surprised? Don't be. My files contain several accounts, news clippings among other sources, of outbreaks of violence in traditional African communities where witches are accused of making men's genitals disappear. Frequent localities for these occurrences are the Northern Province of

South Africa, where witchcraft is rife; and Nigeria, where population pressure and resource stress and relative deprivation factors run high. (Nigeria and South Africa are also the places where news of events in society are most likely to make it to a formal medium that would be on my subscription list, as opposed to places in Africa where there is less media network sophistication — but that's another matter and adds to the point rather than detracting from it.)

Lest you think, though, that the phenomenon is restricted to traditional African society, I must fix your attention to the fact that the emasculating power that medieval witches were believed to possess had a name. It was called *glamour*. The application of the word, and not so much its meaning, has migrated into our own culture — attaching itself to women of bewitching appeal or beauty and to movie stars. These are the women who beckon to men, all the while reinforcing the knowledge that they, the glamorous, are unobtainable. This is the very essence of the frustration of desire, in other words, impotence. It is the dynamic that underpins much of the cults of celebrity that became such a prominent feature of the 20th Century — and show no signs of abating.

Taylor tells us: "The themes of violence and impotence run through the sexual life of the period in a horrid counterpoint, and ever more repellent steps are necessary to evoke somehow the shadow of the vanished potency." He leads the trail of disclosure along the path of these repellent steps: " ... but the *Schadenfreude* of the Age of Reason went even further: there were many who could only obtain the necessary *frisson* by seducing children far below the age of puberty." He then gives examples from the literature and activities of the time.

But wait. We cannot arrive at our destination without completing important parts of our journey.

We are tracking cycles of matrism and patrism in the evolution of society.

The matrism of the 18th Century gave way to the patrism of the 19th. The exaggerated patrism of the Victorian age exerts so strong a fascination on contemporary minds and is so well known as to require little description. Tales of the subjugation of women and fear of their sexuality — to the extent of dressing the legs of tables and pianos in the cause of modesty (quite true) — have entered popular legend. We made the acquaintance earlier of the ultra-patriarchal Lord Salisbury, who regarded all Englishmen and women outside the aristocracy as children whose best interests he was charged to protect.

In the 20th Century the wheel turned again and the West entered its most deeply etched period of matrism ever. The first half of the century was the transition time, and the struggle between the matrist and patrist forces became catastrophic. The masculine drive to power flared excessively and perversely in ultra-patrists: Hitler, Franco, Stalin — the bad fathers opposed by the good fathers: Churchill, Roosevelt, De Gaulle. This interplay was, in itself, a re-enactment of an earlier transition, the one to the Age of Reason, when the opposing fathers were Cromwell and Charles I, authoritarian, militaristic patrist and idealistic matrist, respectively.[4]

The second half of the 20th Century became a monument to matrism: the most permissive sexual age of all, women's liberation, blurring gender differences in dress styles, the rise of welfare societies, *laissez faire* politics, the pursuit of research, inquiry and knowledge, the glorification of spontaneity and exhibitionism, hedonism and the revival of religion that offered direct experience in the place of obedience to a remote spiritual authority. And, lest we forget what this enquiry is really about, a bourgeoning indulgence in child sex.

This brings us to noting one last similarity between 18th Century matrism and our society today, before we tie it all down to what we are seeking: an explanation for the grotesquery and barbarity being seen in sex crime in South Africa today. This last similarity is erotica and pornography.

Sexually graphic material is dependent on a medium, of course. So, in times when there has been no printing, no video and no Internet, the vehicles for prurient material have been absent. Not entirely, though. Twenty-two thousand years ago cave men (appropriately, I suppose some feminists might say) etched erotic poses on cave walls recently discovered in western France. Tiberius liked his pornography on vellum. So, we should not say that erotica and pornography would not have been popular in times where there was no convenient way of passing them around. But the fact remains that it was in the 18th Century that graphic depictions of sex started to become popular. A little-known subset of prostitution, brought to our attention by Taylor, was the availability of "posture girls" for the delectation of voyeurs.

Today, the adult film business is a multi-billion dollar industry to rival any other, with its own "Oscar" ceremonies and fan clubs adulating

---

[4] It would be entirely wrong to read these views as the *only* explanation of Hitler and other contemporary tyrants. Consciousness and behaviour are stacked in levels of reality. This is a discussion of *one* of those levels.

(glamorous?) stars; and pornography is the only consistently profitable and, thus, the most innovative, sector on the World Wide Web. The present day is a climax of the 18th Century's eroto-graphic dreams.

Right, that's the territory. Now let's see what kind of explicatory structure we can raise on it.

In the first place, the understanding that South Africa has entered an age of intensive — and, probably, accelerating — matrism is in itself enough to provide the explanation we are looking for. Incest, and rape of the mother, comes along with matrism. The two are characteristics always found in one another's company. It's as straight forward as that. The collective male psyche of society feels threatened. At the perverse end of its response reflex it hits back by reasserting lost authority through rape of the female archetype, the mother. This is why rape is not limited to women as objects of sexual desire, and is frequently directed at mother figures.

The random violence of Western society today, and South African society in particular, is a replay of the chaotic undercurrent of violence in the streets and ghettos of 18th Century England. Bands of young men are prowling the streets of today to manifest in violence the impotence that lurks in their unconscious and gnaws dully at their consciousness.

Devitalised voyeurs devour the perverse glamour of pornography to fill the void.

And, in the lassitude of the psyche, the extremists are propelled on behalf of the collective conscious they serve to the ultimate *frisson* of sex with the children that belong to them, or to their society; it's the same thing.

Let's be clear about this. The perpetrators of the crimes are the receptacles into which you and I pour the small elements of perversity that reside and swell in each of us. We do have the perversity. It is in the good and bad universality of things, in the yin and the yang, in the north and the south of our souls, in our light and in our shadow. It is the way reality, and we along with it, is made. The perpetrators expel and expiate the grotesqueness that is part of us all. They do it for us all.

If you're still reading, let's continue.

Why the need for expiation by the few for the many should be higher in some societies than in others will be clearer when we absorb the work of DeMause, shortly.

For now, here's part of the explanation. South Africa has recently emerged from a patrist past, and retains powerful elements thereof. This means that South African society has not produced its own pornography.

In addition, opportunities for the expression of deviationist sex have been limited or non-existent. Mind, I am saying the opportunities for expression of deviationist sex has been limited. Deviationist desire has been in plentiful supply.

South Africa has not — until recently, anyway — had the strip clubs, the sado-masochistic rendezvous, the meeting places for dominatrixes and their willing submissives, the orgy venues that are found in many advanced Western matrist societies. Even 18th Century society provided in this respect. It means that South African society has not had the benefit of the safety discharge function that such places and practices offer. It has been a dam without sluices. No wonder it has overflowed.

We have strayed, and must return to our line of argument. We left it when we said that the matrism of our age was in itself enough to explain the sexual violence and child sex of our place and time. There is more. South Africa, through most of the second half of the 20th Century, was significantly out of step with Western society. Self-evidently, African society was different. African society moved on its own evolutionary cycles and, for the modern period, at least, has been overtly patriarchal, where the social ascendancy of the male was beyond question. Several patrist distinctions can be found in traditional African society, the abhorrence of homosexuality being the main one. Afrikaner society, too, was markedly patriarchal. The European settlers brought protestant puritanism with them to Africa; then, cut off from the social evolution of Europe, it stuck to them. Afrikaner society, even that in which I grew up, was one of the most extreme patriarchies in the occidental world. The English-speaking sector of the settler population retained stronger European links than their Afrikaans compatriots, but they in no way kept pace with the evolution of the West.

A Rhodesian delegation led by Ian Smith, some 30 years ago, flew to Geneva[5] for crisis talks. One reporter filed a story about how the Rhodesians *looked*. The reporter was intrigued by their outmoded appearance — toe-capped shoes, wide jacket lapels, short-back-and-sides haircuts. One could pick the Rhodesians out of the European diplomatic, political and journalistic crowd by sight alone. In the same way that their very appearance had lagged behind the march of Western styles, so had their attitudes, their thoughts, and their social values. The same was true for white, English-speaking South Africans.

[5] I am only reasonably sure the locality was Geneva. I am relying on memory in this case.

The sum of this is that South Africa was a redoubt of patrism in a rapidly evolving age of matrism in Europe.

Then political change came to South Africa — quite literally, overnight. The exiled leadership of the banned African National Congress (ANC) returned to South Africa to establish their hegemony over African society, at first; and soon thereafter, over the country as its new government.

The critical factor is that the ANC leadership was, almost without exception, made up of sophisticated people who had become substantively Westernised in their outlook during the 30 years the leadership was exiled. This leadership made it its first priority of government to establish a matrist overlay on a still-deeply patrist society, black and white.

Whereas the civil liberties and practices that characterise matrist society had unfolded in a process of organic growth in Europe, the constructs of matrism were imposed on South Africans in a mighty, blinding sweep. From authoritarianism the society lurched to libertarianism. From one of the world's most oppressive political constitutions, the country leaped to one of the world's most enlightened. Homosexuality was sanctified in that constitution. Moreover, at least one acknowledgedly gay man was appointed to the judiciary to guard and apply the constitution. From a traditional role in the background, women moved without intermediate steps into positions of power: women variously became ministers or deputy ministers of security, agriculture, defence, housing, telecommunications, health and foreign affairs. The South African parliament, once the most patriarchal, vaulted again without an intermediate stage to the fourth greatest female representation in the world — after Norway, Denmark and the Netherlands.

All these matrist innovations shared one important characteristic: they were a superimposition by authority on a patrist social body.

It is difficult to come to any other conclusion but that the collective psyche of society was thrown into turmoil. The great shift from patrism to matrism, had it taken place organically, at a natural pace, would have been disruptive, anyway, for a society as resource-stressed as South Africa. As it has happened, the tremendous, forced, artificiality and speed of the quasi-transition has wreaked terrible havoc on the social fabric.

These observations should not be misread as a suggestion that the changes were not innately desirable, or that they should not have happened, or that the classes most susceptible to the disruption could have, or should have, resisted the changes. Not at all; at every level of society a move to enlightenment was long desired, and welcomed when it happened. It is simply that there has been a great misunderstanding of the true qualities of human nature, and the disruptive potential of the changes was grossly under-estimated and misunderstood.

When we stop to think it all over, we find that we can readily accept that an individual cannot successfully alter his or her nature quickly and easily. Much less, then ... and this is where our understanding broke down catastrophically ... can an entire society change quickly, easily, at the wave of a legislative fiat. On the contrary, when a society is hurled into psychologically destabilising circumstances, you can expect trouble. And we got it.

The rape of the innocent is the price of our ignorance.

Catching DeMause

I believe that the insights of Gordon Rattray Taylor are so important for our comprehension of our social ills — which, permit me to repeat, is our first step towards a solution to them — that I want to move on to the next part of the discussion about these infestations presented by two of Taylor's concluding remarks. In a summation he says:

> Before the Christian era, there existed two royal inroads into the unconscious: religion (meaning group experience) and sex, and these two were commonly combined. With the establishment of the Christian Church, the road of sex was closed to traffic, and the road of religion was heavily policed. The Protestant church, without opening the road of sex, gradually denatured the religious ceremonies until they offered little appeal to the unconscious. Today, the position has been substantially reversed: many people have abandoned the pursuit of religious experience, so that sex remains for them the only route to the unconscious. It is this that gives sex its disproportionate importance in our films, books and newspapers, and as a subject of gossip; this is why the perverted and anti-social manifestations today emerge as sexual crimes rather than in forms sanctioned by religion, such as flagellation. Always coupled with Eros we find Thanatos, for the penalty of the failure to love and create is the irresistible need to hate and destroy.[6]

The natural questions to arise from these views are: What is the future course of events likely to be? And: What can be done? Taylor ends *Sex in History* in this way: "The river does not change: it only becomes more and more characteristically itself. In the same way, we in the West seem incapable of finding new modes for the expression of our fundamental needs to love and hate, to build and destroy; we can only express them in a manner

---

[6] G Rattray Taylor, op. cit. In Taylor's mythological referencing, Eros is the light, creative face of the sexual impulse. Thanatos is the dark, destructive face.

which is ever more characteristic of what we have always done. We are ruled by the dead."

If one bears in mind that Taylor wrote in the early 1950s — the first edition of *Sex in History* was published in 1954 — the progression of events since then not only dramatically underscores his basic thesis, but validates his gloomy outlook.

In Taylor we have a cogent explanation for the violence we know in our time, and the nature of sex violence in particular. But is Taylor right? This is a question worth asking because it is critical that *we* should be on the right track in searching for understanding of the maladies of our lives.

So let's attack the matter from different angles; two more, in fact.

Over time I have devised a rule of thumb for testing the validity of ideas. If I find that different approaches from the perimeter of a subject lead to the same central conclusion, like spokes of a wheel lead one from anywhere on the rim to the hub, then I'm looking at the right wheel.

Psychohistorian Lloyd deMause has written extensively on the history of child abuse. In an essay in which he pulls together his views,[7] DeMause relates the surprising extent of child abuse in the history of society. He deems it "humanity's most powerful and successful ritual" and "the cause of war and social violence".

These are sweeping claims. Our discussion here, however, is not a suitable place for a detailed examination of their validity. Instead, I will give a précis account of DeMause's argument, liberally infused (and for this I hope I will have his indulgence) with what we have already established in this discussion about the functioning of social stress.

DeMause encapsulates his theme: "The main psychological mechanism that operates in all child abuse involves using children as what I have termed *poison containers* — receptacles into which adults project disowned parts of their psyches ... "

Let's take this at face value for the moment, and explore the area that DeMause leaves open for speculation — where the disowned parts of the adult psyches may come from.

Poverty is not only an economic malaise. It is a psychological disease. Poverty substantively emasculates the male. His role of the good father, who feeds, clothes, educates, entertains and indulges, is undermined by poverty.

---

[7] Lloyd deMause, "The History of Child Abuse", *The Journal of Psychohistory,* 25:3, Winter 1998. Also available at http://www.psychohistory.com.

The capacity to provide is closely bound with the masculine identity. "I need to be a man," a homeless man who had invaded land told a reporter who asked after his motives. "You cannot be a man without a home." The home he was building of found materials against government threats of eviction was for his wife and four children.[8]

Equally, the female's maternal identity is undermined by poverty. She is frustrated by being unable to provide properly for her child.

You and I may shake our heads in disbelief and condemnation at people who brutalise children. But we must remember that, when they do it, they are transgressing a fundamental law of nature — successful perpetuation of the species. They are also violating a fundamental trait of human nature — compassion for the child. Therefore, we should be more terrified of the force that is making them do it, than we despise them for doing it. Let's stay with the argument.

The corrosion of the primary instincts to care for offspring, effected by poverty, cannot occur without producing phenomenal stress within the individual. The stress will transform into guilt — and the guilt, as guilt does when it becomes unbearable, will demand transference.

The transference will quite credibly manifest as abuse — a kind of deep, blind, unconscious, primitive revenge, if you will — directed against the cause of the sequence of negative emotions: the child.

This is a dynamic present in many psychological observations, and cited by DeMause: parents who have not experienced love themselves, misinterpret their child's screaming as a refusal by the child to love them, just as the world has refused to love them, and just as their own parents refused to love them ... and they lash out at the child.

The child has become their poison container. The parents' pain at being unloved is projected into the child.

A chain of potently dangerous events is set in motion in abusive scenarios: abused children grow up into violence-prone adults; violence-prone adults form violence-prone classes; and violence-prone classes form violence-prone societies if the poverty from which the sequence originated is sufficiently pervasive.

DeMause, then, is a spoke that leads us to the same hub that we encountered by following Taylor — the abused child in a society with a high inclination to violence. Admittedly, Taylor is giving an account, essentially, of aberrant sex visited upon children, while DeMause is talking

---

[8] Louis Oelofse, "Confrontation looms, warns PAC", *Cape Argus*, July 9, 2001.

about abuse in a more inclusive sense. No matter, it doesn't diminish the argument. In fact it leads us to the work of the Swiss psychotherapist Alice Miller. In investigations that have resonant implications for the understanding of violence in South Africa in particular, and of the nature of social violence in general, Miller has attempted to draw psychological profiles of tyrants, and has written on the political consequences of child abuse.

Many worthy thinkers have written on violence in society. The majority work through the orthodoxy of explaining violence: they distinguish between crimes of need and crimes of greed and they describe the breakdown of values and social structures in economically stressed environments. But when it comes to explaining the wilful infliction of suffering, Miller notes, they fall silent.

Miller takes up the question that has nagged us all in various degrees of insistence: What makes respected members of society suddenly, and apparently uncharacteristically, act like monsters — or endorse those who do? The question is especially tantalising at the level of group behaviour, and Miller tackles it there.

She focuses on the citizens of Germany during the anti-Semitic horrors of World War II. Again, I have little doubt that Miller is teasing out questions we have all nursed, not least present-day Germans themselves. Are the Germans somehow different? Is there some inherent flaw, or *was* there some inherent flaw in their character which allowed them to go along with something that we could not envisage ourselves countenancing?

I have long cherished a view of George Orwell's that I read as a teenager — if memory serves, in an essay titled *England, My England* in the Penguin collection *Inside the Whale and Other Essays*. Purporting to explain why Nazism arose in Germany and not in England, Orwell says the reason is that if a group of men in outfits goose-stepped along an English street, the English would have laughed.

Like all the best humour, Orwell's remark points to a hidden truth. Once you've heard what Miller has to say, you'll know what it is.

Miller dismisses the explanation that the holocaust can be fully explained by anti-Semitism. Her grounds — good ones — are that virulent anti-Semitism existed in many other countries at many other times without inflating to a holocaust. Anti-Semitism, in addition, rode at high tide in Germany in World War I without leading to the excess of cruelty and barbarity it did in World War II. There must be a reason.

Miller goes back in time to the childhoods of the Germans who perpetrated or acquiesced in the holocaust. She draws attention to the fact that the turn-of-century era in Germany had a "Dr Spock" of its own. His name was Schreber. Dr Daniel Gottlieb Moritz Schreber wrote manuals on child rearing that had a pervasive influence on German parents of the time. Some of these tracts went into 40 printings, indicating that their ideas impinged on an entire generation. The ideas are chilling.

Miller and other modern psychologists have referred to Schreber's views variously as "a systematic form of torture with long-term effects" and "systematic instruction in child persecution".

In grossly inflated scientific euphemism Schreber advocated that infants be subjected to "physically perceptible admonitions". That means he advocated beating babies. Schreber assured his trusting audience that "such a procedure is only necessary once, or at the most twice, and then [the parent] is master of the child for all time. From then on, one look, one single threatening gesture will suffice to subjugate the child". Schreber advised this method from the very first day of the child's life — to inculcate obedience and to teach the baby not to cry.[9]

When the Schreber manuals were not advocating such extremes, they reflected the mores of the time, which were conveyed in other child-rearing literature, and are not much less disturbing. Parents were advised against the indulgences of kissing, cuddling and stroking, and the supposedly disastrous effects of spoiling. The prevalent ideal, says Miller, was rigor and severity. Emotional deprivation was its dark side.

In recent decades much work has been done that demonstrates the deep damage wrought on personality development by emotional deprivation, in animals as well as humans. Death results in severe cases. Miller's provocative point is that persons who were between 30 and 45 years old in wartime Germany were an entire generation profoundly damaged by emotional abuse and deprivation.

The abused child generally has a set pattern of reactions. The impulse to maintain a loving link with the parent dominates all other responses. In a tragic paradox, the impulse can be intensified by abuse. If there is no "enlightened observer" through whom the child can transfer its psychic pain, such as a sympathetic other parent, for example, then the psychic pain is internalised. Deep in the unconscious the child formulates a

---

[9] I have relied on Miller's quotation of Schreber from her article "The Political Consequences of Child Abuse", *The Journal of Psychohistory*, 26 (2) Fall 1998. Also available at http://www.psychohistory.com.

revenge fantasy. The fantasy may lurk below the level of awareness, until it is awakened.

Miller's suggestion is that a familiar figure to that generation of Germans, the cruel father, in the form of Hitler[10] and the state, sanctioned a collective catharsis of revenge — in an orgy of hatred and the destruction of human dignity.

Miller pursued the issue further, and found a study based on interviews with 400 witnesses to atrocities against Jews. The purpose of the study was to examine the exceptions to the rule — of which there were many: Germans who, like the now-immortalised Schindler, risked much to save Jews. The study Miller found is titled *The Altruistic Personality: Rescuers of Jews in Nazi Europe*.[11] It concluded that the only difference between those that persecuted Jews or stood by, and those who acted to stop the persecution or rescue its victims, was the way the persons had been brought up by their parents.

Millers views can be stated in this way: the values and methods by which generations of children are brought up has a direct bearing on the types of political systems they will endorse as adults — if we understand politics here to mean regimes ranging from the extremes of tolerance to tyranny.

Therefore, in the case of England, where meaningfully softer conditions of child rearing prevailed at the time, the goose-steppers would quite understandably be met more with mirth than mania.

In present-day South Africa, where child abuse ranks among the worst in the world, the implications are sobering, to say the least. An extrapolation from the researches of Taylor, DeMause and Miller, with which we are now acquainted, does not suggest that abused children in this society will grow up to be tyrants — although this cannot be discounted, and the likelihood that they will perpetuate the private tyrannies that have been visited on them. It does mean, though, that they are likely to be more inclined to support a tyrant, should worsening social conditions produce one, as such conditions produced a Hitler, a Mussolini and a Stalin.

At the very least, widespread child abuse in South Africa presages a society of tomorrow infested to epidemic proportions by violence-prone

---

[10] Hitler's own father, who abused him mercilessly while Adolf's weak mother cowered, was half Jewish.

[11] The work is not well referenced in the copy of Miller's article I have worked from. She refers to the authors as "the Oliners".

and criminally-inclined persons, all driven as much by a yearning for nameless revenge as by need and desperation.

When that time comes we will no doubt scratch our heads over the escalating plague of crime. Will it still be regarded as eccentric to look back at the childhoods of the generation of rapists, batterers and murderers ... being brought up amongst us now?

Hidden patterns of crime

We're in a discussion here on crime in society, and we've strayed far off the beaten track of such discussions. People like DeMause and Miller are careful to point out they are not saying that the explanations they offer are the only explanations for complex phenomena such as child abuse and forms of criminality. I believe, however, that without embracing a perspective such as they bring to the matter, we cannot comprehend this great challenge to our future in its entirety. Further, I say again, the tracks we've been on have not served us well. So let's stay for a while longer on what are still the by-ways of thinking, for they may soon be the main avenues of understanding.

The essence of our discourse is that we are peeling away the upper layers of impotent convention to expose the underlying patterns and mechanisms that create the realities that confront us. An astonishing example of just such deep-level idea mining has recently appeared, mainly in professional journals.[12] It is the inflammatory research of two American economists, John J Donohue III and Steven D Levitt. Their work, which they claim is "purely descriptive, not prescriptive" has been greeted with condemnation, outrage ... and fascinated interest.

This is their story. Donohue and Levitt decided to tackle the intriguing dramatic drop in crime levels in United States cities since the early 1990s. Donohue and Levitt were aware of the explanations forwarded for the decline: innovative policing (New York's famous "broken window" approach), tougher sentencing,[13] a decline in usage in some drug categories, an economic boom, etc.

Donohue and Levitt felt these explanations did not fully satisfy. For one thing, the downturn has not been uniform; for another, the downturn

---

[12] "The Aborted Crime Wave?" *Scientific American*, December 1999. *New York Times* reported it on April 14, 2001. The full study was to be published in Harvard University's *Quarterly Journal of Economics* in May 2001.

[13] It is interesting to note that, while crime levels are down on 1980 levels, the prison population of the USA is higher than ever.

appeared in places where there had been no changes in policing methods, like Los Angeles.

The two researchers set off with two known factors: the crime downturn began in 1992; and nearly all crime is committed by a surprisingly narrow social segment — males between the ages of 18 and 24.

Not being criminologists, thus not being trapped within the conventions of the discipline, the two economists had a flash of non-expert inspiration: they decided to go back to the time when the first of the 18-year-olds who did not turn into criminals were born. Their intuition was that they might find something in the social environment of the time that influenced the upbringing of the youngsters who might otherwise have turned out criminals, but did not.

They found nothing.

Fortunately, they did not abandon their intuition. They went even further back, to the time the non-criminals were conceived. This took them to 1973, and there they found a glaring social innovation: legalised abortion.

An astounding thesis presented itself: being unwanted played a meaningful role in promoting criminality in society. The corollary: a preponderance of children who were wanted promoted greater social harmony through lowered levels of anti-social behaviour and values.

Donohue and Levitt followed where their findings took them. They found that the uneven downturn in criminality graphs followed the 18-year lapse according to when different states adopted legalised abortion (different states did so at different times).

Also, states with higher rates of abortion showed greater rates of crime reduction. Donohue and Levitt reasoned, further, that the dynamic should extend not only to crime, but also to the manifestation of other social ills associated with the youth, like teenage pregnancies. It did, according to preliminary results.

The two investigators concluded that the use of abortion for preventing unwanted children in society could amount to as much as 50% of the explanation for decreased crime.

It's easy to see that outrage was triggered. Donohue and Levitt claimed that they had no agenda for or against abortion … and I might as well join them in the same disclaimer. Like many people, I am caught in the uncomfortable dilemma of fully endorsing a woman's right to choose, while regretting, deeply, that it should be necessary to do so.

Donohue and Levitt, as you may expect, have detractors who are numerous and vociferous — and they are not only anti-abortionists. Other academics have pointed out that children born to mothers who wanted abortions, but did not proceed with them, have a high likelihood of growing up in single-parent environments in which poverty and violence are present. Therefore, they are saying, the factors that promote criminality in the individuals concerned come after birth, not before.

For my part, it seems those that argue in this way are merely fleshing out the definition of unwanted, by describing what it entails. The point stands, I believe.

If the direction of the argument does not amount to an endorsement of wholesale abortion-on-demand, you may ask what it does amount to. My own conclusion is that it tells us we are on the right track in looking for the origins of crime deep within ourselves, our societies, what we think, and how we live; and that we will not make headway in the fight against crime until we find ways of tackling it on these levels.

Let's leave this part of the discussion, then, with a brief look at a group of people who are doing just that — tackling social illness at the level of its underlying patterns and causes.

Jeanne Miranda, an associate professor of psychiatry at Georgetown University, led a group conducting a study of poor people suffering from depression in the ghettos of Washington in 2001.

Her study was focused on the link between poverty and depression. We, however, have already become acquainted with the link between depression and crime through the ideas of Oliver James (chapter one) and we started the discussion in this chapter with the mechanisms of social stress and how they lead to depression and the conflictual behaviour patterns that flow from that depression.

According to a report on the Miranda project,[14] about 42% of heads of households receiving aid grants to families with children meet the criteria for clinical depression. The report states: "Depression rates are very high all around the world among people with hard lives, and these people tend to be disproportionately poor."

In the course of the Miranda study people who did not regard themselves as mentally ill, and who would not ordinarily have sought medical intervention, were encouraged to present themselves for treatment. Great changes were charted in the lives of individuals who progressed from angry resentment at being induced or enticed to the programme, and from despair at the hopelessness of their situations, to positive and energised

[14] Andrew Solomon, "A cure for poverty", *New York Times,* June 5, 2001.

persons taking charge of their circumstances and making meaningful changes in their personal situations.

Along the way, a simple yet reverberating insight surfaced. The report states it like this: "Popular wisdom holds that you need to address unemployment before you start worrying about the fancy business of the mental health of the unemployed. And greater prosperity is a good trigger for recovery. But it is perhaps easier and equally reasonable to treat the depression itself so that these people can alter their own lives."

The Miranda project was still under way at the time of writing, and conclusive results were not known. But from what we know already, I daresay we can make a confident prediction: the crime propensity of the individuals who pass successfully through the Miranda programme will be significantly lessened. That would mean, simply, that through intervention at the level of state of mind the Miranda project — or any like it — is a method at least as effective as policing in combating crime, and a method surpassing any other anti-poverty measure.

Adding injury to insult

The insights of Rattray Taylor, Lloyd deMause and Alice Miller may be read together as an explanation of a mystery in South African crime that has intrigued criminologists. The mystery has to do with the very nature of crime — or a large body of it — in South Africa, which differs in a significant way to similar crime in other parts of the world. It is a mystery that cannot be measured, so it is frequently overlooked by scientists driven by a need to calibrate and document. But there is no mistaking its presence.

It works like this. In the commission of a crime, a certain degree of violence is often necessary. In most cases elsewhere than in South Africa, the degree of violence applied is ordinarily no more than is necessary for the successful execution of the crime. This is a rough and un-quantifiable assessment, and relies anecdotally on the judgement of experienced police officers and criminologists. But it makes sense. Using more violence than necessary works against, not for, the criminal. It increases the seriousness of the crime. Thereby the criminal multiplies the severity of punishment, should he or she be caught; and no extra gain is acquired. So, judging and limiting the degree of violence in the crime is a form of instinctual risk management on the part of the criminal, and keeps the risks, to a certain degree, in the criminal's control.

We've all seen enough movies where the bank robbers react in panic, anger or dismay at finding themselves in an unforeseen level of involvement after one of their number has lost his or her nerve and shot someone in the robbery. The risk and rewards dynamic of the crime turns negative.

Tragically, in all too many cases, perhaps the majority, this dynamic is missing in South African crime. All too often the level of violence applied far exceeds that which was needed to complete the crime successfully.

When cars are hijacked, their owners are not merely held up — they are beaten or shot; often as an apparent "afterthought", according to some survivors and police.

When farmsteads and homes are robbed, it is frequently not only a robbery or a hold-up. Homeowners are frequently subjected to extended torture.

For this reason comparisons of some crime statistics — car hijacking, for example — with other countries tell only an incomplete story.

Where does this quotient of extra violence come from? What drives it and what are its origins? These are the questions that are frequently posed on this subject.

Of course, answers are forwarded, and post-apartheid payback figures prominently — not, I am sure, without good cause — in the speculations. I, for one, remain unconvinced. I don't think it explains enough of the phenomenon. It is an explanation based on a supposition that appearance of the phenomenon is in crimes inflicted on whites by blacks. I am not sure, however, that were a measure possible, it would show that the phenomenon does not occur in crimes perpetrated by blacks on blacks, or whites on blacks, or whites on whites. In fact, I believe that farm attacks by blacks on whites are more than equally matched by the horrendous inflictions of violence and suffering on blacks by whites. The fact that these are invariably triggered by insignificant misdemeanours suggests, again, that there is an underlying origin of the violence.

The work we have surveyed in this chapter provides, to my mind, a much more profound, inclusive and satisfying explanation. Taylor has demonstrated, through examples in history and a brilliantly constructed theory, the historical inevitability of the phenomenon. DeMause and Miller have shown how revenge fantasies become unconscious passions in people who grow up in the circumstances that so many millions of our children have done, and do, and, sadly, still will.

Bang gangs

We've slipped the moorings that held us to routine views of crime, so let's face another off-field assertion, this time concerning criminal gangs.

Criminal gangs are not symptoms of communities in decay. Gangs are how segments of communities organise themselves *after* they have decayed.

This perspective is detectable in a study on urban street gangs and organised crime by Irvin Kinnes for the Institute of Strategic Studies:[15] "Information from the Gang Unit of the SAPS (South African Police Service) suggests that gangs have become socially organised after the transition to democracy and communities that have played host to these gangs have remained socially disorganised." The broad approach of our discussion thus far is also reflected in a supplementary finding by the study: "The fact that gangs have become more organised in this period reflects the social status frustration which marginalized sections of the population experience as a result of the unequal distribution of wealth."

The true story of the hidden nature of gangs and gangsterism is revealed in the clash of the "good" gang versus the "bad" gang on the notorious Cape Flats, probably the most dangerous killing field in all the urban world.

The "good" gang we have already become acquainted with — Pagad, the professed vigilante group whose acronym stands for People Against Gangsterism and Drugs. When we left off our examination of Pagad last, we noted that it was a manifestation of the logic of society fracturing under the stress of inadequate and declining resources. We also noted there were further dimensions to the Pagad phenomenon and that we would return to the subject. So here we are.

The "bad" gang was a gang called The Firm, which became the leading element of a gangsters' organisation called Core, an acronym for, believe it or not, Community Outreach Forum. (What follows will make a lot more sense to you if you start getting used to such paradox.)

Since we are already partially acquainted with Pagad, let's look a little more closely at The Firm. It was headed by one of the country's most notorious gangsters, Rashaad Staggie. He was to die, bullet-ridden and in flames, amid the chaos when a Pagad mob laid siege to his home in the seedy Cape Town suburb of Salt River. By at least one account — that of his younger brother in the court case that followed his death — The Firm was aptly named. Staggie junior told the court they sold drugs worth up to R150 000 (about US$18 000 or about £13 000 sterling) from the house on a

[15] Irvin Kinnes, *From Urban Street Gangs to Criminal Empires: The Changing Face of Gangs in the Western Cape. ISS Monograph Series* No. 48, June, 2000.

regular day. Before his own death, Staggie's name was linked to numerous others.

To you and me, Staggie epitomises the bad guy in every way. But there are plenty of people, not criminals and not drug takers, who think differently. And what we can deduce of Staggie's own perspective defies the easy categorisation you and I might make.

Staggie junior told a reporter during an *in loco* court inspection of the murder scene, alongside the accused, that he felt no special anger or hatred over his brother's death. That's our business, he said, blithely. We're gangsters and we deal in drugs. It's dangerous business. We know the risks. This is how we live and this is how we die.

Staggie's own behaviour before his death was nothing short of amazing. One of the things he was renowned for was his practice of driving down the street of a decayed residential area in his fancy car. He would cruise slowly, and pull to a halt. He would beckon the children, ubiquitous in such streets. Go into the houses, he would tell them, and tell the people that Staggie is going to drive down this street.

Off the children would go to do the big man's bidding and Staggie would retrace his course down the street — still cruising slowly. But now the level of expectation and excitement was feverish, because the people knew what to expect.

Staggie and his henchmen would throw money out of the car windows.

According to Kinnes, Staggie could seed a street with anything around R20 000 in a single block.

The actions of an anti-social monster? Not quite. Self-interest? Of course. Were the same residents, stuffing money into their ragged vests, also terrified of Staggie? Sure they were. But the easy demonisations that you or I might entertain are starting to blur.

They go positively out of focus when The Firm, and Staggie, become the leaders of Core. At this time Staggie was running a loan scheme for the poor from a shop, and supplied bread to the needy. Core itself put it about that it intended to invest its money, would consider development projects in the community and offered to build a preschool for one community. It made donations, Kinnes tells us, to churches, charities and football clubs.

In 1996, at the height of democracy novelty fervour in South Africa, Cape Town residents, such as me, gaped and reeled in bewilderment at the spectacle of the gangsters marching alongside their low slung drug-mobiles, in a column of about 3 000, on parliament to demand their rights.

The phenomenon remains very much alive. It was not a peculiarity associated with Staggie alone. Another drug kingpin, Colin Stanfield, who has been apprehended with millions of rand in cash, was prosecuted in mid 2001. Scores of supporters turned up outside the courts, ordinary folk, housewives and beer-bellied men, waving placards proclaiming Stanfield a hero and a saviour.

All that remains is to factor in another competitor for the hearts and minds of the people — the police. By all accounts they split roughly down the middle: some with the gangs; some against the gangs; some for or against one or more gangs. A recipe for social mayhem.

If you're getting sensations of pre-set value systems cracking up before your eyes then, firstly, you are not alone and, secondly, you are getting the point.

The point is a simple one: nothing is gained by dismissing the gangs as the enemies of society and putting the cops on them. The gangs are part of society. It's just that society is fragmenting and separating into layers and sectors, each operating on its own evolving value system, and interacting with other sectors in complex ways. You may think you live in a layer that is not contaminated by the gangs. But that's only what you think.

The Checkpoint Charlie Challenge

It's the way we think that matters, I think

If a single motive can be said to guide modern Germany it is an effort to atone for the Germany of the past. In pursuit of this goal the German government has an extensive foreign visitors programme. What one may wish to know about the inner thoughts of modern Germany is laid bare, on request. My own request was to be exposed to everything about the reunification of West and East Germany that could be interesting or useful for someone from a divided society to learn. Here, in the next pages, is the best of what I learned.

The German border guard unit wore perfunctory, non-descript uniforms. Germany detested the border between East and West that divided Germans for the duration of the Cold War. West Germany did not want to accord the border the recognition of being monitored by either its army or its police, so the low-key border guard was created. The Berlin Wall etched itself into the imagination of the world as a symbol not only of a people divided, but a division in the human spirit. The Wall itself ran through Berlin but the East-West border segmented the entire Germany.

Because of the wall's divisive insult to the human spirit, the human spirit responded to the challenge of the border in ways that were glorious, tragic, poignant, exhilarating, inspiring, agonising. This can be readily seen in a visit to Checkpoint Charlie, the principle crossing point, where a museum houses many of the exotic, imaginative, desperate methods employed by those who refused to abide the wall, and overcame it ... no, transcended it.

Often, as in the following anecdote, it was only once the division had been transcended that the extent of the spiritual wound wrought by it in the consciousness of Germans became apparent.

One Cold War day, at a point along the border where both Western and Eastern guards spent much time within hailing distance of one another, the officer commanding the Eastern guard transmitted a rare, but not unfamiliar, message to the guards on the Western side.

Communication was not uncommon at all between the West and East guards. They learned to recognise one another as individuals, gave their opposite numbers nicknames and, ultimately, devised systems of discreet signals.

The East German officer's message was something the Westerners welcomed and prepared for, without actively encouraging. The officer let it be known he wanted to come across.

He wanted to abandon his life in the East for the lure of the West.

Acceptance of his intentions was automatic on the Western side. He was asked to delay while his West German identity papers were prepared. In the event, his defection was set for a particular Friday afternoon.

It took place without undue incident. It is not unlikely he had either the co-operation or good wishes of his compatriots at the border post.

He was immediately issued his identity documents. He was asked, seeing he was a military officer, if he would submit to a debriefing.

The East German had expected nothing less and he agreed.

He was then told, it being a weekend, the debriefing would take place on Monday. He was checked into a hotel, and given an amount of cash. He was also given a telephone number, and told to call it if he needed to. An intelligence officer would respond.

Late on the Saturday the phone rang.

"Okay," said the East German, "what's going on?"

"What do you mean?" asked the intelligence man.

"Well," said the East German, "as far as I can make out, I am not being followed."

"Correct," said the West German.

"And," said the East German, "I have ID documents, a passport, and cash."

"Correct. What of it?"

"Well," said the East German, "I could go the railway station and catch a train to Paris, say. Or I could go to another town. Or just disappear. No debriefing."

"That's right," said the West German.

"How can this be?" cried the bewildered East German.

Patiently, the former communist's new circumstances were explained to him — and this became a dimension West German authorities became adept in dealing with. The Easterner was told: "All these things that are troubling you are the meaning of your new life in the West. You can, indeed, go to Paris, or anywhere you choose, without getting permission — nor anyone knowing. In fact, it's nobody's business because you are a private citizen now. As for the debriefing, you have been asked to participate in it.

It can only take place with your agreement. You cannot be forced to do it. You have, as we say, the right to remain silent. We would, nevertheless, appreciate your co-operation. You see, in the West the opposite of what you are accustomed to in the East applies — your rights as an individual supersede those of the state, not the other way round."

The lesson we can extract from the poignant responses and expectations of the East German is that consciousness, containing within it the view of the self, is malleable and it is shaped to a large degree by politics and the society surrounding it.

Let's stay in the fascinating realm of the re-unified Germany a little longer.

Later during that visit to Germany I delighted at a laden lunch table in the many interesting tales of a tweed-jacketed, jolly professor who expanded on his studies of re-unification.

His group had investigated the spending patterns of newly liberated East Germans. There had been an expectation that the quintessentially Western attractions of cars, sound systems, televisions, videos and the like would be the most sought after.

The results of the investigation showed that these goods were indeed sought after. But they were not the most sought after. The greatest expenditure category for those adjusting to a Western life was clothing. Furthermore, the bulk of the expenditure was on men's clothes, not women's. This was a surprise, but one that made sense on further inquiry. The reason, it was found, was that men, primarily, were the competitors in the free economy of the West. Eastern men were catapulted into a mode of competitiveness that had become alien to them in their period of quarantine in communism. They thus manifested a deep psychological need to *look* as if, for starters, they were in the contest. Their self-consciousness about their dowdy appearances was greater than the attraction of the gadgetry of trendy home lifestyles.

It is instructive to note, in these anecdotes, that 45 years earlier, the Germans had been one undivided people with a unified character. The social and political circumstances that subsequently structured their lives turned them into different people, with different outlooks, prospects and capabilities.

Yes, capabilities. The Eastern regions of Germany are today struggling to catch up to the West and perform at similar levels. The medium-term prospects are not encouraging. Like physical wounds, psychic and social wounds are quickly inflicted, but slow to heal.

The trinity of tomorrow

We left the preceding chapter with a view of fragmenting society, fragments that are increasingly characterised by the value systems that distinguish them, locating different parts of society in different phases even different trajectories of evolution. In this chapter we will look at those value systems, and attempt to identify them and understand their effects on the way we live, especially in multi-phased societies like South Africa.

Even earlier in our discussion, we noted that a visitor to our planet would register the gulf between the rich and the poor as the great divide of humanity, and the underlying matrix of its political troubles. Clearly, an apportioning of humanity into only two categories is a distinction made mainly for purposes of argument, and to aid comprehension. At this juncture, we must refine the view another degree.

It seems that the world is gravitating to three major blocs of humanity, with many sub-sectors. Walter Truett Anderson describes it best in *The Future of the Self*:

> This world is no longer divided between two great power blocs and two great ideologies, as it was in the mid-twentieth century. It is, rather, a world divided along countless fault lines — economic, geographic, cultural, religious. It is a world of postmodern people happily doing their things; of modern people still obsessed with progress, economic gain, and organizational bigness; and of premodern people getting trampled and getting angry.[1]

In countries like Sweden, Ireland and Zambia, for example, the postmodern, modern and premodern are largely consistent throughout their societies. Sweden is largely postmodern, Ireland is largely modern, and Zambia is largely premodern. In countries like Brazil, South Africa, and India, however, the three modes of existence occupy the same space and are intertwined in complex ways. These ways create friction, and manifest in social destabilisations like crime and labour restlessness.

The homogenous groups above, I have had to qualify with the word "largely". The reason is that, particularly at the postmodern level, as in Sweden, the picture is changing. Swedish sociologist Professor Hans Zetterberg estimates that about 25% of the Swedish population is distinguished by emerging values that are in conflict with those held by the majority. In the United States new data are emerging that show an increase in segregation at the levels of school, work and residence. In Britain in 2001 a series of street riots, with a distinct racial and social class

[1] Walter Truett Anderson, op. cit.

overlay, revealed a surge of conflict and anger. In Paris and other French cities with large immigrant populations from former colonial possessions, entire districts are considered no-go areas by the police, to be entered in only the most exceptional circumstances.

Indeed, the emerging picture of fracturing suggests a social application of Mandelbrot's self-similarity patterning, whereby global categorisations are reflected right down through the level of countries and cities ... and, if one wants, probably also in districts within cities.

The implications of the fragmentation are difficult to overstate or over-dramatise. Some futurists now are speaking of a time, not too far off, when the broad scope of humans may come to appear as members of differing species. It's not as far-fetched as it sounds.

The wealth gap has metamorphosed into a health gap. In the last 25 years the World Health Organisation has registered nearly 30 previously non-existent, or undetected, diseases — including HIV, Ebola virus, Creutzfelt-Jakob and Hepatitis C. Researchers in the anthropology of disease think we may have entered a third epidemiological transition. The first accompanied the Agricultural Revolution, the start of the era of settled communities, which gave infectious diseases greater opportunity to reach greater numbers. The second came in the late 19th and 20th Centuries when advances in medical science and public health curtailed those diseases, and chronic and degenerative diseases superseded infectious diseases as the top killers.

The developed world benefited most, unsurprisingly, from the successful fight against infectious diseases, but considerable advances were made also in the developing world. Now it seems the developing world has become the platform for a resurgence of infectious diseases, many of them in mutated forms leapfrogging over medicinal barriers — others appearing in previously unknown guises.

The focus of the assault from the microbic strata is in the developing world, where epidemics — such as that of the HI virus — are surging.

The most dramatic feature of the epidemics is that they are altering not only the health of individuals and societies. They are shortening expected life spans. They are degrading physical stature through their absorption of bodily resources that might otherwise be more profitably spent. They are reducing the economic capacity of whole communities and societies by killing and maiming primarily in the economically active age groups. They are inhibiting intelligence and skills levels by hastening and intensifying the malnutrition that normally accompanies them; by eroding education through contagion of teachers and administrative personnel; by the shorter life spans that curtail learning and the transfer of skills ... and a myriad further disruptions that provoke or leech on one another. It is no exaggeration to say that for these entire communities and societies, survival and civilisation are at stake.

At the opposite, northern, pole of the health gap, where the privileged reside, nothing of the sort applies.

The developed world is entering the biotech age. The key to nature's blueprint for life has been found in the decoded genome. It's now a matter of time as humans learn to manipulate the code — thereby joining nature in being the designer of life.

One of the first steps is simple replication. We say to nature: anything you can do we can do, too. Animals, accordingly, have been successfully cloned; and at the time of writing, at least one clinic was singing up customers who wanted a cloned baby.

A senior biochemist confessed in conversation he would not be surprised if human cloning had already been experimented with in social environments where regulation and monitoring were not well out of government's hands.

While cloning itself seems an awesome concept to embrace now, the steps to a technology beyond cloning are already being taken — steps that will relegate cloning to the tentative, even crude, initial experiments in what will have become sophisticated genetic engineering.

Cloning of the entire genome of any individual is destined to be replaced by more sophisticated design interventions in aspects of an individual's genetic make up.

Stem cell research is promising to allow specialists to manufacture organ-specific tissue such as heart tissue, for example, to replace weak or damaged existing tissue.

The decoding of the genome has, additionally, opened the way for the fast-track identification of genes that carry human defects, like birth abnormalities and inherited diseases ... even inherited predisposition to disease like, possibly, heart disease. Once the culprit gene is known, it will require a technique already in development to "knock out"[2] the offending gene from the genome.

More complicated, but firmly located on the probability landscape, is the prospect of "knocking in" desired genes — offering the possibility of

[2] *Knock out* and *knock in* are the terms employed by biologists.

breeding a human with any of a portfolio of desired qualities, from brawn to brains.

In the here and now manifold advances in medicine are offered by present biological breakthroughs. From a more thorough understanding of disease and life processes to individually tailored therapeutic interventions, present-day developments offer a quality and length of life undreamed of — even during the great advances of the 20th Century. The generation to benefit from all this is already with us. My stepson's three-year-old son, Luca, is part of a privileged generation that will be the first to see both the start and the end of a century — this one.

The contrast between the south and north poles of the health gap are awesome. As this century matures, they will in all probability become grotesquely exaggerated.

You can see what those futurists with their admittedly exaggerated claim about humanity sub-dividing into different species are getting at.

In all probability, the majority of humanity will occupy neither the north pole of postmodernity, nor the south pole of premodernity. The majority will be a rumbling, grumbling, morphing, squalling, living buffer between the two. It will be like a giant transit lounge of humanity: accepting new arrivals in the form of societies emerging from premodernism; losing others on the backslide from modernism to premodernism; and observing the very, very few graduates from modernism to postmodernism.

These transitions are not only possible — they will happen. But the great clock is working against societies hoping for onward transition. The reason is the gulfs that will have to be crossed are becoming wider all the time.

To a significant extent these gulfs are the existing fissures that define the world today: the Judeo-Christian West with matching Eastern nodes in Japan, Singapore and, to a lesser extent, Hong Kong; the Islamic strongholds in the Near East, North Africa, Pakistan and, increasingly, India; the anomaly of a hybrid, rising global power in China; and the African and Latin centres.

Each of these has a characteristic collective attitude and agenda. Each conceives its purpose in a different way. Each has a differing scale of what matters most.

Our purpose here is not to go into a detailed examination of these differences. To grasp the point clearly, simply conduct a short thought experiment: think of what the Finnish are trying to achieve for themselves and how they are going about it; then contrast that with what the Taliban are trying to achieve for Afghanistan and how they are going about it. Now you've got it. The rest come in gradations of intensity, but the principle remains.

Our purpose is to recognise that these differing ends and means are pursued through different value systems. These value systems, or sets, arise as a product of the unique attitudinal orientation of a group. The value set evolves and re-enforces the group's uniqueness; soon it becomes part of the definition of the group's distinction; the value set then becomes the process through which the group pursues its vision of itself and its development.

Highly theoretical? Yes, it is. Let us then observe the practical example of such differing value sets in operation in our political lab — South Africa.

You only think you think you know what I think you know

It is common for whites in South Africa to proclaim themselves Africans. Indeed, it is a claim that carries a certain daring cachet.

There is good cause for it. The majority of whites were born on African soil. Most of them, probably, have never been to Europe. My own ancestor arrived at the Cape in the 1690s. If time is the measure, that makes me, and others like me, natives of Africa — nearly as much as it would make Pilgrim descendants American, and more than it would make settler families in Canada, Canadian, or in Australia, Australian.

Yet I, and others like me, by and large, have seldom taken meals with Africans and have never slept in an African home. I, and others like me, speak no African language; if an African came up to one of us and wished us a pleasant day we wouldn't know even *which* African language we were being addressed in. I, and others like me, were culturally nursed on *Noddy*, *The Famous Five*, *Biggles*, *Huckleberry Finn* and *Batman*.

I was educated in English (I mercifully managed to avoid playing cricket) and I studied the philosophies of Hobbes, Locke and Kant, and I learned the literature of Shakespeare, Milton and Dickens.

I once spent an afternoon in the company of an African colleague at an African community sports event. There was no other white-skinned person there but me. There was much merriment in the crowd and frequent gales of laughter. At no stage did I have any idea at all what was amusing the crowd.[3]

---

[3] My sense of cultural alienation was only deepened when, on the drive home, my colleague, Charles Ntuli, explained that the crowd laughed at the losers in the often chaotic races that were run.

So, while on a certain rational level I and the others like me are Africans, for me to claim that I am an African *in the same way* that my black compatriots are African is patently absurd.

Culturally, attitudinally and aspirationally, I am European. My habits and manners are more like those of, say, a Belgian than they like those of, say, a Zulu. The things that please me and displease me, if one could weigh them all, probably would end up resembling more those of the Belgian than the Zulu. Finally, and most importantly, that to which I aspire will in the final analysis resonate more closely with the Belgian than the African.

The best I can say about myself and my lineage in Africa is that it has made me unlike my European progenitors in some ways, but less so than it has left me unlike my African compatriots. In its greatest distillation: I am of Africa, and I am in Africa; but I am not African.

I am not unaware of the inflammatory nature of this view, nor of how I must expect to be pilloried for it.

In one of his better known speeches, South Africa's second democratic president, Thabo Mbeki, poetically proclaimed: "I am an African." It was more than a statement of the obvious. It was an affirmation of something potentially great and something desirable and necessary. It was a noble sentiment, and was perceived as such. Am I, then, and others who I damn along with myself, to be excluded, by my argument, from this noble aspiration?

I do not have a ready answer, nor an easy one.

By the same measure, after Mbeki claimed in another speech, for which he has been castigated without mercy, that South Africa was constituted of "two nations" — one, essentially, black; the other, essentially, white — am I to be understood as a supporter of his view?

While I accept that his critics rightly feel he did not express the ideal of a united society to which we all aspire, he unquestionably described what existed, and one can do no other than support the view. [4]

The nub of it is that my view and its antithesis, and, possibly, your view, and all the other views that exist on this matter, are conflictive. And that's just my point.

If you're still with me we can proceed on the basis that there is, indeed, such a thing as the Western mind set, and such a thing as the African

[4] Mbeki places emphasis on an economic interpretation of his words — one nation black and poor, one rich and white — in which there is room for statistical argument. I have placed a broader interpretation on his words, which I believe is not inconsistent with his intention.

mind-set.[5] Both are conspicuous in South Africa. The African mind set has hegemony in politics. The Western mindset has hegemony in the economy. Those of us who wish to see a successful future unfold in South Africa will want to understand the differences so that we may celebrate them, and respect the contribution that each can make to a vibrant national life.

Just as the underlying rationale of this discussion has been until now that we cannot solve our problems until we understand them, so the rationale now transforms into a vital variation: we cannot love or respect our differences until we understand them; and we cannot employ them as the generators of the third consciousness we must reach if we are to be saved — a subject we will discuss in due course.

The quintessence of difference between the Western view of life and society and the African view of life and society is contained in the relative values ascribed to individualism on the one hand, and collectivism on the other.

The West has made the sanctity of the individual the centrepiece of its civilisation.

African civilisation has made the good of the group its central focus.

The individual, in the meaning applied here, is a peculiarly Western invention. It is difficult for Westerners to step outside of the self to appreciate the full import of this.

Walter Truett Anderson[6] draws on the work of others to illustrate this basic, yet difficult to grasp, point. He goes first to Clifford Geertz:

> The Western conception of the person as a bounded, unique, more or less integrated motivational and cognitive universe … is, however incorrigible it may seem to us, a rather peculiar idea within the context of the world's cultures.[7]

In order to reinforce the notion of individualism's birth in the Western cultural crucible, Anderson quotes Saul Bellow, whose political incorrectness may be excused by his time of writing:

> Now, as everyone knows, it has only been in the last two centuries that the majority of people in civilised countries have claimed the privilege of being individuals.[8]

---

[5] It is my experience in engaging with many types of audiences on these ideas that the deniers tend to come from the Western mind set, while the African mind set welcomes recognition of one of its long-standing gripes.

[6] Walter Truett Anderson, ibid.

[7] Clifford Geertz, *Local Knowledge: Further Essays in Interpretive Anthropology,* Basic Books, New York, 1983.

[8] Saul Bellow, *Mr Sammler's Planet,* Viking, New York, 1969.

African culture, as did so many others, walked a different path in those two centuries.

Now, in the global village,[9] the paths have come together, and a social conciliation is needed. Nowhere is their confluence more greatly felt than in South Africa, and nowhere is a conciliation more needed.

In the Western view, society and its institutions are creations to be utilised by the individual for his or her own good.

The schools and universities are not generally thought of as existing for the elevation of the entire society; the view is rather that they are there for individuals to realise their potential and to prepare for careers.

The law is there to protect the individual and his or her property, and there as a recourse should any of the individual's rights be contravened. It is only in an academic context that the law is viewed as a characteristic, and an achievement, of society as a whole.

The economy is seen in Western eyes as an opportunity to advance the individual's material well-being. It is incidental that society as a whole would prosper if a critical mass of individuals makes use of the opportunities offered by the economy.

Politics is there to regulate the above activities, and ensure they work to the maximum advantage of the maximum number of individuals. It is axiomatic in Western politics that individuals select politicians, parties and governments on "bread and butter" issues — that is, on measures of how well the individual's material wants will be catered to. Voting on grounds of the common good of society is a distant, secondary consideration at best.

This overriding sense of individualism is located, too, in the institutions that exist to foster the above interests. As a result, the institutions themselves are perceived as having degrees of individuality. This means that political institutions are seen as properly separate from economic institutions, and both are seen as properly separate from legal institutions.

The African view does not ascribe the same value to the separation of powers in society among social institutions. The activities of society are seen in an indivisible whole. There is one social corporate body with many arms and legs. Those arms and legs must work in unison. This predicates success in society, just as a human body could not function if its arms and legs each had its own mind and agenda.

---

[9] The term was coined in 1962 by the Canadian theorist Marshall McLuhan.

The Western view sees political parties, lobby groups, government, businesses and business organisations, special interest associations, the media, the artistic establishment, the professions and humanitarian organisations as co-existing in varying degrees of constructive conflict of interests. Out of the balance of interests, out of the programmed conflict and the means for channelling it, arise the harmonisation of the social agenda. Or the greatest possible degree of it.

The African view is uncomfortable with constructive conflict on this level.

Flowing from the foregoing, the Western mind sees divergence as productive. Ordered conflict produces the energy on which the social engine runs.

The African mind regards divergence as destructive. Success is to be found in uniformity and cohesion.

The root is to be seen in politics. As the 10 000 lives lost in South Africa's political transition attest, there has been a catastrophic failure to distinguish conflict from violence.

In the negotiating chambers of the four-year transition to democracy, the parties manoeuvred for precedence and policies. Out in the streets, the political debate was hacked and blasted in fearsome bloodletting.

Because the Western attitude holds that divergence energises society, democracy is externalised. Different political parties represent different points of view. The parties contest and struggle fervently among themselves. But there is sense that they are all engaged, ultimately, in the overarching process of governing society. This sentiment is most easily seen in the concept of loyal opposition.

Because the African attitude holds that divergence endangers social cohesion (not difficult to see; it's almost tautologous), African democracy is internalised.

By and large, the post-colonial politics of most African countries have been straddled by a single, large party, with insignificant parties remaining on the periphery of the political arena. More often than not, the large party had its origins as a liberation movement.

Frequently, these large parties tolerate a degree of differences internally that is similar to what a Western configuration would enjoy among its different parties. The best example is closest to home. The ANC has a tradition of robust debate within its ranks, and at its councils. A familiar observation of insiders is how much diversity of viewpoint was voiced even under the leadership of as august a figure as Mandela. The decisive feature, however, is that the debate and divergence is contained within the party.

The African practice of internalised democracy does not manifest out of nowhere. It has its roots in the traditions of tribal and clan politics (as unpopular as it may be to draw attention to this heritage). The clan chief would preside over a council of elders who would hear disputes within the clan, and decide on actions the clan would take in various matters.

Accounts given to me by those who have been involved in such proceedings reveal that a great spread of opinion is indulged and debated; whereafter the council arrives at a collective decision under guidance of the chief. Voting is unknown. Consensus is manufactured.

Once more, the point is this: the breadth of the debate may, in fact, be as wide as it may be under any system, including any Western system, traditional or modern. But it takes place within the confines of the social body. The possibility that the divergent opinions could be *organisationally* distinct, and accordingly represented, simply does not arise.

In a similar way, in the politics of present-day South Africa, for example, the concept of loyal opposition cannot properly be said to exist. The governing party displays no sense of governing in conjunction with its opposition. The sense is rather that those who set themselves up in opposition do so to undermine the governing party, which must strenuously resist such opposition lest the national good be undermined.

It is a commonplace of South African politics that the president seldom meets with opposition leaders, and never to discuss policy or national strategy.

Of course, there are many reasons for a real animosity between government and opposition in South Africa. The trend of this argument is not to be taken as the only reason.

It simply is so that the atmosphere in the South African Parliament is distinctive for its real air of enmity. Furthermore, the extent to which the atmosphere differs from the parliamentary norm in the world is revealed in so small a thing as the introduction of applause by the democratic government.

To my knowledge, applause for members' speeches — which sometimes is even indulged in the public gallery — is unknown in the Westminster system and its derivatives in America and Europe.

The applause suggests to me the warm presence of African communalism, whereas its absence speaks of a chillier Western air of impersonal business. That is to say, the applause makes me uncomfortable.

The watershed between Western individualism and African collectivism permeates many other spheres of society.

In the commercial sphere the veneration of individualism causes the Western mind to see business as private enterprise. The prioritising of the communal good causes the African mind to see business as a social enterprise.

The Western attitude can be typified as follows. It is my decision alone to manufacture widgets on my property. I am free to offer to potential employees the wages they freely agree to work for, and which allow me to pitch successfully against my competitors in the labour market for the best workers.

Likewise, I am free to charge for the widgets what the buyers' market is prepared to pay. And I alone am entitled to pocket the profit that is created by the difference between my costs of land, labour and material, and the price I get from the market. That is, if there is a profit. If there isn't, it's me alone who bears the consequences of the loss and the obligation to settle the contracts I have with my employees.

If any of my employees do not like the arrangement, or feel they could do better, they are free to do so. They may set up a widget plant right next door, so to speak. This frequently happens. Moreover, it is an important part of how the system works.

The African view says: Whoa! Wait a minute.

Firstly, are the widgets what we really need now? Could our efforts not be better spent on something more useful and rewarding? Let the appropriate authority adjudicate.

Secondly, a grossly unfair, even inhuman, historical process places you in the privileged position of being able to afford the land, the factory and to employ the workers.

Thirdly, we know what you widget makers do. You get together on the golf course, or wherever you congregate to hatch your dastardly plots, and you simply agree not to exceed a certain ceiling in the wages you will offer in this "free labour market" you extol.

Fourthly, that profit you pocket is created not by you alone. The workers have an equal part, at least, in its creation. They should therefore benefit directly from them.

Fifthly, as far as our supposed freedom to go off and become widget makers ourselves is concerned, refer to our comments under "secondly", above. Furthermore, in terms of the ramifications of "thirdly" and "fourthly" above, our chances of becoming widget makers are closer to nil than to anything else.

Okay, I am aware that I have provided as much a Marxist critique as an African one — but, hey, collectivism is collectivism.

The African way embodies a view of the subordination of individual interests to the common good that flared only briefly, in historical terms, in European civilisation in the little more than half century of Soviet Communism.

The essence to note about the opposing arguments given about attitudes to economic enterprise is that the Western approach is based entirely on the entitlements of the individual, while the African approach is based entirely on concerns of the communal good.

In practice, these divergences can produce strange results.

A businessman of my acquaintance had his wholesale undertaking brought to its knees after several profitless years caused by endemic theft by workers. When he finally threw in the towel and paid off 250 workers, they danced ecstatically in the loading yard.

I was bewildered. Can it be, I asked myself, that these people cannot see they are plunging themselves into dire circumstances through their self-engineered ejection into a job-starved economy? How is it that people can act so contrary to their own interests?

It took my (Western) filters a long while to let through the realisation that the workers had greater pleasure in their collective victory over the capitalist than they had fear for their individual fates to follow.

In Namibia, I travelled into the remote reaches of Hereroland to visit a man with the unforgettable name of Uahuapirapi. He had become an outstanding example of Western entrepreneurship in a tradition-bound African society. He had created a dairy herd and was supplying dairy products widely in the region. Many thought Mr Uahuapirapi was a brave new sign of the way things needed to go.

I found a very unhappy man. Uahuapirapi was thinking of giving up the venture. The cost to him in personal happiness was too great. He explained: In order to husband his herd effectively he had to proclaim it his and his only; also, he had to declare within his society (the Western rules had no problem here) that the farm he conducted his business on was his property, his asset, and no-one else's.

In doing these things, he violated his society's deeply held notion of communal ownership of land and, he led me to understand, cattle. The profits he made did not negate the opprobrium and ostracism he suffered as a result. It just didn't seem worth it to him.

In a third, no less astonishing, example, a number of the world's large pharmaceutical companies went to court in South Africa to protect their right to price their drugs — in this case, anti-Aids drugs — as they wanted, and to protect their patent rights.

The South African government defended, claiming that the exigency of the Aids pandemic and the restricted resources of a government such as itself overrode the arguments of drug manufacturers. In doing so, the South African government spoke for a host of non-governmental organisations, activist groups ... and a substantial portion of world opinion.

It was a straight fight between the right to profits and the right to life.

It's difficult to believe, I know, but the pharmaceutical companies either didn't realise that this is what the fight was about, or they did, but decided to engage anyway. Either way, they were doomed. Even if they were to win, their victory would have been consumed in the flames of public anger and contempt.

If one clicks the fight one notch up the interpretive scale, the perspective becomes even more revealing: it was a contest between the ethos of the developed world and the ethos of the developing world. It is instructive to note that the ethos of the developing world won an outright moral victory, no matter what the intricacies of the settlement between the parties contained. We shall need this knowledge at a later stage of our unfolding discussion, which we will soon reach.

It is worth noting something else about this early high-profile moral victory of the developing world ethos over the ethic[10] of the West: the victory, as celebrated and as meaningful as it was, was a bitterly hollow one in practice. The South African government won the right to supply inexpensive variations of the pharmaceutical manufacturer's products to the country's Aids victims — something it had no intention of doing, and had not done up to the time of writing.

But we'll get to this when we talk about a hybrid consciousness embodied in a value system amalgamated of the Western mind and the African mind. For now, we continue with our examination of the differences.

---

[10] In this case the ethic is the right to profit. Dismissing it as unfeeling materialism could have disastrous consequences. The great advances in medicine are generally made by private companies, not by governments. The companies need profits to conduct further research and to attract shareholders.

They are present in attitudes to employment. In the Western mind, employment is a function of business performance. In the African mind, it is a social entitlement. It is clearly to the good of society that all who seek or need employment should have it; therefore it is up to government and business to provide it.

This fundamental dichotomy of viewpoint underlies much of what bedevils labour relations on the shop floor, and what warps communication between (Western-minded) management and (African-minded) workers. It is also a growing divergence of attitude threatening to generate a final political split between the ANC and Cosatu. The separate attitudes underpin their separating views on privatisation. The ANC believes the market should be allowed to determine the level of employment. Cosatu believes the social entitlement should be preserved.

The Western view believes the profits of business are the entitlement of the owners, the shareholders. The African view is that they properly belong to those who produced them, the workers.

Ambition, seen through Western eyes, is what makes the system tick. African eyes view it with suspicion. The striving for individual reward carries in it a sense of the betrayal of the common good. This view commonly manifests in wage bargaining when management is surprised to find their proposals of individual merit recognition rejected. In education it comes to the fore in "pass one, pass all" student campaigns against the academic elitism of university administrations.

Leadership, accordingly, in the Western view, is vested in individuals. In the African view it is vested in a class of individuals. This can be detected in the popular political rhetoric about "the leadership" and "the leadership cadres".

The media, in the Western emphasis, exists in constructive antagonism to the other estates of society. It has a watchdog role, as the cliché has it. The African emphasis is on the media's role in nation building. It is, or should be, a partner, not a referee. This fundamental split can be seen at work in the persistent miscommunication between the media and the South African government, and the rise of animosity between the two estates. The two met in a summit in mid-2001 to resolve their differences. Nothing useful was achieved, and no common understanding emerged. The fundamental divergence in attitudes, each belonging to a different value system, is the reason why.

In the broad social arena the Western attitude rewards uniqueness, regards the individual responsible for his or her self, and is cynical towards politics. The African attitude favours conformity, regards the government as responsible for the well-being of the individual and, according to the South African social analyst Lawrence Schlemmer, has an "overbelief" in politics.

Finally, there is an intriguing paradox.

Westerners are, on a personal level, cool, remote and constrained. They affect an air of indifference in their dealings with one another. Western society is more successful and enjoyable on an institutional level than on a personal level.

Africans, by contrast, are warm, spontaneous, informal and expressive. In their dealings with one another they are caring and are more likely to regard their neighbour's problems as partly their own. On an institutional level, however, African societies tend to be damagingly dysfunctional.

Racism — growing or going?

In South Africa today you can hear something mightily strange. You can have people, all kinds of people, tell you there is more racism in the country now than there ever was before.

What could they be talking about?

How could there be more racism in the new, free society than there was under apartheid, the synonym for institutionalised racism?

That's just it, really. In the past the racism was formal and overt. In a sense, one didn't have to speak about it, it spoke for itself; one didn't have to look for it; it looked for you.

Now the formal superstructure of racism has been removed, but many black South Africans feel — and some whites agree with them — that the sentiment that supported the superstructure lingers undimmed. In fact, in as much as white society has suffered a tremendous loss of status and face, it may even have a new ingredient of resentment added to the racism mix.

The biggest difference in South African society, apart from the abolition of apartheid itself, is that the voice of black South Africa is being heard as it never has before.

Black South Africans dominate the government and the country's television and radio broadcasting. They have significant positions in the press, in business and academia. This was not so under apartheid. This is thus the first time the country is getting it straight about what blacks feel.

In truth, if we were to try to measure today's racism against yesterday's, there wouldn't really be anything appropriate to measure it against. Not properly, anyway.

But wait a minute. Why are we talking about this? Wasn't the idea about getting rid of apartheid precisely that we could put the issue of race behind us; stop obsessing over it, to use the modern idiom; and just get on with the job of doing what has to be done?

The answer, alas, is no.

The nation's president has stated more than once that he believes the country's biggest problem is racism. Parliament's chief whip, caught up in an imbroglio over a car he was alleged to have received improperly as a gift from a company seeking government arms contracts, claimed that the press coverage of the issue was motivated by racism.

I must say that the president's assertion about racism strikes me, for one, as strange. I accept that it is his perspective on the country's ills. Keep in mind, however, that this land is facing Aids, the greatest pandemic known in modern time; is being crippled by poverty of staggering proportions; is being undermined by crisis-level unemployment; is assailed by one the highest murder, assault and rape rates in the world. In the light of the foregoing, the president's identification of racism as the biggest problem needs special attention.

And, if the governing party's chief whip[11] genuinely believes that the press's interest in a *prima facie* case of wrong-doing on his part is because he is black-skinned, then the issue of racism is going somewhere very strange indeed.

If, in the alternative, the chief whip does not genuinely believe that his physical appearance is the reason for the public interest in his behaviour, but that a cry of racism is a plausible rebuttal anyway, the society is going somewhere even stranger with the issue.

Whichever way you cut it, South Africa, facing the monumental challenges that it does, cannot afford a government that grossly misunderstands the nature of society, its direction and its needs. For, should a misunderstanding of racism misdirect an understanding of other serious social ills, the odds could become unwinnably stacked against South Africa.

So, let's begin with a question. Could it be that a lot of what passes for racism is, in fact, something else? Could racism have become, in many instances, no more than a convenient cudgel to be used for any general

---

[11] Naturally, he may not be chief whip by the time you read this. Or the matter may have been cleared up in some way. Clearly I am using these instances to illustrate a malady that supersedes the particular and the personal.

purpose? And, therefore, are we not in danger of letting a serious ill languish unattended simply because all and sundry has been called, mistakenly, by its name?

A cogent thinker who has had some interesting things to say about racism is Dinesh D'Souza, a researcher at the American Enterprise Institute.

D'Souza was a senior domestic policy analyst in the Reagan administration and, as such, is associated with the conservative stream in American politics. What this means, in effect, is that D'Souza belongs to school of American thought, on this topic, that says race can, and should, be transcended. He set out his ideas in a landmark book, *The End of Racism*.[12]

The book was much debated, and pitched D'Souza against the liberal establishment, which went along with progressive, and even radical, racial thinking in America. The liberal school held that race was too real a matter to ignore and should form the basis of public policy. One of the best-known outcomes of this thinking was the now-abandoned policy of affirmative action.

South Africans get a dizzy sense of going back in time when confronted with the American progressive notion of making race the basis of policy. It's uncomfortably close to the shaky rationale offered by the proponents of apartheid.

In this sense present-day South Africa reflects elements of both the "transcend" and the "recognise" schools.

The South African government seeks to stamp out racism, yet embraces meaningful segments of the progressive movement: affirmative action is one of the primary policy planks of the government.

The logic of this confusion can lead one into curious avenues of thought and attitude — such as when the South African Minister of Sport slammed merit as a principle of selecting national sports teams. If one rests one's weight metaphorically on one foot, one can quite easily see what he means: historical disadvantage has deprived certain racial groups of the ability to compete on an equal footing, and should thus be compensated through inclusion driven by broader considerations. Fair enough.

But if one shifts one's weight to the other metaphorical foot, it seems quite bizarre to send a national sports team into the international arena, while consciously having handicapped its ability to win, or perform to maximum potential.

---

[12] Dinesh D'Souza, *The End of Racism*, The Free Press (Simon & Schuster), New York, 1995.

Ah, how the value systems clash!

South Africa is picking elements from both the conservative and the progressive streams, apparently by impulse, and without articulating a clear vision of a racial policy.

To the extent that racial policy exists, it is haphazard, and drawn from contradictory value systems. For this reason, no South African has a ready grasp of what our attitude to race should really be. Should we be post-racists and deal with race by starving it of the oxygen it gets through acknowledgement and recognition? Or should we acknowledge and recognise it, and manage society accordingly? Or a bit of one, and a bit of the other? If so, which bit in which case?

Just as visible as the confusion is the underlying cause — our fear of talking about these difficulties, engaging our differing views ... and emerging with something we all understand and co-own.

So, let's see what we can learn from D'Souza's investigations.

D'Souza begins by driving home the fact that African American society is in trouble. African Americans comprise a disproportionate segment of America's poor. More than 65% of African American children born each year are born to single parents.

According to how we have already come to understand the dynamics the increasing gap between the *haves* and the *have-nots*, the problem in America is worsening. The proportion of African American male high school graduates who go on to college is lower today than in 1975. There are more young African American males in prison than in college.

The Johannesburg *Sunday Independent* reported that in 1979 the lowest socio-economic quarter of American society was four times less likely to receive a college or university degree than the remaining three quarters; in 1997 the lowest quarter was 10 times less likely to do so.[13]

D'Souza notes that when racial liberalisation got under way in America in the 1960s there was a widespread belief that racism would soon be conquered.

Clearly, this has not happened — to the extent that many African Americans now reject integration. D'Souza asks why.

He notes that the first reason is that the civil rights movement succeeded in assuring formal equality, but meaningful equality continued to elude African Americans as a whole. Equal rights did not produce equal

---

[13] *Sunday Independent*, Johannesburg, April 26, 1998.

results. For individuals there may have been a balanced relationship between rights and results, but not for the whole.

Then, as a good researcher should, D'Souza asks why, again.

That's where the going gets tough.

He divides this difficult part of the inquiry into several penetrating questions.

He begins by asking whether racism is a peculiarly Western idea. It is, he says. "Contrary to popular impression, racism is not universal." He says racism arose in the modern era of the West partly as a bid to explain "large civilisational differences that could not be explained by environment". The good news, he says, is that since racism has a beginning, "it is conceivable that it might have an end".

Was slavery a racist institution, he asks? No, he says. It was practised for thousands of years in virtually all societies, including Africa, where it survives today. In America, American Indians and free blacks owned thousands of slaves. What is uniquely Western, D'Souza argues, is the rise of the abolition movement.

Why did white liberals and black activists abandon colour blindness as a basis for law and policy? D'Souza says this was because the civil rights movement adopted the assumptions of cultural relativism — namely, that all cultures were equal. The civil rights movement focused on one great problem African Americans faced — racial discrimination, while ignoring an equally serious one — cultural factors (you can read: values) that inhibited African American competitiveness. This led to unequal results, which, in turn, led to affirmative action and racial preferences as means to fight inequality.

D'Souza asks: Why have charges of racism multiplied while clear evidence of racism has declined? He says there is a civil rights establishment that has a vested interest in making "exaggerated accusations" of racism. Quite literally, many jobs depend on the existence of racism.

Why is the black underclass worse off while the black middle class is better off? This is where the rubber, as they say, hits the road. D'Souza speaks directly:

> ... blacks with better skills and motivation have moved out of their old neighbourhoods, taking with them middle-class norms and social and financial resources. Consequently, in the inner city, civilising institutions such as the church and small business have greatly eroded. Moreover, the civil rights establishment has a vested interest in the persistence of the underclass, because the scandalous pathologies of poor blacks create the public sympathy that legitimises continuing subsidies *to the black middle class* (my italics).

Does contemporary liberalism have a future, D'Souza asks?

> No. Many white liberals are so embarrassed by low levels of academic perform-
> ance and high levels of criminal and antisocial behaviour by blacks, that they are
> destroying liberal institutions such as free speech, race neutrality, the legal pre-
> sumption of innocence, and equal rights under the law *in order to compel equal
> results for racial groups* (my italics again).

Is racism the main problem facing African Americans today? No, says,
D'Souza:

> The main contemporary obstacle facing African Americans is neither white rac-
> ism, as many liberals claim, nor black genetic deficiency, as Charles Murray and
> others imply.[14] Rather it involves destructive and pathological cultural patterns
> of behaviour: excessive reliance on government, conspiratorial paranoia about
> racism, a resistance to academic achievement as "acting white", a celebration
> of the criminal and outlaw as authentically black, and the normalisation of ille-
> gitimacy and dependency. These group patterns arose as a response to past
> oppression, but they are now dysfunctional and must be modified.

Then D'Souza interrogates himself: Are you saying that racial discrimination no longer exists?

> On the contrary. Evidence for the old discrimination has declined, but there are
> many indications that black cultural pathology has contributed to a new form of
> discrimination: rational discrimination. High crime rates of young black males,
> for example, make taxi drivers more reluctant to pick them up, storekeepers more
> likely to follow them in stores, and employers less willing to hire them. Rational
> discrimination is based on accurate group generalisations that may nevertheless
> be unfair to particular members of a group.

It is easy to see how D'Souza became the butt of claims that he was legitimising racism, especially when he talks of "rational discrimination". But
an honest reading of his argument does not support that accusation.
Besides, it is most unlikely that he, a person of colour himself (he is an
Asian American), would sweet talk racism.

Some of the parallels with South Africa are striking. Others are more
opaque; and there are some critical differences.

The matter of equal rights not producing equal results is cause for
thought. In South Africa, the blame for unequal results has been placed
almost entirely on historical disadvantage — in other words, the runners
in the race for success started at different times, and thus the early starters
have more experience than the late starters.

---

[14] Charles Murray co-authored, in 1994, the notorious *The Bell Curve: Intelligence and
Class Structure in American Life*.

Of course this is valid. But if South Africa genuinely wants to overcome these handicaps, it must scour the values discussion, of the sort that we have had above, to make sure there are none of the "cultural pathologies" D'Souza talks about present in this country. For, if there were to be such pathologies, then the responses of affirmative action and the entire empowerment programme — involving practices such as preferential contract awards and transactions in business — will ultimately fail because they do not address underlying problems.

What D'Souza has to say about multiplying charges of racism while racism itself has clearly declined has a meaningful import for South Africa. A dependency "industry" of racism is not present to the same extent. But the same end result is attained. This is done through the fact that allegations of racism have become a ubiquitous instrument of political interaction. The allegations serve many purposes — *vide* the chief whip — and are useful in achieving many ends. It is thus in the interest of many politicians and, to a lesser extent, others, to maintain a certain level of racism.

One can see, from Mbeki's ranking of racism as the country's number one problem and from the frequency with which he and other politicians allude to it, that imputed racism has become an important political instrument. Further, the more the governing elite needs to deflect attention from its doings or misdoings, the more it is likely to wield this instrument. And this, in turn, means that the vested interest in keeping a commensurate, legitimising level of racism alive will ensure greater racism.

D'Souza's observation that the African American middle class has geographically pulled away from the underclass, taking with it "civilising institutions", including small business, is, to my mind, the heart of the usefulness of his analysis.

The fact that the African American middle class experiences reduced levels of discrimination tells us that the chief cause for discrimination is differing value systems. The African American middle class adopts the values and behaviours of white middle class America, and the only difference soon becomes skin colour; and skin colour alone is not sufficient to justify, provoke or maintain discrimination.

Conversely, where discrimination exists, it is primarily a function of contrasting value systems colliding, rather than race *per se*.

What D'Souza has to say about the future of liberalism is, too, something we need to pause over. I think he casts the net too widely, for there are many other aspects to liberalism than the race issue; but let's give him the benefit of assuming he means liberalism *in this respect*. The equivalent in South African context is the rigid political correctness that has arisen.

It has arisen partly as a fear of eliciting the ready accusation of racism, which, as we have seen, can end a career or a business or a contract or a relationship. It is perpetrated by considerable sections of the media. It stifles discussion, such as this one. It stifles honesty, and it pushes the goal of a genuinely non-racist, contented society that much further away. It attacks the spirit of freedom that is the core of liberalism. Yet it is wielded, most often, by those who most proclaim themselves to be most liberal. It threatens the liberal tradition in South Africa and is made more pernicious by its masquerading as liberalism itself.

When D'Souza asks if racism is the main problem facing blacks today he is speaking, across the Atlantic, directly into South Africa's perception of itself. He makes it clear he believes it is the value systems, giving rise to negative behaviour patterns, that are the main problem. Because it is these that *cause* a reactionary discrimination.

While one might take issue with D'Souza on many fronts, his achievement, to my mind, is that he successfully removes what we call racism from a skin colour terrain, and moves it to where it belongs, a values terrain.

I find it hard to believe that people could be so crass as to discriminate on the basis of a person's skin colour. You may have concluded by now that I have a sceptical view of the judgement faculties of my fellow humans, but to believe that would be downright contempt. It is for this reason that the entire discussion on values has so far referred to Westerners and Africans, and African Americans, except where inappropriate; and not to "whites" and "blacks", except where quoting D'Souza (which is another of my criticisms of his critique).

Similarly, then, I assume that there is no-one so misguided as to think that D'Souza is saying that negative values are the only values poor African Americans have, nor that all poor African Americans have negative values.

He is making valid generalisations about classes of people. The argument does not apply to individuals, of whom there may be any type or number of exceptions. This is another demonstration of the fact that this is a values issue, not a colour issue.

It is interesting to note, too, the experience of African Americans in Africa. Many such persons migrated to South Africa after the democratic transformation of 1994. In their minds, it seems to me, they reckoned a black thing was happening in the motherland. In South Africa they had the prospect of a developed society run by blacks.

When they arrived — and this is a lament widely heard — they were dismayed that there was no "black thing" happening in South Africa. Because, of course, there is really no such thing. If a "black thing" exists at all, it is a flimsy and insubstantial thing.

An African thing was happening in South Africa. And the *arriviste* were shocked to discover that they were Americans, not Africans. The pigmentation they shared with Africans was incidental at best.

Before we leave D'Souza we must register one vitally important difference. He is talking about an African American minority in American society. Africans constitute a large majority in South African society, in fact the ratios there and here are an inverse of one another.

The reason there is a degree of parallelism between the experiences of African Americans and Africans is that the Western value system enjoys a considerable hegemony in South Africa, exceeding what would be suggested by numbers.

What we can further conclude is that the positive elements of the African value set are struggling to break through the membrane of Western values to take their rightful place in their own society.

Personally, I am genuinely looking forward to the day.

But, before that sun shines on us — and we will talk more about it in a short while — let us dwell a little longer in the shadow.

An important insight is provided by one of the great minds of the 20th Century, that of Sir Isaiah Berlin. As a Latvian Jew and Professor of Social and Political Theory at Oxford after World War ll, Berlin's mind grappled with the problem of Nazism — its origins and its true nature.

In his collection of essays, *The Crooked Timber of Humanity*,[15] Berlin describes the rise of what he calls "a kind of nationalist resentment" among Germans. He finds its beginning in 17th Century Germany's awkward relations with its fellow-European nations. In an age of Newton, Rubens, Galileo, Descartes, Vélazquez, Elizabethan drama and Louis XIV's grandeur and the creation of France as the centre of the arts, Germany had little to offer. " ... apart from architecture and the isolated genius of Kepler, original talent seemed to flow only in theology ... " says Berlin. "Life and

---

[15] Isaiah Berlin, *The Crooked Timber of Humanity: Chapters in the History of Ideas,* Fontana Press, London, 1991.

art and thought remained profoundly provincial." Then he describes what this led to.

> The attitude to the German lands of the advanced nations of the west, particularly of the French, seemed to be a kind of patronising indifference. In due course the humiliated Germans began feebly to imitate their French models, and this, as often happens, was followed by a cultural reaction. The wounded national consciousness asserted itself, sometimes in a somewhat aggressive fashion.
>
> This is a common enough response on the part of backward nations who are looked on with too much arrogant contempt, with too great an air of conscious superiority, by the more advanced societies. By the beginning of the eighteenth century some among the spiritual leaders in the devout, inward-looking German principalities began to counter-attack. This took the form of pouring contempt on the worldly success of the French: these Frenchmen and their imitators elsewhere could boast of only so much empty show. The inner life, the life of the spirit, concerned with the relation of man to man, to himself, to God — that alone was of supreme importance: the empty, materialistic French wiseacres had no sense of true values — of what alone men lived by. Let them have their arts, their sciences, their *salons,* their wealth and their vaunted glory. All this was, in the end, dross — the perishable goods of the corruptible flesh. The *philosophes* were blind leaders of the blind, remote from all conception of what alone truly mattered, the dark, agonising, infinitely rewarding descent into the depths of man's own sinful but immortal soul, made in the semblance of divine nature itself. This was the realm of the devout, inward vision of the German soul.

This "counter-attack" that Berlin speaks of — which is a campaign of attitudes, and is clothed in the "nationalist resentment" — festered through the years that followed to rupture the membrane of civilisation and erupt in the toxin of Nazism in the early 20th Century.

The parallels with the present day are disturbing, if one replaces the France of that time with the West of today, and Germany similarly with Africa. The West has its arts, its science, its wealth and its "vaunted glory"; Africa has "soul".

The danger is that if a lesson is not taken from history — in this case it is a history that has played over and over — and a balance between wealth and soul is not achieved, something could go seriously wrong.

The attitudinal counter attack of Africa could soon be driven by "a kind of a nationalist resentment" and its outcome will probably not be a duplication of Nazism, but it will be something ugly. This is unavoidable. What's more, the early signs are here, plain to see once you know how to see them. When we turn our attention to Zimbabwe, we shall see some of them at work.

This force in human affairs, like other forces, does not work in isolation and is seldom solely responsible for the probable outcomes that the historian Hobsbawm talks about. This attitudinal reaction to perceived inferiority ordinarily combines with resource stresses on other levels of reality — stresses such as poverty, unemployment, the relative deprivation of Oliver James, and corroding social fabric — all of which South Africa is experiencing.

These are conditions in which societies frequently produce a demagogue, a symbolic figure that embodies the frustrated, subliminal humiliation and anger of the populace. It's when that figure provides a means of discharging that subliminal humiliation and anger that society tips into madness.

The evidence litters history. Czeslaw Milosz, in his dark, poetic 1950s account of totalitarianism in *The Captive Mind*,[16] sees the same dynamics at work in Russia, a nation which, he says, "has never known how to rule itself, and which in all its history has never known prosperity or freedom". He sees Isaiah Berlin's perspective in Russia's fraught relations with the world and itself: " ... Russia's inferiority complex, which leads her to demand constant homage and assurances of her unquestionable superiority."[17]

It is not to say, however, that with our imperfect analytical tools we are reading the historical signs correctly. It is not to say that a march towards demagoguery and madness is inevitable. Not at all. But the signs are here, and this is a reading of them that we ignore at our peril.

The signs are here, I say? Certainly. They are to be found in placing Berlin's insight as template over our own experience — and they can be seen even more clearly at work if we broaden our perspective to a wider interpretive angle. Let's take "Africa" to mean not only Africa itself, but the developing world as a whole.

Let us see the values of the developed world in conflict with the values of the developing world. Suddenly the passionate anger and hatred of the devout Islamic world's "counter attack" on the godless West snaps into focus.

Comprehension becomes ours. In the shadow we find the means to understand the madness that grips the world.

[16] Czeslaw Milosz, *The Captive Mind*, Penguin Books, Harmondsworth, 1985.
[17] Listen to the SABC reporting the next time President Mbeki visits abroad, or a trade mission travels, and you will witness a nation indulging in just this sort of "constant assurance".

The secret thoughts of Africans

Africans won't tell you this, but they know something about the thoughts of Westerners that Westerners don't know themselves. It's a thing you have to be African to know. However, seeing as you've got this far, you're entitled to know it, too.

Africans know that Westerners will only give them their invisible stamp of approval once they, the Africans, have become Westerners with black skins.

It's in the way the West looks on Africa. It's a way that may be indulgent, contemptuous, dismissive, charitable, avaricious, patronising, or just plain duplicitous. It's a look that is never just square, and without an agenda. And the agenda always remains unspoken, even though it permeates every interchange.

The agenda says: you know what you must do; you must conform to our norms; you must be like us. Until then, you can come into the club, but you must sit at the table reserved for you. The bar is for members only.

And if you're an African, you know about the rules for membership. Oh, you don't know what they are, because no one will ever tell you that. You just know they're there, that's all. That's the sting in it.

Until there is some great declaration, until there is some honest meeting, some profound resolution, the unspeaking African mind will smart under the discrimination of unarticulated Western disapproval.

For this reason, somewhere in their secret thoughts, Africans sometimes wish the Westerners among them would ... how should one put this? ... go someplace else.

For this reason a new level of anti-white sentiment is detectable in Africa today. Where once it was hidden, it is now making erratic appearances. These appearances flow from the extremists of Africa but there are ominous signs that, as is so often the case, the extremists speak with the murmured and muttered approval of the middle mass.

At present, it is Mugabe of Zimbabwe, a despot who fantasises an African pastoral idyll, and Qaddafi, arch-foe of the West, who are speaking loudest. Mugabe has referred to whites as "dogs" and Qaddafi has urged them to leave Africa.

No one in Africa has said, up to this time of writing, that Mugabe and Qaddafi speak for Africans — but no African has thought it important enough to say they don't. On the contrary, at the closing meeting of the Organisation for African Unity in July 2001, African foreign ministers drafted a resolution praising Mugabe and his sanction of the illegal seizure of white-owned farms, and Qaddafi is the moving spirit of the OAU's successor body, the African Union.

In South Africa itself, nothing quite as crass is said — but the frequent and patently inflated cries of racism have led many whites to feel uncomfortable about what lies unsaid just below the surface of articulation.

Perhaps it is this very sense of disquiet, rising from their unwanted intrusion, that causes whites to exaggerate their patriotism, to express groundless beliefs that "things will come right", and to leapfrog the contradictions of the claim "I am an African".

It's at this point that African antipathy towards white Western arrogance and moral shallowness reaches an apogee.

The issue is the way whites want blacks to join them in projecting a collective amnesia.

One could see it this way: whites ensured blacks were shackled before the whistle blew to start the rush to the great banqueting table of resources and opportunities; then, when they had garnered the best for themselves, they feigned a great epiphanic realisation that it was wrong to have shackled the others … rushed over to remove the bonds and said: let's share what remains equally among us.

Who wouldn't feel aggrieved?

It gets worse. When blacks draw whites' attention to the gross moral imbalance of it all, whites say: "Yes, but that's in the past, old chap. Let bygones be bygones, now, and lets get on with today. Look ahead, not back." There's a defensible sentiment in there somewhere, but it doesn't change the fact that you've broken a competitor's leg, then invited him to a race. "Let the best man win," you cry.

The white response to black anger is so banal that a good number of whites have come up with an artful dodge to get around the whole uncomfortable business. It's called "the apology".

It's a brilliant ruse, and it works like this: you go up to the bloke whose leg you broke; you slap him on the back and you say: "Sorry about breaking your leg like that, old Bean. It was a bit off of me, I must say. But chin up, now. Starter! Let the games begin!"

The profound remove of Africans on this topic was illustrated in a bid to launch a nationwide apology among whites, when blacks looked on silently, one couldn't help thinking, in a mixture of amusement and dismay.

If one is not African, one can only imagine, additionally, how deeply galling it must be for the victims of apartheid to listen to its upholders today making tub-thumping speeches about the disgraces and evils of racial discrimination.

Heck, even I can feel it.

If, however, those apologetic whites had committed themselves to creating and maintaining, say, a free university, then we might have been talking about something different.

The final secret thought of Africans that I know of is their profound sense of betrayal. No, not their betrayal by their white Western counterparts. That we've dealt with above. I mean their betrayal by other Africans — the African elite of South Africa.

To illustrate this I need do no more than turn to this morning's newspaper,[18] as, doubtlessly, you could do yours when you read this. A short report at the bottom of page one details how the top two men in the premier black empowerment company, New Africa Investments Limited (Nail), earned R2.9 million each, over a 15-month period. But, the report went on, they had resigned after the company's share price had fallen 40% in the period. The report goes on to say they sold their shares in the holding company for R70 million and will get half each of an R80 million restraint of trade they granted the company.

Now, let's not misunderstand one another on this point. There's nothing wrong with a black elite. In fact, one of the very things wrong with this country has been the absence of such an elite. But this is an elite that has been created virtually overnight. And what an elite! The amounts of money that now flow within it are stratospheric and, I dare say, would raise eyebrows even in the august trading houses of The City, London, or in Fifth Avenue.

A beneficiary of this hyper-empowerment of my acquaintance went from battling on a monthly salary of R4 000 at a "struggle organisation" to a personal worth of about R40 million (in share options) in a matter of months.

The largesse that the South African elite is passing round within its increasingly self-defining ranks is wholly out of place for a developing country with a market the size of South Africa's.

It's a pathology of entitlement in overdrive, and it has a critical audience.

No, not a foreign, Western audience of disapproving investors. That's an important audience. But the critical audience is within South Africa.

---

[18] "Nail chairmen took home R2.9m each", *Business Day*, July 24, 2001.

It is the millions of hapless souls who thought post-apartheid empowerment might mean an improvement in their lives, too.

Instead, their circumstances have demonstrably worsened. There are fewer jobs for them, there is greater homelessness, and there is greater poverty. They are freer but less secure than they have ever been. They have greater freedom of choice, but less to choose.

The collective psychology of the majority of South Africans will be the main influence on the developments of the future, and understanding that collective psychology is the first step to understanding what that future might hold. Collectively, the majority of South Africans have been on a mighty roller coaster ride in the last decade: from the traumatised self-image apartheid instilled in them, a brief flaring of great hope illuminated the African soul, to be followed by a bitter disappointment in those hopes. Where will the roller coaster's momentum take it next?

A prominent black columnist dwells on the conundrum. Stirred by a government that he sees as able "to produce big and beautiful plans but which fails to see them through to implementation", Mathatha Tsedu[19] asks if South Africans "must accept that we have a predominantly black government that oversees the preservation of white privilege and which is only able to get blacks some crumbs ... ?"

The not-so secret thoughts of an African

I place the section under this headline in parentheses. I am not sure why I am including it, except that I am going to enjoy reporting it to you. It concerns the thoughts of an original and entertaining man. They are thoughts that are the very antithesis of anything you will encounter on the formal level of South African political life today. They are the thoughts of a minority; but I suspect it is a large minority, and it may be growing. It is an instance of traditional African patrism rampant.

They are the thoughts on the country's plague of crime, held by John Magolego, leader of a vigilante movement called Mapogo-a-Mathamaga, which Magolego told a security conference audience means "the brown spots of the leopard".

Magolego's group ferrets out those they deem to be wrongdoers, gives them a perfunctory hearing — usually just an opportunity to name accomplices — then administers a beating with a traditional *sjambok*. Magolego

---

[19] Mathatha Tsedu, "Black Eye", *Cape Times*, March 27, 2000.

says getting the names of accomplices is as easy as getting water from a sponge — "you just have to squeeze" a little bit.

He says tracking down perpetrators is straightforward. The word "suspect", he says, is "not in our dictionary". The community usually knows who the criminals are, Magolego says.

In any event, his mistrust of the justice system runs deep: "We've got to find you guilty before the magistrate finds you not guilty."

Furthermore, the criminals are usually rich enough to afford lawyers and, as everyone knows, "the lawyer will dance in your mind until you are puzzled".

Magolego deals confidently with anxieties that Mapogo-a-Mathamaga may get hold of the wrong person. "We say: 'Bring us the right person. Until you do, *this* is the perpetrator!'"

And as concerns the much-heard criticism that the vigilantes are not chosen by a legitimate social process, he scoffs: "We have selected ourselves because we prefer to hate crime."

He maintains Mapogo-a-Mathamaga has been successful in eradicating crime in areas it is active. Where you find a lazy housewife you will find cockroaches, he explains. Mapogo-a-Mathamaga is not a lazy housewife, he adds, almost needlessly.

Finally, in a truly post-apartheid reversal of perceptions, he sympathises with the white businessmen and farmers who are switching their hopes and allegiance from the police and courts to John Magolego and his cohorts. He sees them as a cornered minority, assailed by criminals and abandoned by the authorities, and says they support him "because they realise that I am the only one who realises that they are a human being, just like me".

I laugh merrily, along with the rest of the audience, at his rhetorical flourishes and his outrageous flouting of the conventions of social justice.

It's not a good sign.

The secret thoughts of whites

This incident occurred many years ago, in my earliest years of reporting. It happened at the Johannesburg newspaper, *The Star*, a fine paper in the South African liberal tradition. *The Star's* downtown offices face onto Sauer Street, and one day Sauer Street was turned by the city council into a one-way street.

The news editor, who was an honest man who prided himself free of prejudice, asked a reporter, who was an honest man who prided himself free of prejudice, to write a puff piece for page one.

The reporter wrote: "From today Sauer Street becomes a one-way going out of town."

He gave it back to the news editor, who sent it to the copy taster, who was an honest man who prided himself free of prejudice, who passed it to a sub-editor who was an ... you get the idea.

No sooner did the paper appear than *The Star* was deluged by callers saying Sauer Street had been made a one-way *going into* town.

You see, the entire white-collar editorial floor staff lived in the northern suburbs of Johannesburg. The statement, thus, that Sauer Street was a one-way street going out of town was as true as it was unremarkable. But for people living in the southern suburbs, which included Soweto, and where the majority of *The Star's* employees (and, probably, readers) lived, the opposite was true.

I took this to be a lesson in how prejudice lies buried in our perception, and I have always carried it with me ... the lesson, not the prejudice.

The impact of this is that the prejudices that all of us carry lie beneath the level of awareness. Those of us, white, black, whatever, who admit this and those of us who deny it — we all have it equally.

It's perhaps just a little more irritating in those who deny it most fervently but display it in their unconscious actions. I call it the Beetle Bailey syndrome as a result of a cartoon sequence my colleagues gleefully related to me when I worked on a community newspaper in a newsroom where I was the only white reporter.

In the cartoon the preppy, waspy, young white lieutenant is belabouring the phlegmatic, black, Lieutenant Fuzz with a full discourse on how free he is of prejudice.

"Yeah," interjects Lt Fuzz, "racial stereotyping is nothing more than a fallacious epistemological construct founded on an equally erroneous empirical dialectic."

"Hey," cries the preppy lieutenant. "I didn't know you guys could talk like that!"

"Jes' flushin' ya out, baby; jes' flushin' ya out," responds the laconic Fuzz.

In just such a way do the most well-meaning of whites find themselves perplexed and bewildered when they are brushed aside by blacks — because they are wholly ignorant of how, in their gushing eagerness to appear "liberated", they have isolated the black person, in subtleties and nuances of conversation, as "the other".

The most interesting thing about white Westerners in South Africa today, however, is "where they are at" in respect of dealing with their fall from social, political and economic supremacy.

In one sense it is not a pressing, and not a manifest, problem because Western values still maintain hegemony as the mind set everyone, including blacks, has to ascribe to and aspire to in order to be deemed a success. Furthermore, while whites have lost total hegemony in the economy, they have not lost it entirely. The economy remains a white-driven estate, albeit one that is subservient to the political management of a black majority government.

Beyond and beneath these qualifications, however, lies the truth that whites have moved on from mastership to having to work hard at a rationale for their hanging on to a corner of national life and national consciousness.

The dichotomy of experience was expressed by a minister of the Gauteng provincial government, Mondli Gungubele, commenting on a newly created national day: "To whites Freedom Day is a reminder of the day their own liberty and symbols ended. For blacks April 27 marks the beginning of freedom."[20]

A remarkable thing about Gungubele's observation is that there are so few signs of it to be seen. Of course, it is true that April 27, 1994 was the day the entire country was freed — whites in their own way, too; but on a purely factual level, it was indeed the day their special privilege and the symbols by which they lived, willingly or unwillingly, came to an end. Gungubele is right.

It is remarkable, additionally, that there are so few signs of the effects in Afrikaner society, in particular. For it was in Afrikaner society that the extremism of white reaction was located ... and appears to be no longer. At any rate, it does not appear to exist at the intensity it did before. Where has it gone, and why?

At one level the answer is quite plain. The black apocalypse feared by the extremists did not materialise. Far from it. Black rule has been characterised, more than by anything else, by its humdrum ordinariness; it has proved to be neither especially better nor especially worse than that of the Afrikaners themselves.

[20] *Mail & Guardian*, April 28 – May 4, 2001.

But I think there is something deeper than that. I can only conclude that we now know that white society in general, and Afrikaner society in particular, followed docilely the rule of the dour old Afrikaner patriarchs, not because they were white, but because they were patriarchs.

The wish for a father figure was stronger than the fear of "the other".

So, when Nelson Mandela — the arch father figure, radiating unbendable, old fashioned values and symbolically doting on children — took the place of the Afrikaner fathers, he rescued the psyche of the nation — white, black, whatever — by not only stepping into the father figure need ... more than that, much more than that: he replaced the bad father image with a good father image.

When one applies this template to the South African experience one realises how double-lucky South Africa was in its transition; and its miraculous escape from all-out civil war becomes easier to understand.

When people speak, as they like to do, of "Madiba[21] magic" it reveals they sense a metaphysical dimension to his presence, and it is doubtless this that is being referred to.

A tantalising set of questions presents itself in the post-Mandela era: Has Mandela-ism done its work, and the nation can move on? Or does the need remain, and, if so, does his successor, Mbeki, measure up to the requirement?

I believe we are too much in the situation to give answers in a proper perspective. History will have to do that for us. For the time being, however, it is difficult to sense an affirmative answer emerging.

There are disturbing manifestations in the course Mbeki has followed. In the unmistakable impression he has created of being more interested in his global, non-aligned and African agendas than in South Africa itself, he has presented himself in the figure of the absent father. His cool and remote personality, with his tendency to be analytical rather than emotive, emphasises his absence on what Rattray Taylor calls the experiential level.

The fact that Mbeki has mis-diagnosed the nation's illness in HIV/Aids, and has thereby been unable to empathise with the sick, who number in their millions, has exacerbated the un-feeling image. A psychologist may extract childhood resonance from intriguing public remarks by both Mbeki and his father, Govan, about how their political circumstances enforced

---

[21] Madiba is the clan name for Mandela, from the region of his hometown, Qunu, in the Eastern Cape.

remoteness between them. The same dynamic seems to be playing itself out in Mbeki's inability to "connect" with the nation he leads.

The upshot of all of this is to leave the white Western state of mind in a limbo of unknowing, and a sensed, but not articulated, yearning for a resolution that remains forever out of reach.

In this miasma, and driven by the experiences of crime and declining opportunities, whites are leaving the country in significant numbers. No one knows for sure what these numbers are. There is no obligation on South Africans departing the country for good to state that that is what they are doing, and one may readily imagine the emigrants would keep their options open by not declaring their intent. Inquiries at popular destinations for South African immigrants always show many more South Africans arriving for permanent residence than the South African departure figures show. The ratio can be two-to-one or more.

The exact figures don't matter. The immigrants fall into the higher socio-economic brackets and the country is being bled of homegrown know-how that is not being matched by immigrants from elsewhere. One survey showed that around 41% of top business executives would take the opportunity to leave the country if they were presented with one.[22] It is here that the invisible, but true, damage of emigration lies.

It is a condition that goes back, curiously, to medieval monasteries. It is known as acedia. I reported it in *When Mandela Goes* and repeat it here because of its relevance, and because of the degree to which it has grown since then.

'Acedia' is the Latin word for a state of sloth or apathy. I have also called it the departing monk syndrome, because that is how it is triggered. An individual monk may become dissatisfied with the conditions in a particular monastery. For some time he voices his displeasure, then he leaves. The interesting thing is not in the leaving of the monk, but in what he leaves behind him.

The remaining monks are plunged into a state of acedia. The departure of the monk has set off their own disquiet. They suspect that he has seen deeper and further into the nature of things than they have, and that they should be doing what he is doing. Whatever the case, they are plunged into uncertainty and lassitude.

White South Africa is acutely acedic; it is suffering a bad case of departing monk syndrome. The symptoms are the lack of domestic investment

---

[22] *Business Report,* August 31, 2000.

and the flight of capital. Plagued by indecision, whites do not commit more than they need to in order to maintain holding operations in their domestic and business lives. If they are fortunate enough to be able to, they export their capital[23] while they themselves linger in limbo. Leading the way in this regard have been some of South Africa's biggest corporations. Rembrandt, SA Breweries, Anglo-American, De Beers, Liberty Life, Old Mutual and scores of lesser-known entities have effectively exported themselves by relocating their main operations outside South Africa.

The spiritual suspension that characterises the state of mind of most of white South Africans was compounded by the failure of the Truth and Reconciliation Commission to affect a genuine catharsis, at least among whites. The TRC's primary achievement was to provide a forum for victims of apartheid brutality to have their stories heard — thereby helping, in some small way, to alleviate their burden. But that's where the focus remained, in the main.

The TRC saw an appalling parade of the thugs of apartheid, the torturers and killers, the blunt human instruments and evil footmen. With rare exceptions, those in whose name they operated appeared only to make exculpatory political statements.

The result was that whites wrote off those who did appear as mavericks who had overstepped the mark. This treacherous minority, who so nearly gave all of us a bad name, deserves whatever punishment is heaped on them: that was the sentiment.

The TRC failed to reveal the true dynamic of such situations. It has been demonstrated by the historian Ian Kershaw in his exhaustive biography of Hitler, and description of his time.[24] Kershaw's account of fascism in Germany reveals not how much Hitler did in the perpetration of evil — but how little he needed to do. Most of the horrors were committed by others in his name, others who wished to please him. Nevertheless, Hitler remains the great "legitimiser" of the evils of Nazism.

Just so in apartheid. The excesses were committed without direct orders in many cases. They were committed by those who knew what would be tolerated, or even actively or passively approved. Those in whose name the excesses were committed, are not exonerated.

---

[23] According to the Finance Ministry, 73 814 people sent R17.4 billion out of the country between July 1997 and December 2000. This was substantially higher than the value of foreign investment in the period.

[24] Ian Kershaw, *Hitler: Hubris 1889–1936 (vol 1)* 1998, and *Hitler: Nemesis 1936–1945 (vol 2)* 2000, both W W Norton & Co, Inc. Scranton, USA.

Yet, this dynamic did not surface at the TRC proceedings.

As a consequence, the paradoxical effect was to reinforce white evasion of collective culpability. This, in turn, means that white South Africa has not yet confronted itself over apartheid and cannot achieve "closure".

In this way, the Western mind in Africa floats between moorings. It is beset by a suspicion that it is needed, but silently resented; it is uncertain about its beliefs and unresolved in its intentions. It is Waiting for Godot.

South Africa's binary brain

South Africa's problems have always been cast in terms of black and white, right and wrong, left and right, stay or go. The divisions have been starker, and more absolute, than they have been in societies at a greater degree of equilibrium.

Additionally, it seems that our brains work most easily in polar opposites: we understand our spatial world in terms of up and down, above and below, in front of and behind, north and south, east and west; our moral universe in terms of good and evil, right and wrong, heaven and hell; even ourselves we see as happy or sad, loving or hating, accepting or rejecting, conforming or rebelling.

The trouble is, life's not like that. Living comes in shades of grey.

But the South African experience, combined with the natural construction of our thoughts, has led South Africans into the quick sands of a thought trap. South Africans, perhaps more than others, are prone to think in bi-polar terms.

Therefore, you are either with us or against us; you are a friend or you are an enemy.

Once again, South Africa's history makes it easy to understand this foible of thought. You could only be for apartheid or against it. You couldn't be a little bit for, or a little bit against it. You either believed that black South Africans should have the vote, or they shouldn't have the vote. There wasn't a true half measure.

As a news reporter in those times, it was sometimes a passing amusement to me when I realised that some in the white National Party took me to be an ANC partisan, and some in the ANC took me to be a National Party partisan. It seemed that no one was open to the most plausible view — that there were a great many people who were, quite properly, partisan to neither group, and that I was a member of that group.

I realised early in my career that no political party was ever likely to have an exclusive lien on moral correctitude. I was happy to serve, instead, the ethics of journalism, where it mattered not *who* was right, but *what* was right. It seemed to me a much nobler thing.

The trap of bi-polar thinking has persisted into the present day. It is a significant inhibitor to positive social intercourse.

The us-and-them pattern of thought places people in the political arena on either side of a divide that cannot be breached. It causes an excessive sensitivity to criticism, for any criticism that does not come from within your own camp comes, by definition, from your enemy and is therefore an attack. The attack has to be repulsed. The critical ideas are seldom weighed.

It impedes a constructive understanding of political opposition. It discriminates where discrimination is not wanted. And it robs the whole of a vitality it could have by embracing its differing parts.

The view that holds "if you're not with us, you're against us" deprives the national debate of intellectual depth. This happens when any critic of the new society is automatically dismissed as a proponent of the old. Little or no room is made for the truth that the new society had the choice of taking on many forms; and it is not axiomatic that the form it has chosen is the right one.

The drift of the intellectual life of South Africa is threatening to violate Adlai Stevenson's definition of a free society: " … a place where it's safe to be unpopular".

Vibrant debate and constant vigilance are the hallmarks of sound progress.

The birth of a third consciousness

A prominent psychiatrist and Jungian analyst, visiting from America, lectured in Cape Town not long ago. He spoke with depth and insight about how the South African experience had impressed itself on him. In the course of doing so, he made this remark: "The First World has lost its story."

His point was that in South Africa he had found a place that *did* have a story. One's intuition leads one to a ready understanding of what he was trying to convey; and, I daresay, one agrees readily.

There is something about the sterility and the ennui of life in the West that tells one that the story that has been told — and it's a great one — is now over. There is something about the quiet desperation of Westerners in their search for salvation in everything from drugs, kooky religion to status possessions that tells one they've lost the plot. In fact, the fact that "losing the plot" has become a popular idiom tells one a lot.

The novelist V S Naipaul has castigated Britain as a mediocre society that "celebrates its mediocrity". Another commentator, in a memorable phrase, referred to modern Britain as "superficially sophisticated". The writer P W Martin[25] says the West has made freedom its lodestar, and has pursued it without question, but has yet to face the question of what it wants the freedom for.

> When freedom is threatened we spring to its defence. But when freedom is secured we are at a loss what to do with it. As a consequence we win the wars but lose the peace. If we are ever to win the peace we have to know what freedom is for.

Martin wrote this in 1955. We are more alienated from the answer now than we were then.

There is a consensus among the great historians that Western civilisation has passed its apogee. The greatest student of civilisations, Toynbee, believes ours has arrived at "a time of troubles". He and his like believe that the West has some while since stopped making meaningful civilisational advances. We have come to confuse technological progress with civilisational advance. Hobsbawm believes our age is in the grip of technologically sophisticated barbarism.

Neither of these thinkers believes that Western society is at its end, that in time to come its great cities will be cold embers that a future civilisation will pick over. Rather, the expectation, voiced so eloquently by Jung, is of a great spiritual revival.

Spurred by such a revival, humanity will enter a new phase in the evolution of consciousness.

But where will it come from? What will the mechanism be?

The African value set could be the catalyst. The potential, at least, is there.

Bizarre? Impossible? Ridiculous?

Maybe.

Then again, the notion is well established that social progress is made when two great cultures collide and form a hybrid. The hybrid is energised by the best each of the constituents has to offer, as well as by the pruning away of the dross of each. There is both destruction and creation in the meeting of cultures, traditions and values. This is the essence of rebirth.

---

[25] P W Martin, *Experiment in Depth: A study of the Work of Jung, Eliot and Toynbee*, Routledge & Kegan Paul, London, 1987.

A hybrid consciousness produced by the present collision of Western and African[26] values would downplay mechanistic efficiency for a little creative spontaneity and fun.

It would produce a view of society as an interdependent organism rather than a first-come-first-served race between materially avaricious individuals.

It would produce a more humane society in which happiness would be regarded as great a good as profits.

It would produce an economy in which *what* is made would be as important as how much money is made from it.

I am not talking about swapping one set of values for another. I am talking about a process where each influences the other, and produces a third. And I am only too painfully aware that there is very little in Africa right now that suggests there is any plausibility to this idealistic notion.

Yet I believe there is a certain inevitability about it. I know, as I am sure you do, that the West must re-new itself; and that behind the façade of chaos, brutality and moral corruption that Africa currently presents to the world its root values are pure and fine — and that they await rediscovery.

We just have to make room for it, that's all. It will happen by itself.

I see it happening already. I see it happening in a yearning for religion that reconnects with the spirit of the human and of nature, I see it in a rising tide of humane politics, I see it in the decency revolution. I see it, especially, where one may see everything first, in art. I see contemporary Western music searching for its roots in Africa. I see the painters of the West seeking the symbols borne in ethnic art. I see sculpture, literature and psychology in a great search for the inner being.

I believe with Jung that "the artist is the unwitting mouthpiece of the psychic secrets of his time".[27] I believe with Czeslaw Milosz that

> The average citizen of the West has no idea that a painter in a garret, a little known musician, or a writer of "unintelligible" verse is a magician who shapes all those things in life which he prizes.[28]

In the great hybridisation of culture and consciousness that almost certainly lies ahead, the greater task is Africa's. It must put its many houses in order. It must borrow from the West that which it lacks — social order,

---

[26] You can read "developing world" if you wish. In fact, I think you'd better.
[27] C J Jung, op. cit.
[28] Czeslaw Milosz, op. cit.

the sacredness of public trust, and the worth of enterprise — before it can give its own gifts in return.

Will this happen?

I wish there were someone who could tell me for sure.

The Snakes and Ladders Snag

Inside the Impotence of Politics

In the upper reaches of the board game of Snakes and Ladders you may come into contact with the jaws of a serpent. Its bite will send you tumbling down again to the lower reaches of the game, meaningfully impeding your progress to the goal.

We encounter serpents at many stages in the game. However, it is only at the uppermost extremity of each beast that the encounter is charged with poison, and it knocks us down.

In life, if we recognise the beast for what it is in our early encounters with it, before it could do us serious harm, we might deal with it there, before it grows beyond manageable proportions. Our failure to do this condemns us to suffer its poison eventually.

The same is true of politics. The business of politics we find in the upper reaches. There the beast that we have encountered several times before becomes dangerous, capable of inflicting wounding bites that frustrate our progress to our goal, and even reverse the progress we have made to that point.

So it is that many of the issues of politics, the behaviour of parties and voters, and the political course that societies take ... or fail to take ... have their origin in the kind of things that we have been examining up to now.

Ideological disputes between political parties begin their existence as shortages of resources, and assert themselves as underlying disagreements on how to make sure everyone gets a fair share of what life in the society has to offer. The greater the shortages, the more intense the conflicts; and, by extrapolation, the more resources decline in proportion to the number of people wanting their benefit, the more conflict intensifies.

Crime, we have seen, rises from great civilisational shifts of patrist societies to matrist domination; and from the type of childhood the nation's people experience. High levels of crime lead to lower levels of financial investment in an economy; this leads to fewer resources, which increases conflict and induces higher levels of social stress, which produces damaging childhood environments and upbringing practices, which create a more violence-prone society, which becomes conducive to rising authoritarianism, which stifles the human spirit, which inhibits enterprise, which produces poverty, which takes one back to the crime you started with … for the chain reaction to begin again, soon becoming a downward-spiralling vortex.

A nation unable to agree politically on its priorities emerges from a clash of values. Different value sets place different degrees of value on different aspects of social and economic life. National energy is consequently drained from the economy and cultural life and directed into the political arena. There the struggle to resolve macro-disputes takes place.

This diversion of energy — caused either by resource-apportioning conflicts or values clashes — is why many poor societies are consumed by intricate political conflicts and divisions while rich societies present a more humdrum political face.

A society that lacks confidence in its ability to succeed is the eventual product of a society with low levels of mental health, frequently characterised by endemic levels of sub-clinical depression.

A society that lacks the will to transcend obstacles it encounters is a result of the states of mind that accompany depression: a pervasive sense of helplessness, and the victim syndrome, which induces its subject to believe his or her condition is the doing of others.

Low economic performance is in many respects no more than the lack of the sheer physical vigour in a nation pandemically in low health, or sick with Aids, and hobbled by the shortened life spans that come with the conditions.

An economy lacking in know-how for technological advance is the product of the emigration of its educated classes — driven by fears for personal safety and a sense of being unwanted. In this regard, it is worth noting that the brain drain arises as much from a feeling of social alienation as it does from the purely materialistic considerations of the migrating individuals — for any psychologist will tell you that a sense of belonging is a more powerful impulse than a sense of well-being.

For these reasons, in this chapter, we must walk in the shadow of politics so we may come closer to understanding why politics has failed us.

The failure of politics

The South African government defends its delivery record, particularly in the provision of electricity, water and telephones — and, to a lesser extent, the broadening of schooling and primary health care. The details can be found on the government's web sites[1] although the government is decidedly reticent to draw attention to its performance, admitting coyly that it needs to be "speeded up".

The problem with assessing the positive aspect of the government's provision of resources and services is that it rests on a subjective measure: What would have been the reasonable minimum one could have expected from an only moderately capable government in the circumstances? And, thereafter, what could one fairly call extraordinary effort and performance in the extraordinary circumstances that pertain?

One thing is plain, there is no comprehensive development policy. Development gambits are *ad hoc*. Grand plans are floated, then not implemented. Moratoriums are placed on civil service recruitment, then reversed. Extensive retrenchments of teachers and other vital civil servants are launched; when the damage becomes apparent, they are abandoned, not fixed. Job creation summits are held without any follow-through.

The dire need to haul in the inequalities and retardations imposed by apartheid is not driven by an integrated campaign — which might ignite the imagination of the wanting population and inspire the bureaucrats who need to do the work.

There was one. The Mandela government came into power with a Reconstruction and Development Plan, with its own ministry. However, the ministry was quickly abandoned and its minister, Jay Naidoo, former high profile Cosatu chief and architect of the "rolling mass action" that many say did most to bring the white government to its knees, forced into obscurity.

This uncommon political excision and execution was never — and never has been — properly explained.[2] For a while Mbeki insisted the RDP had been taken under his wing and continued, albeit without the fanfare. But this didn't wash, and the acronym "RDP" quietly dropped out of the government's vocabulary. In 1996 the RDP was followed by the Growth, Employment and Redistribution (GEAR) programme which shifted

---

[1] The primary government site is at http://www.gov.za. The government's communications agency is at http://www.gcis.gov.za.

[2] The only consistency I can find in this development is that a string of other political figures with a profile such as Naidoo's — Ramaphosa, Madikizela-Mandela, Phosa, Sexwale, Jordan — all suffered unfortunate political accidents, and found themselves without purchase, in Mbeki's rise to the presidency. When it came to selecting a successor to Mandela a curious situation existed: there was only one viable candidate, Mbeki.

emphasis from delivery to investor courtship. However, by 2001, when there had been far less than the envisaged growth, declining employment, and the only effective redistribution had been to the new super elite, GEAR became the instrument of acrimony within the governing alliance. Suffering a similar fate to the RDP, it was quietly starved by inattention and laid to rest.

There is an additional problem in measuring civic progress in South Africa, and places like it. Absolute numbers tell one little — it's the relative numbers that matter. This means that it may sound impressive to hear that a certain extension of services has taken place, but it may sound less heartening when the progress is placed against the size and growth rate of the need.

The unhappiest example of this is in housing. The provision of a million dwellings in the first six years of ANC government failed to achieve what the party's first housing minister, Joe Slovo, quietly called "freezing the backlog". In other words, the need grew faster than the provision in that time — and there were consequently more homeless people at the end of the exercise than there were at the beginning.

The picture gets even murkier. Population growth — the main driver of escalating need — is being affected by Aids deaths. It's not a crude matter of reducing numbers; it's a case of evaluating the number of people being born, against the length of time they live, what their needs are in that time, and how this changes the population profile (shortened life spans means more of the population is younger).

Some commentators are making deductions that reduced numbers will mean bigger service provision gains — but they could end up in an awkward pickle. The tobacco company Philip Morris in 2001, ethically blinded by self-interested rationalising, argued that early deaths of smokers was one of the positive effects of cigarette smoking because of the saving on health care, pensions, welfare and housing for the elderly. Thus, arguing that real gains are being made in delivery because the growth in numbers is slowing down, or that there are fewer adults, is to enter a similar moral territory.

The outcome is that, without a development plan, and in the face of endlessly complicating variables, there is no viable way of measuring the government's performance. Suffice to say that the subjective opinion in the country, across the board from the intelligentsia to the impoverished, is that the government has failed to deliver satisfactorily. The government's own faltering admissions in this respect complete the impression.

It would be easy to produce here an extended account of the failure of policy and performance in South Africa today. Nothing, however, would be gained thereby. The instances themselves are covered thoroughly in the press.

Additionally, I have attempted to make the character of this discourse not a bid to win a political argument, but to search for understanding. Moreover, the broad trend of political failure did not originate with the post-apartheid government. This government merely failed to halt and turn around the decay that had set in long before it came to power. This is a discussion not so much of the failure of government, or a government in particular, as it is an examination of the failure of politics itself.

This caveat, nevertheless, does not change the fact that the combined failure of politics and the government has left developing societies, South Africa in particular, with very real problems.

The failure of politics has left South Africa with a decaying justice system.

The political management of the society has failed to stimulate a labour-absorbing economy.

In the fight against Aids the government has produced only a low-key preventive campaign. There is no treatment policy.

Politics has failed to provide a moral compass in the ethical wasteland left by apartheid. The government is reluctant to pursue suspicions of corruption — such as in its mammoth arms deal — with convincing vigour; it closes ranks round embattled members of the ruling party; and it places solidarity above morality — as seen in the case of the disgraced cleric, Alan Boesak, convicted of stealing money intended for the child victims of apartheid, yet embraced by cabinet ministers ... including one who had just relinquished the portfolio of justice.

In the absence of a moral compass, cynicism and despair flourish. A sense of common purpose becomes impossible to attain. The corrupt ethic of "get it while you can, before someone else does" infects the entrepreneur, the bureaucrat, the police officer and the civil service technician.

In sum, the failure of politics has edged both the South African civic body and the governing elite into a dreamlike state, wherein they execute pre-programmed motions of government and doing business, all the while upholding the conspiracy of not admitting things can't go on the way they are for much longer. Our actions are plunging us deeper into crime, unemployment, poverty and civic decay.

We don't understand why this should be. We are doing what we were taught to do. Some of us are trying very hard, indeed.

We don't know what else to do, so we keep on doing it.

The eyes of Thabo Mbeki

One does not need great powers of imagination to see things from Mbeki's point of view as he contemplated his succession to Nelson Mandela.

He would have asked himself how he could avoid being compared to Mandela, and found wanting. How could he prevent the unfolding of history judging him a failure when the nearest yardstick was the towering figure of the icon of liberation?

The answer would have come without too much difficulty: don't compete on the same terrain.

Mandela had filled, and expanded, the role of the great conciliator. He was a father figure that straddled South Africa's racial divides, giving each sector of the fragmented nation something and someone to admire. He has been a monument of unmoving moral solidarity. He presents the same face to each human and to all of humanity.

Nothing of this kind lay in the path that history would unfold before Mbeki, and Mbeki knew it. To begin with, he was too young, by far. Commensurately, one got the impression, he was in a greater hurry; and, not to put too fine a point on it, he projected the image of a much angrier man.

Nobody really minded. In fact, most welcomed it. It seemed right that South Africa should move from the necessary but ephemeral business of reconciliation and setting the mood for material progress — and get on with the job. The idea of a more down-to-earth manager in the presidency who wouldn't mind stepping on a few toes to meet targets had a special kind of appeal to a nation — and a world — that wanted to do business.

In 1996, at the adoption of the new South African constitution, Mbeki made a self-defining speech in which he repeated five times the refrain, "I am an African."[3] He pulled no punches in the speech but the parts that were left unsaid were understood as clearly as those that were said.

It was understood that one could not embody the spirit of Africanness without having an agenda to settle with the West; the West that had trampled Africa underfoot and segmented it with borders that suited Western requirements and ignored African realities; the West that thereby bequeathed to today's generation a cauldron of broken societies, violence

[3] The speech text is available at http://www.gov.za/awards/mbekiafrican.htm.

and anger that the West now snottily expects Africans to put an end to; the West that saw Africans only as units of work, maintaining a vested interest in their not rising beyond lowly forms of labour; the West that callously shattered indigenous social structures by founding huge commercial exploitations of African resources, which depended on migrant labour.

The decision seemed, in a way, to make itself: President Mbeki would be cast as "Mr Delivery", and the moniker attached itself to him. He began his presidency with a major overhaul of the structuring and procedures of the presidency. He installed a "shadow cabinet" — low-key advisers on each portfolio of government business — reachable in his own corridors. He grouped interconnected portfolios so that, for example, if the department of health built a clinic, the department of public works would be there to build a road to it, and telecommunications to supply a telephone line.

Mbeki prepared the ground by highlighting the need for delivery in his public utterings in the lead up to his presidency. Sometimes he raised eyebrows; usually he roused much interest and anticipation: he said very little had changed for ordinary South Africans in the first years of ANC government. It seemed like the forthright self-criticism of a brave and unblinkered man. His rhetoric pushed home the broad scope and drama of the urgency of delivering "a better life for all", as an ANC slogan expressed it.

Mbeki said when the poor rise up "they will rise up against us all"; he quoted the African American poet Langston Hughes answering his own question: "What happens to a dream deferred? It explodes."

However, this was only part of the Mbeki make-up. There roiled inside him a paradox.

Could it be that when he proclaimed so fervently "I am an African" he was reassuring the part of himself that was not?

From the age of 20, in 1962, Thabo Mbeki was in exile for nearly three decades of his adult life until the unbanning of the ANC in South Africa in 1990. Mbeki studied economics in England, underwent military training in the Soviet Union, and, although he spent many of his exile years in Africa, his focus of activity was in diplomacy on behalf of the liberation movement.

The Mbeki of today bears the stamp of this background. His gentility, his fondness for fine tailoring, and his care to project a sophisticated and erudite image are a Western overlay to his African heart.

He is the epitome of the new, globalised African. He is the hybrid of values.

And here, as the Shakespeare he likes to quote, has it, lies the rub.

His two-sided make-up makes him ideally suited to intercede with the world on behalf of Africa. But it also renders him short of a man of the masses. His inability to identify viscerally with working class Africans, never mind the rural classes, is, by common consent, a political weakness.

Accordingly, there is a growing perception that the poor, the landless, the jobless and the sick are no more than poetic presences in Mbeki's speeches, there to facilitate his working of a grand agenda that is only now becoming clear.

The Mbeki presidency began on a disturbing note. His inauguration cost a staggering R47 million ($5.7 million; £4.3 million). A substantial amount of this had been solicited from big business; nevertheless, such was the amount lavished on the ceremonies.

What was one to make of this?

Imagine the alternative. The money, both public and donated by business, is used to build a school, a clinic, or a small housing development. The inauguration is held there. The new president says: let all take note — we mean what we say. Upliftment is the priority. Ceremony must wait. This is the way it's going to be.

Speeches and action would have docked. The nation — and that part of the world that cared — would have sat up and taken notice. Here was a leader of Africa in the making and worth watching.

Yet the answer that would resolve his statements with his actions had to hang, suspended. At any rate, the disproportionately lavish inauguration was just a single incident. Over-hasty interpretations can mislead.

So the country, and parts of the world that remained interested, watched and waited.

As it happened, Mbeki's presidency was only months old before it started to become fully clear how he intended to distinguish his regnum from Mandela's; and when delivery was spoken of, just what he had in mind delivering.

Mbeki, it turned out, was a man with a very big plan indeed. It was breathtaking and visionary.

It might also prove to be foolish over-reaching that will end in disappointment and ruin.

Mbeki's ambition was to elevate the status of the developing world. What he had in mind was not the mere upliftment of a single country, his own. He wanted to change the balance of power between the entire developing world and the developed world. He wanted to break the pattern that condemned the rich and the poor to different destinies.

It would entail reforming global institutions, for which he aimed to lobby. His primary instrument was to be the galvanising of Africa into a great leap forward. For this, he would spearhead the creation of a blueprint.

Just as Newton claimed his achievements came because he stood on the shoulders of giants, so Mbeki resolved not to attempt to fill Mandela's shoes, but to stand on his shoulders. Mbeki would lift his sights from South Africa itself and make himself the agent through which the current order that divided humanity was changed.

The hybridisation of values now had an agent and a plan.

Looking back, one can see the progression of the vision. In a paper for the Institute of Futures Research,[4] Stellenbosch political scientist Philip Nel, working with Ian Taylor and Janis van der Westhuizen, wrote: "His eagerness to don the heroic mantle of a global campaigner for the developing world was already in evidence in Mbeki's speech to the Twelfth Summit of the Non-Aligned Movement in Durban in August-September 1998."

The researchers then trace the maturation of the vision through a meeting of the Commonwealth Heads of Government in South Africa in 1999, where Mbeki got the Westerners to endorse a declaration on "globalisation and people-centred development". The line moves through various negotiations with the Group of Seven most developed nations, to his address to the United Nations General Assembly, also in 1999, where he boldly told the gathered community that the principal global institutions had to reform, to the Africa-European Union summit in Cairo in 2000, and again in the same year in his opening of the Non-Aligned Movement Summit in Havana.

The culmination of phase one came in July 2001 at the summit of the heads of the G8 (the Group of Seven plus Russia) in Genoa when they endorsed a broadly stated New African Initiative, the main thrust of which is a "new partnership" between the developed world and the developing world — in this case Africa.

Nel, Taylor and Van der Westhuizen quote Mbeki from his budget vote in Parliament in 2000 as he provides a synopsis of his view and ambition:

> At the centre of all engagements I have mentioned is the critical question of our time, of how humanity should respond to the irreversible process of globalisation

---

[4] Philip Nel, Ian Taylor & Janis van der Westhuizen, "Mbeki's Global Initiative: the Limits of a Reformist Agenda", *Political Issues*, 10 (7) July 2000. Nel, Taylor and Van der Westhuizen conclude that Mbeki may, in the final analysis, be co-opted to a re-packaged and re-phrased but substantively unchanged globalising agenda of the North, and may thus serve its ends by ensuring better Southern compliance with it.

while addressing the fundamental challenges that face the bulk of humanity. These include poverty, underdevelopment, the growing North–South gap, racism and xenophobia, gender discrimination, ill health, violent conflicts and the threat to the environment. These problems cannot be solved except in the context of the global human society to which we belong. We must and will actively continue to engage the rest of the world to make whatever contribution we can to ensure that the process of globalisation impacts positively on those, like the millions of our people, who are poor and in dire need of a better life.

This engagement must necessarily address, among other things, the restructuring of the UN, including the Security Council, a review of the functions of such bodies as the IMF and the World Bank, the determination of the agenda and the manner of the operation of the WTO and an assessment of the role of the G7. Central to these processes must be the objective of reversing the marginalisation of Africa and the rest of the South, and therefore compensating for the reduction of national sovereignty by increasing the capacity of the South to impact on the system of global governance.

Here we have an African who is setting out to change the way the world works. He wants to kick start, or at least add decisive impetus, to the reform of global institutions; and he wants to re-make the existing global order in which the rich nations relate to the poor.

Is Mbeki an African Don Quixote tilting vainly and a little comically at the windmills of established world order? Or is he a product of his age, personifying in his vision the great hybridisation of values the world must, and is, moving towards for its renewal of spirit and hope? Is he simply doing what *someone* has to do? Is he drawing Excalibur from the stone?

Does, therefore, the gratitude of history await him, or ignominy and ridicule?

Let us realise, as we confront these questions, that our interest in the answers is not because we are merely intrigued by Mbeki's moment in history, but because his fate — to a greater or a lesser degree — is the fate of us all. If the events of which Mbeki is a personification proceed to a satisfactory conclusion, we have hope; if they do not, then the fate we explored in earlier chapters — the irreversible fracturing of humanity into three great constituents, on separate trajectories, and living in ever-greater fear of one another — is our certain end.

Let us register, too, that if you accept the way in which I have set out the evolution of values, the clash and eventual resolution of individualism versus collectivism, then you see through the eyes of Mbeki:

The challenge we face is to achieve the cohabitation in the global conduct of human affairs of the concept of human solidarity and the principle which governs the modern societies of the North, that the search for personal gain and advantage is the only viable and proven engine of progress and human fulfilment.[5]

The doing and undoing of a visionary

We have entered a terrain where the questions pile up more rapidly and urgently than we can sort through them. It's not surprising. We have ignited the root question of our time. In this we are in agreement with Mr Mbeki. Like an incandescent firework, the root question spews against the darkness a dazzling myriad of lesser questions.

Does Mbeki have the personal make-up and qualities to realise the vision he has dreamed and drawn?

Can he pull off the global agenda *as well as* what would amount to the miracle of turning South Africa from its course of disaster? Or will the first take care of the second?

Is Mbeki not perhaps convinced that South Africa is on a track to success and that the country must now more or less get on with its business by itself while he pursues a higher mission?

What will Mbeki's reaction be if — or, as I believe, when — South Africa's internal politics threaten to disrupt his grander, global agenda? Will he resort to extraordinary measures to prevent the break-up of his party, alliance, and government — measures that will give the lie to his claim of being the spokesman for the great new partnership of values and practices? Will he be reduced to nothing more than another African oligarch trying to hold a fracturing nation and economy together while staying in power?

Will he be able to withstand, politically, the assault by a political voice that will surely arise within South Africa — a voice that will say to the millions of desperate ones: It's all very well that you have a president who is trying to save the world ... but we will save *you*. Mbeki wants to give the South a better deal with the North ... but we will give you a job, a roof, and food to eat.

I cannot pretend that I can answer these questions. They are the intractable questions of our time and place. Yet each of us must devise a sense of where things are going. Without such a sense not one of us can plan a sensible course into the future. So, in what follows, I shall recount some of the things that have presented themselves to my attention in this regard,

[5] Mbeki at the opening of the G77 South Summit in Havana in 2000. Quoted by Nel, Taylor & Van der Westhuizen, *ibid.*

so that the burden of answers may be taken on by a more responsible authority — you.

Several unusual events characterised Mbeki's entry to the presidency — apart from the sheer profligacy of it.

The first passed without any comment. In putting together his first government, Mbeki — who had been deputy president in the Mandela government and was commonly acknowledged to have been running the administration for some time — created a ministry for intelligence.

Every country has a department for intelligence, but it is usually a part of defence or, less desireably, part of police. Few countries have ministries of intelligence. That Mbeki wanted one suggested a presidency that would prize information above normal levels. This was curious. South Africa has no national enemies. If anything, the new democracy was the darling of the world, and the star of Africa. Furthermore, time has shown that — as far as one can tell — South African intelligence has played little or no role in fighting international crime, drug smuggling, or the like.

Also, within months Mbeki had signed into law an amendment to the Intelligence Services Control Act. The Act provided for an intelligence oversight committee to be a parliamentary watchdog over intelligence activities. The amendment, however, allowed Mbeki to control what the oversight committee was told, and what it could say.

What, then, was the nature of Mbeki's uncommon and urgent interest in intelligence? And why was it so strong that he would signal to careful watchers, through the creation of a ministry, that there was stuff he needed to know, badly?

Before a year was out, some directional signs appeared. The new ministry was caught in a bungled surveillance rigged to record comings and goings at the German embassy in Pretoria. And the Democratic Alliance, the main opposition party, claimed that its parliamentary offices were bugged.

Could presidential paranoia explain the appetite for information? Was there something in his political make-up that led him to mistake friends for traitors and to see mortal enemies where there were merely democratic challengers? Circumstantial evidence tilted in this direction, especially when further signs of high-level paranoia revealed themselves. We will return to them shortly.

A second perplexing event occurred when the Mbeki government was only days old. The newly appointed premier of the Mpumalanga province boasted to reporters that politicians frequently lied, and that he considered this quite normal behaviour. There was an outcry. Corruption and dishonesty was a high-profile issue and Mbeki and others had made several public promises about how they would not tolerate it.

How brilliant this was, I thought. Here providence offers the new president a ready-made opportunity to grab headlines that will make people sit up and notice. All the president has to do is say: this is *exactly* the kind of thing I have been saying we will not tolerate. I promise a genuinely clean government that is worthy of everyone's respect.

And off with the hapless premier's political head.

To boot, the miscreant in question was a thoroughgoing nonentity, a leftover from an apartheid homeland government, who surprised many by getting the post in the first place. He was, and time underscored it, utterly expendable. It was all just so beautifully set up, it could easily have been ... set up, if you know what I mean.

To my even greater surprise Mbeki deflected the outcry, saying it was a party issue, and should be dealt with there. He missed the opportunity. Why, I wondered, would a shrewd and capable politician, such as Mbeki was, not grab this golden chance? Was it not so that honour was the single most important perceived asset in South Africa's political armoury, which should be nurtured, not squandered?

Whatever the true answer, the matter went to the party and in the end, yes, nothing was done.

The disquieting signs of a presidency based on confused ethics spilled into the public domain ... and continued to do so at intervals thereafter.

The Dalai Lama visited South Africa. After the freeing of Mandela, the Tibetan spiritual leader became the world's main symbol of human bondage. Mbeki wouldn't see him.

This upset many people of principle in South Africa and the world. Aside from other reasons, Mbeki was displaying a full reversal of the morality the ANC demanded of the world in the time of its struggle.

South Africa was, at the time of the Dalai Lama's visit, engaged in upgrading relations with China, a diplomatic venture that has delivered little of note. In the course of this, South Africa had terminated formal diplomatic ties with Taiwan in order to please the comparatively mighty Beijing. There was no doubt in anyone's mind that there had been pressure on Mbeki to snub the Dalai Lama, and he acquiesced.

In its struggle the ANC called on the world, and the Western trading nations in particular, to put economic expediency aside and isolate the apartheid government, economically and culturally, as a matter of principle. The ANC reserved its most vitriolic criticism for administrations such as those of Reagan and Thatcher, which advocated policies of constructive engagement.

Here, now, was the ANC practising the most dismal expediency. It was putting commercial and political profit ahead of recognising the very ethic that had driven its own struggle.

To appreciate the disappointment of the world's campaigners for human justice, one only has to go back in time, and imagine a head of state refusing to meet Mandela for fear of incurring the displeasure of apartheid's president P W Botha.

The Mbeki government was six months old when it was learned that the former Ethiopian dictator, Mengistu Haile Mariam, on the run from charges of genocide and crimes against humanity, was receiving medical treatment in South Africa. Addis Ababa promptly asked for his extradition. The South African government refused to comply, saying there was no extradition treaty between the two countries. Again, Mbeki remained intractably silent. His office refused to entertain questions on the matter.

Mengistu returned to his exile haven in Harare, Zimbabwe, and told the Voice of America by telephone that the South African government had told him he could come back when he liked.

No comment could be extracted from Pretoria.[6]

Is it fair to isolate these events in the busy rush of government and draw inferences about them? It's a question we need to ask, because much is at stake, and the inference that is arising from this account is a serious one.

My answer is that people act in terms of personalised value sets, just as groups, nations or entire civilisations might. Every action, every word chosen in the place of another, provides a window into that value set. The smallest of windows can afford an outside observer a comprehensive few of the inside of a room. In this way even a single word can reveal a person's history, attitude and values.

The actions under discussion are such windows.

Further, if mistaken impressions have arisen in the tumult of the management of public affairs, then any public figure of repute knows both the need and the way to put the issue right. When this is not done, one is not merely entitled, one is obliged, to ask: What does it mean?

---

[6] South African Press Association, "Mengistu might come back", *Cape Times*, December 9, 1999.

Lastly, when the stakes are this high, there simply isn't room for moral sloppiness. South Africa came within grasping distance of moral leadership of the world. The end of apartheid, the political settlement between blacks and whites, and the secular sainthood of Mandela have been celebrated in song, poetry and literature. Two prominent South African commentators, Frederik van Zyl Slabbert and Heribert Adam, have spoken of South Africa's "moral capital" — and the fact that it is being allowed to drain away.

Certainly, Mbeki and his administration have spoken, and done, more against corruption and dishonesty than any other South African government, and, for that matter, most in the world. Yet if one weighs these actions, they all fall into the category of admonitions, intentions, declamations and regulations. When actions contradict these, the official response is invariably inadequate, at best. The result is that an impression has settled in the public mind that there is a big discrepancy between what is said and what is done.

There's no way around it: doing the right thing is not available for compromise.

When a cabinet minister was rapped by the public protector for making false accusations of a financial cover-up against the auditor general, Mbeki remained silent ... then promoted the minister to the justice portfolio. When the government obstinately refused, in the face of a public outcry, to let its own anti-corruption unit investigate allegations of wrongdoing in its biggest arms deal, Mbeki kept the matter at arm's length ... then replaced the unit's head, a judge, with a party man.

Through all of this a public image of the president formed: aloof from parliament and remote from the affairs of the country, absorbed in his bid to remake the world order, absent as a moral beacon, and making headlines only when he travelled abroad. More and more the impression gained ground that the president found as much to occupy him abroad as at home.

Then the slumbering disquiet over presidential paranoia awoke — and the word was on many lips, even in print. In 24 months of government the president and his office made three substantial allegations of conspiracies against Mbeki.

In one, an international audience gasped as Mbeki and a minister, apparently in a co-ordinated gambit, in separate interviews alleged a political conspiracy against him. Pointedly, the putative conspirators were three figures who had become alienated from the political mainstream during Mbeki's ascendancy.[7]

If Mbeki had implied they wanted to see his political defeat, no one would have doubted it. But he went much further than that. He was definitive that it was a conspiracy, and his minister raised the possibility that his personal safety was at issue.

When nothing followed the accusations that gave them any substance, and the government produced only a discredited scandal peddler as a source, the storm abated ... but the damage it wrought remained.

On several occasions, Mbeki's closest aides stated publicly there was a concerted campaign by the media — note: by the media, not in the media — to discredit him. The media were typecast as white owned, which was only partly true, and perpetuating a liberal agenda — using a label that had become a pejorative in South African political jargon. The accusations of the media conspiracy remained, as such accusations normally do, vague and formless. No specific instances of a campaign were indicated, and no logic of its methods or purposes was alluded to. No complaints were taken to the statuary bodies tasked with adjudicating complaints against the media.

Yet another illustration of conspiratorial anxiety surfaced. This, perhaps, was the most disquieting of all for its overtones of conventional anti-imperialist angst. In two newspaper articles, classic illustrations of caucus leaks and deep-contact reporting, Howard Barrell, of the *Mail & Guardian*, South Africa's most assertively independent newspaper, reported on a wide-ranging address by Mbeki to the parliamentary caucus of the ANC.[8]

Mbeki told the parliamentarians, according to Barrell's sources, that the Western powers were threatened by the rising influence of developing countries in global trade and politics.

This is the standard political hyperbole of the developing world.

Mbeki, however, went further. He said, reportedly, that powerful Western forces, including the CIA, were aligned to resist the changing world order so as to protect their interests. The CIA was involved in the campaign to assert that HIV caused Aids ... and was seeking to discredit him for questioning this view.

---

[7] Ramaphosa, Sexwale and Phosa. *Cf.* footnote #2.

[8] Howard Barrell, "Mbeki fingers the CIA in Aids" and "What the president said ..." *Mail & Guardian*, October 6–12, 2000.

Many people wondered whether the CIA was needed to do what Mbeki was doing himself.

Many people who had started off as enthusiastic believers in Mbeki, or at least willing to give him a chance, then began to wonder if there was not a potentially disastrous contradiction between what was promised and what was delivered.

If the Mbeki presidency came to an end at the time of writing, July 2001, it would be remembered for three things: Aids, the collapse of neighbouring Zimbabwe and the New African Initiative. Each deserves separate inquiry. For it may bring us to see that the South African story, as it is embodied by Mbeki, is set in Shakespearean terms: a lead character who is called to greatness, who can see the path to that end, but who is beset by fatal character flaws that will convert the promise of greatness to tragedy.

While Rome burns

There is something both macabre and transfixing about watching a disaster happen, knowing that nothing will stop it, least of all anything you may do.

It has been in this hypnotic state that the world has watched the country worst affected by the greatest natural disaster to strike humanity,[9] South Africa, twisting in a questioning and a denial of what the rest of the world knows to be true.

Long after the basic physiology of HIV/Aids had been worked out to the satisfaction of the world's scientific establishments — and a dissident theory had been weighed and discarded — the South African government revived the dissident theory. Moreover, the South African government gave the hardcore of dissidents that remained from the intellectual winnowing that had taken place a platform they probably thought they would never see again.

The departure from orthodoxy was lead by Mbeki, and his government — the health ministry in particular — followed.

---

[9] The only two comparable experiences, in terms of mortalities and overall impact on society, were the Black Death of Europe in the 14th Century, and the 1918/19 influenza epidemic. The mortality percentage in Europe was comparable to what is expected for Aids — 18–25%. The influenza killed about 5% of the population of South Africa, and about 6% in the worst-hit country — India. It is, not, however, merely a matter of numbers. The economic complexity and dependency of contemporary societies makes the impact much greater now than then.

Inexorably, South Africa slipped down a barren route of hair-splitting, quasi-learning, semantics, prevarication, refutation and downright wrong-headedness while the virus replicated in the population and the body count mounted.

It was an exercise in avoidance, in classic guise and of epic proportions.

I became intrigued by what the reason could be for this collective denial. I surmised it lay in the fact that there was nothing in human experience to measure the catastrophe by, no conceptual tool with which it could be embraced.

The closest approximations of the experience Aids would bring lay in the plague of the 14th Century, and the great flu epidemic of 1918 and 1919 and all that existed of these were dim memories, stored away in little-referenced academic treatises. So I went in search of these memories to see if their awakening could tell us anything about what confronted us in the present.

I read about the Black Death, the plague that came to Europe with a ragged army of Mongols and Hungarian Kipchaks. With them, the invaders brought a rat-borne infection that killed several of them while laying siege to a Genoese trading post in 1347.

Their commander saw an opportunity, the consequences of which he could not possibly imagine.

He catapulted several of the infected bodies into the Genoese settlement. One can imagine that the Genoese citizens were nonplussed at this strange event. Little could they have known that the invasion had begun — real, but invisible. The inhabitants had no resistance. The greatest microbial assault on humanity up to then was under way.

Charles van Doren[10] recounts the principle changes that followed the plague. The first was in social attitudes. There was a "widespread relaxation of morals" in the wake of the plague.

Six hundred years later Czeslaw Milosz[11] would also write graphically on how the nearness of death banishes shame and decency.

This tells us already that the spiritual degeneration we are witnessing in South Africa can be linked, in a manner greater than we generally understand, and at a level deeper than we perceive, to the Aids pandemic. We might also expect the effects to intensify over the next 20 years.

[10] Charles van Doren, *A History of Knowledge: Past, Present and Future*, Ballantine Books, New York, 1992.
[11] Czeslaw Milosz, op. cit.

Van Doren's second observation reminds us that mere numbers or percentages of deaths do not describe an accurate picture. This is because the total number is aggregated across the population. The fact is that deaths concentrate in particular sectors of the population and the economy, making the devastation localised and uneven. It also renders the effects especially harsh in certain instances, and less so in others. During the Black Death, for example, nearly half of agricultural labour perished.

The shortage of labour pushed labour prices up. However, it also pushed up the price of the food, resulting in inflation that cancelled the effect of their increased earnings.

An incidental effect traced by Van Doren reminds us that the consequences of so great a blow to the social psyche can be utterly unexpected.

The great piles of clothing that were left over from the plague's victims gave rise to a new industry — the manufacture of rag paper. Up to that time all writing was done on parchment or vellum, neither of which were suitable for printing. When Gutenberg started on his invention of moveable type, the market was saturated with thin, pliable, inexpensive rag paper. Without this paper, printing would not have been a viable concept, and might not have arisen ... at least not until paper found its way to the West from China, where it had been known and used for centuries.

Despite the parallels and curiosities involving the Black Death and Aids, I felt there was little to extract. It would be foolish to speculate that Aids would lead indirectly to an innovation anything like printing. Although Aids, like the Black Death, finds its victims mainly among people lower on the socio-economic scale, many studies by business and other sectors have accurately mapped the cost to them that Aids will exact[12] — through the death of workers, teachers, medical staff and civil servants. For instance, an estimated 40% of hospital workers will be HIV positive by 2010; anything between 30% and 45% of miners will be; and truck drivers — a vital arterial sector in the economy — are estimated already to be nearly 60% HIV positive ... at one truck stop a survey team found 95% of the drivers tested proved HIV positive.

It was clear that the flu epidemic of 1918, and its second wave in 1919, would replicate conditions closer, thus be more relevant, to the present.

---

[12] A provocative and interesting attempt to debunk the economic impact of Aids is contained in David E Bloom & Ajay S Mahal, *Does the Aids Epidemic Really Threaten Economic Growth?* National Bureau of Economic Research (USA) Working Paper #5148, June 1995.

After a lengthy search, I found only one thorough study of the effects on society of the scourge of the Spanish flu. It may be the only one. It is a doctoral thesis prepared by the historian Howard Phillips, written (but not published) for presentation to the University of Cape Town in 1984. It is titled *Black October: The Impact of the Spanish Influenza Epidemic of 1918 on South Africa.*

A startling picture emerges for a reader in the 21st Century.

It reveals a society infinitely more far-sighted and responsive to the disaster, as we shall see. It is perplexing that this should be so, especially as we would confidently assume that we now have a more developed and advanced society. That the facts contradict this once more echoes the remarks of Hobsbawm and other historians about our modern barbarism.

The first thing worth noting is that the 1918 flu is hardly remembered. It is not within the normal ambit of general knowledge. Few people have heard about it — and those that have know little of it.

This is curious, as the flu epidemic was the biggest disaster ever to strike the population of this country, even to the present day.

It is the most significant demographic event ever. On a worldwide scale, more people died in the flu epidemic than in World War 1. The situation in South Africa was not dissimilar.

The curiosity of forgetting is further emphasised by the fact that the flu did not occur in the distant past, beyond the reach of inherited memory. My father was born in 1920; so the flu would have been in the young adulthood of my grandfather. Yet I never heard my father, nor anyone else of his generation, nor of his father's, speak of it. By contrast, I heard them speak much of the war.

It is remarkable that the epidemic and the havoc it wrought are so poorly remembered. It is remarkable that there is only one substantial academic study of its impact. This is particularly so if one takes into account the exhaustive analysis of World War I, and the macabre fascination with it that shows no signs of abating with the passage of time.

Of course, World War I was a man-made disaster while the flu was a natural catastrophe. The two seem to capture human imagination in different ways. The war was begun, conducted and ended by humans. Humans had nothing near the same control over the flu.

Nevertheless, it is tantalising to think that the dynamic that has caused us to close our eyes to the flu is the same that is preventing us from opening our eyes to Aids.

The Spanish flu was one of the most aggressive viruses ever known. A victim could be invaded by the virus in the morning — leading, often, to collapse within an hour or two[13] — and be dead by nightfall or the next evening.

The virus was located late in 2000 in six Scandinavian miners who had died of it, and whose bodies were preserved by freezing. This has allowed the first study of the virus. It is worth noting that it was nearly 20 years after the epidemic that medical science understood that the flu was caused by a virus. At the time, the cause was put down to "germs" that flourished in unhygienic conditions. (The fact that the poor of society were the hardest hit created a misleading observational overlap here, but more of this later.)

The flu came to South Africa, from Europe, on two troop ships carrying soldiers returning from the war. The duration of the epidemic was short — the last three months of 1918. The second outbreak, in 1919, was of a milder strain and not as pervasive.

The flu killed an estimated 300 000 to 350 000 people in South Africa, about 5% of the population, which stood at 6.5 million at the time.

Over the next 15 years or so, it is expected that up to 25% of the South African population will get sick with Aids, and most, if not all, of these people will die.

A comparison of the circumstances pertaining to the flu, society's response, and the situation regarding Aids today discloses many factors that have not been thought through, and some that have not been thought of at all. We are still dumbstruck by the numbers in the Aids scenario, and we repeat them like a mantra. The following observations go beyond the numbers and attempt to extract the social ramifications. Again, I am entirely indebted to Phillips for his thorough analysis.

[13] It was not uncommon for people to die in the street.

Contrasts and Parallels between the
Influenza Epidemic of 1918 and Aids in the 21st Century

The Spanish Flu	HIV/Aids
South Africa's present-day Ministry of Health is a direct outcome of the flu epidemic. *Public health matters*, until then, were run out of a small office, resorting under a distantly related government department. The social and economic costs of the epidemic illustrated the need for monitoring and control of disease, so much so that this was placed on a level with other national priorities — such as education and defence, and an independent ministry was created.	There is likely to be a *post hoc* weighing of the effect of Aids. When the cost is counted, the relationship between public health and economic performance will be more sharply appreciated. Public health will enjoy a higher priority than it does today — but that will come only *after* Aids.
Although general *levels of responsiveness* were high, the Influenza Epidemic Commission (a government enquiry established afterwards) found that the authorities, at all levels, were reluctant to acknowledge the scale of the problem until it was too late to do anything effective.	It seems a replay of this dynamic is unavoidable. The way the authorities of today may be judged in time to come makes disturbing speculation.
When the *scale of the problem* was acknowledged, bodies like local authorities found they were ill equipped (expertise, material resources, organisational capacity, etc) to deal with it appropriately.	The local authorities of 1918 can be equated with the NGOs of today in this respect. They are active and willing — but there is no substitute for a campaign driven from a national platform.
Rural political bodies and local authorities were slower to respond than those in urban centres.	The same can be expected through the Aids epidemic.
The lack of a timely *organisational response* to the epidemic was later remedied by the creation of boards of relief for natural disasters. Their purpose was to limit the economic collapse of communities after disasters.	From the point of view of organised welfare, society is much better off today than it was in 1918. However, the threat of Aids is that much greater.
The Cape Town and Wynberg General Board of Aid was established. It was conceived as a permanent and financially secure body to guard against the folding of charities, many of which buckled under the strain of caring for victims and survivors.	There are currently no signs of an organisational response at this level — and there probably won't be until well into the Aids epidemic.

The Spanish Flu	HIV/Aids
The epidemic led to renewed efforts in *cleaning up slums* and providing new housing; in Kimberley the pail sewage system was ended and the city bought a water works. Bloemfontein adopted a new social welfare programme.	First the disaster, then the reformist zeal. Rob Dorrington, an actuarial scientist and leading South African Aids expert, predicts that the "body count" would first have to become visible before people start to react.
The sum of the response in the *political arena* was to move the general issue of social welfare up the agenda. (There were more responses at this level than would be appropriate to detail here.) Phillips characterises this response as " ... an important milestone in the development of an interventionist, white welfare state in South Africa".	Will the fall-out of the Aids epidemic spur the government of the day to greater interventionism in welfare matters?
The flu epidemic became a binding force in Afrikaner *nationalism*. It gave Afrikaners (who made up the bulk of the white poor, a class where the flu hit heavily) a further uniting element in their opposition to the government. (They objected strenuously to the government's handling of the epidemic.)	The main political dynamic in our society is not ethnic (as in 1918). It is the division between rich and poor. Could Aids have a similar effect in entrenching the animosity of the poor (who will suffer most) to the rich?
An important measure of social response in times of epidemic concerns *orphans*. Phillips says " ... the influenza epidemic wrought the single greatest advance in the history of child welfare in South Africa." At government level efforts regarding white orphans culminated in the creation of the National Council for Child Welfare. Churches dramatically stepped up fund raising. The Dutch Reformed Church created seven new orphanages, and enlarged several existing ones. The railways, police and post office all started orphans funds.	There are already an estimated 200 000 Aids orphans in SA. Their number could peak at 2 million, according to some authorities. To date, there is no meaningful response to this crisis.
Not all flu orphans, of course, were caught in the *welfare* net. Many ended up in the streets, courts, reformatories and jails.	The Institute for Security Studies concluded in a recent study (cited previously) that Aids orphans would significantly boost crime levels in SA.
Phillips found the flu did much to pull *rural communities* within the ambit of metropolitan economies.	Aids is likely to have a similar effect as accelerated rural poverty causes an increased migration to the cities.

The Spanish Flu	HIV/Aids
The *demographic impact* of the flu was felt for at least a decade. For example, school enrolments showed declines from 1918 to 1928.	Recent demographic models (Carl van Aardt, University of Pretoria) are showing significant alterations to the SA population age profile.
On the broad *economic front*, the epidemic highlighted the plight of the poor, and made it a national issue (at least for a while).	Increased focus on poverty could be a meaningful influence on public policy-making on a broad front. The costs of dealing with the disease (the present health budget absorbed by Aids alone by 2010) and the demand for government action could lead to significant public policy and budgeting changes.
An example of *policy changes* occurred after the flu as government channelled demobilised troops to farms as labour to underpin agriculture (where labour had been hard hit). Government also allowed farmers legislative leeway to strike lenient wage arrangements with labour — e.g. paying out of harvest proceeds.	This, and many other permutations, could be impelled by Aids effects on labour supply — significantly upsetting current, hard won, relations between government, labour and the private sector.
Labour shortages hit in unexpected ways. Milk and a host of other deliveries, like newspapers and groceries, for example, were disrupted for unexpectedly long periods.	The Road Freight Association recently said that at the present rate of Aids deaths among truck drivers, SA would be out of drivers by 2003.
Ordinances were amended to allow shops longer opening hours. But some shops were unable to sustain even normal hours, and shut. Isolated supply stores in rural areas closed, creating *food shortages*.	The dependency chain is extensive and difficult to perceive ... until it breaks. With Aids set to have about five times the reach of the flu, more far-reaching disruptions could materialise.
The mines experienced serious *labour disruption*. This included unexpected manifestations. Rumours and exaggerations about the disease reverberated back to myth-prone communities ... and all recruiting from Mozambique, for example, came to a halt.	Similar "wild card" repercussions — of a kind that cannot be anticipated — may attend the Aids epidemic.
The labour complement on the mines shrank to 62% in November 1918. November became the worst financial month on record, according to the Chamber of Mines — nearly three times lower than at the time of the great strikes of 1913, playing a significant part in the profitability crisis that culminated in the Rand revolts of 1922.	This is an illustrative example of the knock-on effects of an epidemic, and it would be surprising if similar did not arise as a result of Aids.

The Spanish Flu	HIV/Aids
In Transkei subsistence maize production was depressed 60%. (Commercial planting of maize in hard-hit areas of Transvaal and Natal went down 40%.) *Hunger* followed — with disruptive consequences for social stability, labour migration, etc.	The impact of Aids on social stability is probably greatly underrated at present. Areas like Transkei may be far harder hit in the epidemic — because this time their economies are more complex, thus they involve more dependencies and are more fragile.
Food supply disruptions put pressure on costs and inflation. In 1919 maize exports had to be capped to combat local price spirals.	Supply breakdowns, or cost inflations, can lead to lay-offs, exacerbating unemployment … and increased drain on public finances as funds are diverted from development to welfare.
On the *social front*, there was considerable disruption in communities beset by ignorance and rumours. Phillips reports a rise in traditional witchcraft practices, for example.	There is likely to be a substantial turn to traditional spiritual resources as modern practices are perceived to fail. Early signs of this are emerging. The values gulf and culture gap between communities will widen.
In society at large, the epidemic was accompanied, and followed, by a rise in *spiritual activity*, the practice of religion, and behavioural disturbances like hysteria and nervous breakdowns.	The spiritual stress of Aids, and the toll on society thereof, has not yet been taken effectively into consideration. The impact on mental health, particularly, is deeply worrying.
Depression strikes communities where there has been much loss of life — parents, spouses and children. Phillips reports this from medical and church sources.	Depression reduces resistance to secondary illnesses and produces psychological problems over a wide spectrum. This eventually has a deleterious effect on the productive capacity of a community or society.
The flu illustrated graphically *how diseases travel*: it entered via two ships, then travelled up the railway routes to the main centres, thereafter following social patterns of movement (e.g. sick miners going home to their villages).	Two of the highest Aids infection nodes are the army and the mines. There is a failure in national planning to target these nodes for special measures. A significant channel of infection, also, is illegal immigrantion from the sub-continent. Again, a more pointed plan of action could probably help.
The poor in all communities were the hardest hit by the flu. Present-day thinking ascribes this to low nutrition among the poor.	At least one authority (Carl Albrecht, an independent scientist) believes that since the low nutrition profile of the South African population is a significant element in the spread of Aids, the genetic upgrading of mealie meal, for example, could retard the syndrome, if not the infection itself.

The above observations, as useful as they may be in extending thinking about the ramifications of Aids, leave us without the answer to why the great slackness should prevail. To edge closer to such an answer, we must follow the unfolding of the Aids imbroglio in South Africa.

In 1998 a small group of Pretoria scientists approached the South African government with the news that they had discovered an antidote for HIV/Aids. They were given a hearing by the full cabinet. In itself, this was a surpassingly strange procedure. The fact that all normal steps that would have applied to scientific discovery had been circumvented, suggested that the government attached the highest priority to the matter.

The scientists claimed that their drug, which they called virodene, prevented or cured Aids by attacking the HI virus. The mechanism by which their drug worked, they said, was one that prevented the virus from replicating in the human body.

The government was thrilled with the news, Mbeki in particular. He later pilloried those who debunked virodene as medieval book burners and inquisitors.

Seen from today's perspective, what did not happen is as instructive as what did happen. The virodene scientists were not sent away with a flea in their ear and an admonition to bring a cure for poverty instead — as, effectively, has been done with the world's orthodox medical opinion.

The unorthodox way virodene came on the scene raised the alarm in medical and scientific circles — especially when it was disclosed that the virodene scientists had conducted human trials ... but that the Medicines Control Council (MCC) had never heard of virodene, and had certainly not authorised clinical trials.

Then it turned out the active ingredient in virodene was an industrial solvent. In fairness to its protagonists, it probably did kill the HI virus ... but also everything else. It was a poison.

Why the scientists circumvented a standard medicine development procedure that must have been well known to them has never been explained.

The Medical Control Council accordingly published a warning about virodene and stated that a serious breach of professional ethics was threatened if the manufacturers went ahead with it. Not only that, said the MCC, it would amount to a criminal action if a patient should be harmed or die.

Virodene as a medicine quietly retreated from public attention, but two revealing incidents appeared in the afterwash.

The virodene scientists fell out among themselves over the ownership of their company and went to court. During proceedings a document surfaced that said the ANC was to be granted 6% of the equity of the envisaged company.

Mbeki and the government denied any knowledge of this.

The government, however, was mightily angry at the MCC for putting a stick in the spokes of the wheel of its Aids cure. The heads of the MCC were summarily dismissed, and new executives were put in their place. The matter, however, ended in a stalemate when the newly structured MCC came to the same conclusions about virodene as its predecessor.

The issue then lay fallow for some months, although protest was building over the government's fumbling of Aids policy. The Aids directorate in the ministry of health underspent its 1999/2000 budget by 40%. The minister of health circulated provincial officials with literature claiming that Aids was a conspiracy against Africans perpetrated by the usual suspects, among whom the CIA featured prominently.

The Aids Advisory Council was replaced by the National Aids Council, which enjoyed the astonishing distinction of excluding the country's leading Aids experts and the main NGOs active in the field.

During this time Mbeki was head of the government's ministerial task force against HIV/Aids.

Looking back over these events from the perspective of the present, the shufflings and manoeuvrings suggest that something was brewing.

Soon after Mbeki became president, the bombshell hit.

Mbeki expressed doubt that HIV was the cause of Aids.

He associated himself with a group of dissenting scientists, based mainly in the USA, who believed that the viral cause of Aids had been misconstrued.

The world was thunderstruck. A renegade group who had enjoyed brief prominence while their propositions were examined, and who now could not bring themselves to let go of the disproved suppositions, was one thing. But a government — and of a catastrophically affected country, at that — giving the eccentric group a new lease of life was something else entirely.

Prominent scientists who had been open to a process of questioning and re-examination had rapidly — after resolution of the scientific evidence — distanced themselves from the dissident viewpoint. The never-say-die core that remained was an intellectually motley lot. They didn't have a unified belief. They were united more by their challenge of the emerged orthodoxy than a theory of their own. Broadly, though, they propounded the views that HIV, if it existed, which some of them doubted, was a harmless passenger virus; that deaths ascribed to Aids were a mistaken labelling of deaths due to a range of standard diseases; that, if Aids existed, it was actually caused by the medicines used to fight the HI virus; and that the tests for HI virus were useless and misleading.[14]

When the dissidents came to South Africa at the invitation of Mbeki many people who met them and attended their meetings were struck by their erratic behaviour, quick tempers, and unconventional debating styles. Several accounts of this tenor appeared, most notably a Pulitzer Prize winning series in *The Village Voice* in New York by Mark Schoofs.[15]

One of the dissidents[16] wrote to a South African newspaper claiming that the CIA, the FBI and the National Security Agency of the USA were conspiring in a bid to isolate and neutralise Mbeki and his government. "Millions of dollars", he said, were being spent on this neutralisation of Mbeki and other African leaders, and to "orchestrate" the public media. These views were a striking echo of Mbeki's own lament before the ANC caucus, reported above.

The views still held by dissidents today were dropped by the scientific establishment after the HI virus was discovered in 1983. Up to then, there had been a suspicion that it existed because many aspects of Aids suggested a viral agent as the cause of the infection. One of the principal factors was how the infection travelled in geographic areas or among specific social groups — for instance, Haitians or gays in San Francisco ... or in sub-Saharan Africa.

The discovery of the virus — first achieved, as in nearly all virus cases, by the presence of its antibodies — led to the eventual isolation of the virus itself, and, by today, to a reasonably good understanding of how it attaches itself to CD4 lymphocyte cells, replicates there, suppresses them, and thereby degrades the immune system of which they are an integral part.

Surprisingly, in 2000 Mbeki repeated one of the dissident's outdated axioms: the HI virus has not been isolated.

Mbeki seemed to have forgotten about his earlier enthusiasm for the HIV-fighting properties of virodene.

---

[14] The most cogent of the dissidents, Peter Duesberg, who has since gone on to claim that science has misunderstood cancer, has set out his views at http://www.duesberg.com. A description of HIV as the cause of Aids can be found on the site of the National Institute of Allergy and Infectious Diseases (USA) at http://www.niaid.nih.gov/spotlight/hiv00/.

[15] The series ran under the overall title of *Aids in Africa* in July 2000.

[16] David Rasnick, "SA at the heart of a global conspiracy", *Business Day*, May 9, 2001.

The ferocity of the public reaction to Mbeki's stance must have taken him aback. For he then attempted to blur the issue with circumlocutions. He pointed out that he had never said HIV was *not* the cause of Aids. His view was, rather, that it could not be the *only* cause.

Now, let's go carefully over this bit. If Mbeki was saying that the HI virus could not be the only cause of a depleted immune system, that a host of other maladies, like poverty, malnutrition and others could have the same effect ... then he would merely be stating a commonplace.

If, however, he was saying that the HI virus was not the only cause of Aids — a specific condition of immuno deficiency rising from the actions of the HI virus — then he was dead wrong.

It's simple, isn't it? There are any number of states of immuno deficiency, resulting from any number of factors. One of the states is called Aids, and it results from infection by the HI virus.

You can put it this way, too: if you become infected by the HI virus, you will develop an immuno deficiency called Aids, and, if left untreated, you will almost certainly die.

This is too straightforward to become a major point of contention between a president of a country, his government, millions of people, many of them desperate and dying, an entire civic constituency of non-governmental bodies, an international audience including governments, the world's media, and the global scientific establishment.

There must be something else afoot.

Let's try to clarify it by following the trail of the evidence for a while longer.

The first destination that the evidence leads to is that, post-virodene, Mbeki appears to have lost his enthusiasm for anti-HIV medicines. He and his health minister have stated repeatedly that they will not permit their distribution.

The drug manufacturers have, over time, made several offers of discounted prices, even free drugs and test kits ... which they can easily afford since SA accounts for less than 1% of global pharmaceutical sales and the public relations benefits to a donor would be enormous. All of these offers have met either a cool reception, evasive replies, have been ignored, or simply refused. The record contains too many instances to detail here.

The South African government went to court to prevent the drug manufacturers upholding their patent rights in South Africa, won the concession, then announced the drugs would, nevertheless, not be made available.

There is an exception — nevirapine. In December 2000 an upbeat story in the *New York Times*[17] reported the manufacturer Boehringer Ingelheim saying nevirapine would be made available in South Africa.

At this time of writing, July 2001, it was still being "tested" in selected South African hospitals and not freely available. It is a drug that can reduce the number of HIV positive children born from infected mothers by half, and it is in use in many parts of the world — having been duly licensed by the relevant authorities.

Mbeki has said on numerous occasions he is worried about the toxicity of anti-HIV drugs, like nevirapine and AZT, and implied thereby that he is committing a humanitarian act by withholding them from South African patients.

The simple truth is that the drugs are, indeed, toxic — as are most medicines if taken incorrectly. The anti-HIV drugs are successfully used in many places, including other African countries.

Once more, the facts are too simple to justify a catastrophic misunderstanding.

We bump again into the unavoidable conclusion: Mbeki and the ministry of health do not want existing anti-HIV drugs employed in the fight against Aids in South Africa. This view is reinforced by the fact that a very small adjustment in Mbeki's stance would have put him in the clear with world opinion: if he had argued that the syndrome of poverty, poor nutrition and social oppression that he points to made people more susceptible to HIV infection — rather than that it caused Aids — he would have occupied today an honourable position as a campaigner for a uniquely African comprehensive response to the epidemic.

But this would have entailed acknowledging the primacy of HIV and that, in turn, would remove any logical objection to the use of anti-HIV medicines. Instead he has courted world opprobrium by denying the primacy of HIV as the cause of Aids.

There is one further, significant assumption that we must deal with before we can move on to the next part of our inquiry. It is the assumption that it is proper for Mbeki to express himself on matters of epidemiology, on the physiology of viral science in general and HIV in particular, and on

[17] Rachel L Swarns, "South Africa to distribute $50 million in donated AIDS drugs", *New York Times*, December 2, 2000.

the pharmacology of the medicines involved. It is the assumption, further-more, that it is proper that his layman's opinion should be the measure from which is derived public policy that directly affects the lives and deaths of millions of people.

Unquestionably, it is most improper that this should be the case. It will make a very strange picture, indeed, when the present is viewed from the future, and it shows a country ravaged by a dreadful epidemic ... while its president adopts a quixotic stance against the causes and the medicines the rest of the world understands and endorses.

We must now ask what is so important in this issue that Mbeki would risk his personal standing and his grand vision of remaking the North-South order for it.

The first possibility is that the debacle has arisen out of well-inten-tioned errors of judgement. Mbeki genuinely wanted to embrace the broad scope of the Aids problem. This cannot be true. The elementary facts of the issue are easy for anyone to grasp, as we have seen above. If Mbeki's judgement were so erroneous that he could not grasp that, or that he could not marshal the fine scientists that exist in this country and elsewhere to brief him on the facts, then that profound incapacity of judgement would surely be glaringly visible in many other ways and instances. Since he is clearly an intelligent and capable person, lack of intellect cannot be the explanation.

The second possibility is that Mbeki's anti-Western sentiment goes deeper than one supposes; that he is, therefore, driven by a visceral impulse to side with those who attack Western orthodoxy, especially in matters of vital concern to Africa. So deep is this instinct in him that it blinds even his sense of where his best interests lie. This is not an accept-able explanation, either. It would mean that Mbeki is so much a victim of his emotions that he would let them get the better of his reason, and endanger his good standing in the eyes of his fellow citizens, and among the thinking people of the world. Not likely.

The third possibility rests on one of the most damaging of the mortal sins — pride. Swept up in an excess of hubris, Mbeki miscalculated, and thought he would distinguish himself by bringing an alternative view on Aids to centre stage ... not knowing that it had already been tested and rejected, and believing that, in time, he would be recognised for his moral and intellectual courage. Then, when the bubble burst, the same pride would not let him admit his error, and he did what many a politician before him has done, and will still do — he tried to wriggle out of it. This, too, is not acceptable as an explanation. The reason is simply that it would be so easy to wriggle out of the situation in many more artful ways than a bland admission of fault, if that was required. A "retreat with honour" is not only a noble gesture, it is a standard exercise in political spin doctoring. Such a course of corrective action would have been — would still be — far less damaging that an obstinate adherence to the path of amateur scientific rebellion.

Whichever way you cut it, there is no discernable political advantage for Mbeki on the course he has embarked.

So, if there is no political advantage, what does its elimination leave us with?

The editors of the medical journal, *The Lancet*, embarked on a similar sequence of reasoning to that which we have undertaken here. They test the main arguments and rationales offered by the South African government — and find,[18] in the restrained language typical of such a journal, that they do not stand up to elementary logic. For example:

> Zuma's[19] point that the money saved on treating a woman during the perinatal period would be better spent on preventive measures such as education does not take into account the savings made from not having to treat an infected child.

And:

> Mbeki's explanation that zidovudine is toxic is not in keeping with other risk-benefit assessments of the drug.

And:

> ... the country cannot afford to waste time and resources re-examining issues that have been explored while procrastinating on effective action to limit the spread of infection.

After weighing the evidence, the editorial states: "Why anti-HIV policy in South Africa is taking these bizarre paths is perplexing."

Then the editors raise the only speculative conclusion they can come to:

Is there some other agenda, such as the promotion of locally developed drugs?

Could *The Lancet* be right?

Could Mbeki and his government be caught up in a desperate bid to hold Western medicines at bay while, behind the scenes, work progresses on developing an indigenous drug or treatment?

[18] *The Lancet*, editorial, vol 355, no 9214, April 29, 2000.
[19] Dr Nkosazana Zuma was South Africa's minister of health from 1994 to 1999.

One thing is certain, in a dire situation characterised by obfuscation, double-speak, diversion, puzzlement and illogic — crying out for explanation — this is the only explanation that fits the facts. As far fetched as it may seem, it is the only explanation that imbues the otherwise incomprehensible actions and events with some logic.

As a hypothesis it satisfies all the requirements posed by the problem.

It explains the talk of "finding an African solution to an African problem".

It explains why Mbeki is prepared to put so much at risk for the pursuit of his otherwise inexplicable course of action.

It explains why he can't accept the advice of his own, and the world's, scientists.

It explains why he must keep existing anti-HIV medicines at bay, until such time as an African medicine is available, or ready.

Finally, it is entirely in keeping with his clearly perceptible gambit for a continental, and even a global, role and place in history ... even if South Africa must pay a price for its attainment.

On a personal note: as an explanation, do I welcome it?

I certainly do not. The callousness of its implications are staggering. I arrive at it with the greatest trepidation and hesitation.

Am I aware of the consequences it exposes me to?

I believe I am.

Yet, after many months of assiduous thought and research, have I been able to find another explanation?

I am afraid not.

Eden in Africa

The only template of understanding that sits acceptably on the problem of Zimbabwe is one we have already acquainted ourselves with — the clash of African and Western values. The benighted country, suffering economic collapse, food and fuel shortages, and the breakdown of social order, has seen desperate peasants, shorn of any hope for betterment, invading the lands of prosperous white farmers.

The peasants' actions are driven by a mythic yearning to recapture a rural idyll that once was theirs and Africa's. At some point they and their fathers and mothers had abandoned the idyll for the promise of a new way, the Western way. The realisation has since settled in them that the Western way enticed them, only to taunt them with glimpses into the widows of wealth, while they shuffled in the gutters of the promise.

Now they want back what they have lost.

Their yearning is voiced by a manic dreamer, a despot and dandy, fond of exotic spectacles and commandeered airliners, given to poetic speech rich in pastoral metaphors, who scares the bejabbers out of foreigners. Robert Mugabe is the West's anathema: he scorns its principles and flouts its norms; he calls the whites who tend the country's economy "dogs" and wishes aloud they would leave; he uses the country's army to pursue and protect his personal interests in fellow dictators' lands, he banishes judges and journalists who cross him and he openly enthuses over the peasants' land grabs. He is a hero in Africa.

This is not a gratuitous disparagement of Africa. Mugabe is a hero on his home continent not because he is a despot but because he is thumbing his nose at the West. He dismisses the bleatings of the West and proclaims that he is putting right what they made wrong. He is brazen. He is out there. He personifies the fantasies of others.

Mugabe has offered Africans a fantasy escape from the burden of relative deprivation as described by Oliver James and the persisting psychic pain of labouring under the unspoken disapproval of others, as described by Isaiah Berlin.

The following is typical of the rhetoric of a promised, vanished, dreamed land of rural contentment he imbues his lengthy speeches with:

> We just want our soil, our environment, our everything, including, of course, our wildlife, our birds, even our snakes and insects. Let them leave us alone, with our cows enjoying our sanity, with our animals without the mad cow disease.[20]

The reach of the symbolism projected by Mugabe can be easily detected in the powerful reaction there has been to him and his actions — supportive in the main from Africa and Africans, and condemnatory from the West, including the whites of Africa.

The mood of the invasions spread quickly through neighbouring Namibia and South Africa. The enormous pressure building up from the dispossessed, in South Africa in particular, now had a tag that was spoken easily on the lips of people and written in the headlines that reported and perpetuated the mythological pursuit of the return of African land to Africans.

Nearly half of Zimbabwe's roughly 4 000 commercial farms have been occupied, and the Zimbabwe government intends to seize about 3 000 in total, without compensation.

---

[20] Robert Mugabe, May 6, 2001.

In an echo of Mr Uahuapirapi the land, once seized, becomes subject to collective ownership.

The Zimbabwe experience brought the gulf between Western and African perceptions into stark focus. While the West ranted, African endorsement came from all levels of society, the political and the popular.

In August 2000 the South African Development Community (SADC) formally leant its unqualified support to Mugabe in his actions and aims. In July 2001 foreign ministers at the Organisation of African Unity drafted a proposal in full support of Mugabe.

A Zimbabwean correspondent captured the dichotomy of attitudes in a letter to a South African newspaper: "President Robert Mugabe will emerge a true African hero."

Capturing the essence of difference between the Western mind and the African mind, the correspondent wrote:

> While it is true that what Africa and the rest of the Third World need to lure the transnational corporations is less governance, this is in the form of cheap labour, respect of private property, low taxation and relaxed environmental laws. Unfortunately this system has produced pure capitalists who do not regard the sovereignty of a people or a nation.
>
> Forget about so-called democracy, human rights and rule of law, for they are just like *The Bible* when our land was taken during colonisation.
>
> If the Zimbabwean revolution is not allowed to correct the vast injustices and imbalances of the legacies of slavery, colonialism and neo-colonialism, then in international politics democracy becomes like three wolves and a sheep voting for what to eat for supper.[21]

What comes through strongly is the African sense of the hypocrisy of the West. The veneer of democratic norms and the culture of rights are seen as no more than expedient instruments with which the West now wants to prevent Africa restoring the balance that was lost when the West committed the very transgressions it now accuses Africans of. The correspondent's vivid image of the original land robbers with *The Bible* in their hands conveys the point graphically.

At a formal level, the Zimbabwe government answered Western protests that the land grabs violated the rule of law — by saying that the land issue was not a matter for the courts. This only makes clear that the African mind, in this instance, perceives a level of justice that is above the level practised by the courts and the law. It reveals an African view of the law

[21] Simon Hudebwe, "Mugabe is a hero", Letters, *Mail & Guardian*, June 8–14, 2001.

and the courts as essentially Western cultural implements that have only a limited function and value.

A headline over a column by Mondli Makhanya in the *Sunday Times,* South Africa's largest-circulation newspaper, asked: "What's so special about Mugabe when dictators all around oppress freely?" Another columnist, Mzimkulu Malunga, under the headline "In white venom for Zimbabwe, blacks see snake in SA's grass" in *Business Day*, stated: "This hysteria even makes some blacks wonder whether there isn't something that Mugabe is doing right."

This great dichotomy of views is what Mbeki both saw and felt when he became part of the tempest of emotions. Frustrated whites strained at the leash as they waited for Mbeki to take an implacable stand against the farm seizures — which would appease the norms on which the Western economies in Africa ran.

Need one say that these were the very economies that Africans not only felt estranged from — but which, they believed, had been actively working against African interests. To expect African sympathy for the discomfort of these economies was asking for pie from the sky.

Mbeki spoke dismissively of the "frenzy of fear and hatred" that broke out among white South Africans over Mugabe and the land invasions. He had himself photographed with Mugabe in Harare, walking in public, the two men in a quintessentially African gesture — interlocking their little fingers.

When Mbeki moved, late in the play, to placate his white Western constituency, he chose a gathering of mainly white businessmen in Johannesburg. In a speech that focused on topics other than Zimbabwe, he included a statement that similar land invasions would not be tolerated in South Africa. He paid little heed to the foreign Western constituency.

By this time the debate among whites had veered badly off target, so clouded was it by emotions. The white public mood formed as a cry that South Africa must "do" something about the situation in Zimbabwe.

Quite clearly, there was nothing to be "done". What was required was that South Africa, through its president, its government and its public voice, needed to cement into the West's perception that the dynamics that drove Zimbabwe were either absent in South Africa, or would not be allowed a foothold.

For the reasons discussed, Mbeki was not able to bring himself to do this. There was no course of action that would effectively appease both the African view and the Western view in the controversy. The only stratagem was to keep as low a profile as possible. Besides, a politician, if forced into action, will address his core constituency first, and then lift his sights to those that lie on its periphery. Foreign investment in South Africa, already critically low, fell to the lowest levels it had been for many years.

What do we take away with us from the Zimbabwe experience? What does it tell us about the road that lies ahead? Are Africa and the West on irreconcilably different tracks?

No, Africa is merely defining itself — in this case, through an extremist who draws our attention to a residual attitude. Africa's character and personality, after long slumber during colonialism and the fitful wakening from its oppression, is emerging.

The excesses of Zimbabwe tell us that the great clash of values is not an abstraction restricted to discussions such as this one. It is real, it's chaotic and it hurts.

The state and the union

One of the many dichotomies embedded in the Zimbabwe story is that it was taking place at the same time that African leaders, headed by Mbeki, were forging the most ambitious plan for African development ever seen. On the face of it, the Zimbabwe experience was a contradiction in practice of everything the plan was formulating in principle.

It must have made for more than one awkward moment in the many preliminary discussions Mbeki and his colleagues were having with Western governments — as the Africans explained their high-minded goals, while their fellows were, in their support of Mugabe, formally endorsing the disavowal of those goals.

The development plan occurred in tandem with an innovation in African macro-politics. The ineffective Organisation for African Unity was being remade into the African Union, which originated as a vision of Libya's Qaddafi.

Below the level of politics interesting forces of the shadow of the African collective mind were at work.

Africa, as we have noted, is in the main and in its heart a deeply patrist continent. Indeed, along with the Middle East, it is one of the last refuges of patrism in the post-modern occidental world. Africa, though, is patrist without a father figure at the collective level. To be sure, there are patrists in many sub-societies of Africa, but there is none that embodies the collective conscious. Mandela came close, but stopped short of becoming the symbolic figurehead of Africa.

Of course, one reason is that, until now, there has not really been such as thing as a collective African consciousness. Africa has been too fractured; too disparate. Its ability to communicate with itself has been too limited for it to have a unified character or mind.

This, though, is changing quickly. Africans are now thinking in continental terms, at a level and intensity that they have not before. To be sure, there is now an African Union and a New African Initiative. Behind these lie less visible, but significant developments, such an African broadcasting union and African cultural events like song, arts and film festivals — all signs of an emerging African consciousness.

Consequently, there is a struggle in the shadow to produce a symbolic leader of Africa. The machinations of history as a collective dynamic have already produced the candidates. Mbeki, Obasanjo of Nigeria and Qaddafi are at the peak of the contest — with Qaddafi suffering the clear practical disadvantage of not being presentable in the West. A lower rung is more crowded, with Bouteflika of Algeria, Wade of Senegal, and Mugabe.

Mbeki is the clear favourite. It is likely, in the years to come, that he will become the face and voice that the world most identifies with Africa.

The platform of either his continued rise, or fall (if he escapes the Aids trap), will be the African Union and the New African Initiative, which will in due course come to be seen as different aspects of the same thing.

Its greatest danger lies in the discrepancy between the ethos of the Union and the Initiative, on the one hand, and the pedestrian realities of Africa on the other. The symbolic illustration of Zimbabwe's living contradiction of the spoken aims of the Initiative may never be bridged.

In as much as the initiative is designed specifically as a means of re-ordering the balance of Africa's relationship with the West, this is a most significant problem.

The paradox is driven further by one of the most curious things about the Union — the degree to which it, an African initiative, is an unrefreshed imitation of the European Union. The proposed African Union comes replete with plans for an African parliament and, more amazingly even though more distantly, plans for a common currency.

This may lead to the African Union and South Africa sharing an unexpected characteristic. In South Africa there is a discernable gulf between the attitudes that prevail in government, and in its broad mass of people. We have in an earlier chapter discussed how the exiles who returned to govern in South Africa imported Western matrism — and superimposed it on the inherent patrism of the society. The overt European quality of the manner in which the African Union is conceived may, in a similar manner, just on a continental scale, represent an attitudinal gulf between it and the people of Africa. This would mean a future of conflicts and paradoxes, rising from deep within the collective unconscious of Africa, may bedevil many of the Union's proposed doings.

One early illustration is contained in the proposal for a common currency. However distant the goal might be, it reveals the gulf that must first be crossed. Trying to imagine a set of conditions in which Egypt might be willing to pool its currency with Rwanda, or South Africa with the Congo, for example, reveals the power of the paradox.

In practice, it means the short-term fate of the African Union could be an uncomfortable conflict between perceptions and realities, and between ambitions and achievable goals.

For this reason, the greatest tactical mistake the Union can make would be to set its goals too high. For failure to achieve them will only deepen the cynicism that already governs Western attitudes to Africa. As we have learned from the insights of Isaiah Berlin regarding Germany's response to the condescending cynicism of its European neighbours, the reaction of Africa would entrench a set of responses — for which Zimbabwe is a harbinger — that will drive the continent into a fate that no one wishes for it.

From Problems to Possibilities
New thinking, new ways, new hope

If you don't believe me, believe Albert Einstein. He said: "The significant problems we face cannot be solved by the same level of thinking that created them." South Africa needs a new level of thinking to solve its significant problems. And South Africa's most significant problem is that its dream has died.

The new society came into being in 1994 as a result of a dream, and with a dream. It began as a dream of liberation from racial tyranny and the limitations of mind and spirit that were necessary to maintain the tyranny. Liberation turned it into a dream of development and prosperity.

The language, alone, that accompanied the events of the time, revealed the metaphysical nature of people's experience of them. South Africa was said to have passed through a "miracle". Inside and outside the country, the dream society was called "the rainbow nation". Its leader, in the popular idiom, was said to possess "Mandela magic". It was as if a land of wonder had come, at the end of humanity's most barbaric century, to redeem it.

Nobody thinks like that now. Not Susan Citizen who fantasised that her material struggle would be alleviated; not the poor, the unemployed and the homeless who did not expect that their number would multiply; not the hopeful entrepreneur who anticipated a strong acceleration of economic growth and opportunities; not the investor who seeks reassurance of the long-term safety of her dollar, her pound or her yen; not the idealists of all colours who imagined a more moral civic society; not the plague-ridden who hoped for a nurturing government giving greater care and showing greater empathy; not Mamphela Ramphele, a revered South African anti-apartheid activist who fears returning from her posting at the World Bank to face official lassitude about HIV/Aids and the social problems it is brewing: "I have two sons. I wouldn't want them to come back to a country where they will be at risk at every level."[1] Not even the government, which admits that "little has changed".

[1] Interview with Anso Thom, *Cape Times*, 2001.

South Africa needs a dream. It cannot be without one. Too great an effort is needed to overcome the challenges that face it for any success to come from mere trudging along the demarcated path. South Africa needs a psychic shock. Only this will snap it out of its sleepwalk.

We need to turn now to how this might be achieved. As we do so, we must take in the sweep of our argument until now.

We began by finding that there are unexpected benefits to treating society as one might an individual — by recognising the existence of society's collective mind. The notion is uncommon. It has found limited acceptance in popular culture and academic circles. Yet we are not the first to apply it, and we are in good company when we do. Writing on this topic on the C G Jung Page, John Fraim[2] draws attention to Freud's speculations in *Civilization and its Discontents*. Freud hoped that it might be possible one day to "embark upon a pathology of cultural communities". Freud toyed with the notion that a collective neurosis had settled on society:

> It can be asserted that the community, too, evolves a super ego under whose influence cultural development proceeds. ... The super ego of an epoch of a civilisation has an origin similar to that of an individual. ... If the development of civilisation has such a far-reaching similarity to the development of the individual and if it employs the same methods, may we not be justified in reaching the diagnosis that, under the influence of cultural urges, some civilisations, or some epochs of civilisation — possibly the whole of mankind — have become "neurotic"?

We then moved some way towards Freud's tentative diagnosis by looking at the state of mind of a society under stress. And we looked in some depth into the origins of social stress. Let's bring it all to a head with a brief overview of what is commonly known about the behaviour of stressed individuals, who have developed some degree of depression as a reaction to the stress. The stressed/depressed individual will manifest some and, usually, all of the following:

- *Loss of energy.* The sheer mental strain of coping against the odds reassigns energy resources from the outward and physical to the inner landscape and the struggle of the spirit. Individuals impaired in this way expend as much, or more, energy than unimpaired and outwardly successful persons. They just absorb their strength inwardly ... in order to appear normal.

[2] John Fraim, *The Long Birth of Psychohistory,* The C G Jung Page, August, 2001
http://www.cgjungpage.org/articles/fraimpsychohistory.html.

- *Lowered anger threshold.* Just as a person walking a tightrope would be irritated by wilful distractions, so the coping depressed individual is easily angered by extraneous stimuli.
- *Hair trigger to violence.* As anger and violence are closely associated, so the stressed/depressed individual, pre-occupied with the struggle to cope, is quick to anger, and the anger is quick to spill into violence.
- *Withdrawal to familiarity zones.* Part of coping strategy is to stick with what is known best. Accordingly, the stressed/depressed individual draws back from experiences and terrains where he or she is does not have sufficient self-assurance.
- *Inability to change.* The stressed/depressed individual frequently knows perfectly well what is needed to change his or her pernicious circumstances, and even how to go about it. However, owing to low energy, a tendency to withdraw, destructive flashes of anger and even angry lashings-out — with a range of other knock-on maladies such as loss of confidence, loss of belief in the worth of goals, and so on — the individual simply cannot mount the changes he or she can conceive. Often, talking about the changes in order to convey to others the impression that change is imminent, accompanied by resolutions to undertake the changes and assurances that this will be done ... soon ... take the place of change itself.
- *Displacement activities.* Faced with apparently insurmountable challenges, the stressed/depressed individual will occupy his or her attention with manageable tasks. These will be cast as necessary preliminaries to the main task, or they will be rationalised as suitable alternatives ... and their value will be commensurately inflated.
- *Helplessness and the victim syndrome.* The stressed/depressed individual will finally be overcome by a sense of disempowerment, and the belief that his or her unhappy fate is the doing of others. If others had acted differently, had not deprived the individual of the necessary opportunities, had considered the individual's interests while pursuing their own — we can go on at length in familiar terms — then the individual would not now be in this unhappy condition. The identity of "the victim" is a ready-made one, and lends itself usefully to manipulating the guilt of others, thereby extracting sympathy and concessions.

These states are familiar to all of us. To some degree, at some time, each of us has been some of the way down each of these roads.

. Let us go over the points again, and this time let us imagine we are talking not about an individual, but a society — and not any society, about South Africa.

There is a perceptible loss of energy among South Africans. They simply do not have the levels of entrepreneurship that are found in other, more successful societies. The productivity of South African workers does not compare favourably with world norms. The paucity of energy and enthusiasm is most visible in South Africa's inability to maximise its best shot at economic recovery and prosperity — tourism. The levels of service on which the industry relies, and which succeed more on energy and enthusiasm than on skills and training, remain sluggish and underdeveloped.

The lowered anger threshold and the propensity to violence in South African society speak for themselves. Criminal violence, inter-personal violence and deaths in accidents are among the highest in the world.

South African politics has remained firmly stuck in familiarity zones. The prologue to this work discussed the "political decapitation" South Africa had experienced — a change of government without a meaningful change in society. One of the most remarkable illustrations of this is how the primary concern of the old order has been dragged through to the new order to remain the principle preoccupation — racism. The governing party, in its second five-year term, still likes to think of itself — and be thought of — as a liberation movement. In sum, to the average citizen or visitor to South Africa, who is more concerned with daily practicalities than remote civic theory, the new South Africa is disturbingly similar to the old.

South Africa's ability to change was at a high point in the four years between the unbanning of the ANC and its related organisations, and the end of the negotiations that set the stage for the democratic election of 1994. The atmosphere in the country was electric, and the achievements of the Codesa negotiating forum — which included a total overhaul of the political structure of the society and a new constitution — were monumental. Thereafter the pace of change slumped, and became incremental, at best. The latter-day atmosphere is characterised by summit conferences on unemployment, poverty and racism that achieve little or nothing ... except, perhaps, to deepen popular cynicism.

Faced with the numbing challenges of developing along a path marked out by First World yardsticks, and defeats inflicted by advancing poverty, joblessness and disease, South African has given itself over substantially to displacement politics. The government pushes to front-of-stage its gender liberation, its prosecution of racism and its espousal of abstractions such as Africanism. It has also busied itself with the social implications of gay rights, the banning of public smoking and restrictions on the advertising of alcohol. All of these matters are praiseworthy, of course. But they get disproportionate attention in a society as fundamentally needy as South Africa's. These issues would be congruent with an advanced democracy fine-tuning its civic balances. In a place such as South Africa, in the face of the starving, the sick, the dying, the homeless and the jobless, they are incongruous. It's displacement of political energy.

The victim syndrome is amply illustrated by the persistence in the national consciousness, and in the national debate, of the ascription of blame to apartheid and colonialism for society's present ills. Naturally, this is not to say that either of the two is blameless. Not at all. We have dealt with that. It is rather a matter of the degree to which these ills are dwelt on, and the degree to which that focus on apportioning blame diverts attention and energies from implementing recoveries. A society in better overall attitudinal condition than South Africa is in today would have celebrated its release from its constraints, and would have tackled its recovery with much greater vigour than has been the case.

It may be argued that the preceding analytical lean is a little too heavy on the negative, and that it fails to take into account, adequately, the opposing view: that change on the scale required takes many years to align, that material progress has been made in many instances, that South Africa is on the right road, and that it will reach its goals in time. Regrettably, while there have assuredly been many improvements, they are outpaced by the acceleration of the need. South Africa is not on the right road. It will require significant course adjustment before it is; and, even if it were on the right road, it will not have the time to reverse the critical dynamics at the pace it is tackling them — before it has to face a great reckoning. At best, South Africa is pursuing goals that are receding at a pace equal to, or faster than, the pace at which they are being pursued.

A psychic shock is needed to dispel the miasma.

One of the delusions of the miasma is the expectation that the government must provide; that, indeed, the government *can* provide. The psychic shock must banish this. Truths that have to find their way into the South African mind, in some form at some time, are that: the government can never build a house for everyone who needs one; the government can never provide a job for everyone who doesn't have one; and the better life that all seek has to be created by all, not by some.

Much misunderstanding surrounds this question. Consequently, much of the national debate around issues of "delivery" is misdirected. It has become so much part of the convention that the government itself participates in the delusion, failing to point out that there are clear limits on its ability to "deliver", and that those limits fall short, by a long measure, of satisfying the national needs.

This means the psychic shock must unlock a process of development that wells up from the broad populace.

This does not mean, however, that the government does not have a role to play in igniting the process. On the contrary, it is the agent that must deliver the shock.

Here we bang up against a problem. The government has so eroded its credibility in the public mind that it is not in a position to act as that agent.

Collectively, the government has lost evident possession of the moral compass that society needs and that we identified earlier in our discussion. Instances of official corruption are pervasive in news reports. Dishonesty in high places has become part of the popular myth. It is the stuff of jokes.[3] Movie makers in other countries, when seeking to typecast a baddie, with alarming frequency are coming up with a South African. "Corrupt South African" is becoming as common an expression in some circles as "French chef" or "Italian gigolo".

Individually, the South African president has acquired a serious image problem. If the Mbeki presidency were drawn as a graph in which the horizontal axis measured time, and the vertical axis news headlines frequency, then the majority of peaks in the graph would be made of negative publicity: lavish inauguration, lying politicians, Aids blunders, Zimbabwe mishandling, arms-deal controversies, conspiracy allegations. The only positive peak ranking with the reaches of the negatives would be the New African Initiative.[4]

Politics without a moral compass in a society in which politics is a secular faith creates most invidious social conditions. These were seen with bitter acuity by the Marquis de Sade who, founding a genre destined for misunderstanding — pornography as a moral instrument, wrote from prison:

> 'Tis the manifold misuse of authority on the part of the government that multiplies the vices of individuals. With what face do those who are the head of

---

[3] People complain unnecessarily about the government. Why? We have one of the best governments money can buy.

[4] Mbeki's input to the plan — apparently its major content — began as the Millennium Africa Recovery Plan, known by its acronym MARP or, more euphoniously, as MAP.

government dare punish vice, dare demand virtue, when they themselves provide the example of every depravity on the face of the earth?[5]

Perfidy in government seeps into society and becomes the cause of its
moral depletion. So it is there, at the very top, that the psychic shock must
be administered.

What is it to be?

The psychic shock must fulfil two criteria:

- It must address the heart of the problem, which is belief; belief in its
  many manifestations: belief that government genuinely is committed
  to the cause of upliftment and does not merely say so; belief that
  betrayal of the public trust has, unquestionably, no place in public life;
  belief that every South African is capable of better and is in the process
  of becoming so; belief that the new society is worth having and worth
  striving for.
- It must arise out of action, not statement.

If the psychic shock embraces and achieves these qualities, the vehicle
that is chosen does not matter greatly. It will probably present itself, once
an effective course is set in this direction.

The president could spearhead a campaign to rid, first the administration, then public life more broadly, of those that abuse the ethics of their
position. Like any act that is intended as part of the guiding social myth,
this one must include sacrifices. The guilty must be offered to appease the
god of public opprobrium. It must be seen to happen. There must be spectacle. Only in this way will public anger be sated.

The government must find a way to recant on its mammoth arms purchase. Only through this will it demonstrate that it understands the helpless despair with which the needy have listened to the speeches on ending
poverty, while the speechmakers employ their greatest ever marshalling of
resources for submarines, boats and airplanes to fight an enemy they cannot name or describe.

Let the government, rather, in its actions demonstrate that it recognises
endemic crime as one of the nation's prime enemies; that crime has a
stranglehold on the economy; that it is the single greatest inhibitor of
investment and greatest impellent in the flight of skills. Let all of the country's uniformed resources, including the military, be thrown into this battle

---

[5] Marquis de Sade, *Letters from Prison*, Arcade Publishing, Inc. New York, 2001; translated
by Richard Seaver and reviewed for the *Cape Times* March 27, 2001 by Paul Wessels.

— for it is *this* enemy that must be defeated. If there is a reason why military resources cannot be deployed in this way to a degree greater than present, let it be explained, acceptably, why not.

The president could create an international development corps, as President Kennedy did his peace corps. Its aim could be to establish a "training camp" everywhere there are significant numbers of needy people, and its purpose could be to transfer the rudimentary skills that will enable the workless to create their own jobs. Gardening skills, driving, home handiwork, basic building, cooking, homecraft, childminding — all of these, and many besides, are elementary capabilities that many of South Africa's work seekers lack, and which would significantly enhance the value of their labour ... and their chances of selling it. Serving in such a corps could be made an attractive option for the great numbers of young idealists in the developed world, yearning for just such an involvement and mission.

In the fight against Aids, a similar international effort could be mounted. There would be any number of participants, backers and donors. South Africa could lead the global struggle against the pandemic, instead of trying to hold a substantial portion of the world's efforts at bay. Where it is argued that the administration of the life-prolonging anti-retroviral drugs requires complex regimens that exceed Third World capacities, let South Africa be seen to be leading in innovations to overcome the hurdles. Let South Africans be lead so that they are praised for what they are doing, not pilloried. And if there is another agenda, let it be stated. Let there be honour and clarity where there has been diversion and disclamation.

In the economy, let the ports be free and let the taxes be flat-rated. Let the red tape of bureaucracy be scoured from the system. Let the global economy be embraced and beckoned, rather than resented and rebuffed. Put out a welcome mat for skilled foreigners; for them, let immigration be easy and near-automatic. Create an institute for policy innovation and implement its recommendations without delay. For is there any sensible innovation that could impede the economy more than the deadweights of policy and convention that it already carries?

In its foreign policy let Pretoria lead Africa and the rest of the developing world, from an unassailable moral platform and speaking with one voice, in a campaign against the hypocrisy of the West when it calls on all to allow unfettered globalisation of trade, yet frustrates access to its own markets. In respect of the nascent African Union let there be an end to grandstanding, and let Pretoria lead other Africans in a cohesive effort to return Zimbabwe to the course of development that all other succeeding nations are on. Then let Africa convene its direly needed court of justice — and go after the continent's rapacious rulers. If this should prove too high an ideal to reach, let South Africa be seen to go down fighting honourably for it, scrupulously applying the principles to itself.

Finally, let those who lead South African now realise that if they fail to produce the psychic shock that can reverse current inertia and present perceptions, they merely leave the initiative there to be taken up by someone else.

Moving from quantity to quality

In this discussion we have tried to identify and understand some of the dark pillars on which rest our experiences as a society. We have needed to walk in the shadows of the unconscious that we all share and we have had to explore the commonality of consciousness that arises there from. We have had to grapple with how our personal lives, when aggregated, give a character to our group, our social segment, and our entire society. We have seen how great civilisational tides of attitudes and values are flowing together to create the turbulence of our time — and the possibility of a new outlook within humanity's ranks.

For many readers who have stayed with the discussion this far, parts of the journey may have been unusual, even eccentric — and, at times, just a little cranky. It's something we are all going to have to get a lot more used to as we continue our search for ways of improving our social experience in ways that our thinking up to now has failed to do. In the opening stages of this examination we noted the feeling of many leading thinkers — especially, in this case, Stephen Jay Gould — that our thinking has to change its quality from the analytical to the synthesising, from reductionism to creative accrual, from understanding the parts to recognising that the time has come to understand, also, the whole. This is why our discussion has had to make the excursions it has into macro-trends in history, psychology, the psychology of history, and the role of collective thoughts and attitudes in what has been, up to now, our more mundane appreciation of politics and economics.

If we accept the foregoing, then we are doing no more recognising something that has already started to happen. The world is changing the way it thinks about these topics.

In 2000 the World Bank said the definition of poverty should be broadened from its present meaning of merely "low income" to include "powerlessness, voicelessness, vulnerability and fear."[6] The import is clear. The true poverty of the world's desperate people cannot be understood, or be properly dealt with, until their state of mind is recognised as part of their condition. Writing on the relationship between human capital and economic growth, South African economist Nicoli Nattrass says:

> According to the new "endogenous growth" theory, higher levels of accumulation of both social and human capital are vital contributory factors to per capita income growth. It is estimated, for example, that growth in Korea and Japan was raised by as much as 1.5% per annum by their above-average levels of schooling.[7]

New thinking in development economics recognises that monetary measures are not the only indicators of social well-being. Put another way: economic growth and social development are not necessarily the same thing.

The evolution of these ideas has taken place in recent years. Well ahead of his time, charaterisitically, was the Harvard economist J K Galbraith. At the end of the 1970s, he tackled the nature of mass poverty in a landmark book with the same title.[8] In it he observed how the tools of economic advancement would be brought to underdeveloped communities in the South Pacific — education, health services, work opportunities, etc. These came mainly through minerals exploration by Western companies. When the companies moved on, Galbraith saw, the jungles reclaimed the classrooms and vines entwined what were once the clinics. Galbraith concluded that what was missing was a state of mind in which the local people would *want* the development that was offered to them. And to want it, and stick with it, they had to believe its benefits were worth having. There was nothing about Western values that was as evident to the locals as it was to the Westerners who despaired unthinkingly at the locals.

Then a watershed idea arose within the Gaia hypothesis. A set of calculations were made, which revealed one of those conclusions that is so obvious it takes a genius to think of it.[9] The calculations were based on the fact that an average citizen of the developed world, an American, say,

---

[6] *Friday at Noon*, Issue # 348, September 15, 2000, Institute for Futures Research, Stellenbosch.

[7] Nicoli Nattrass, *Labour-demanding Growth: Lessons from International Experience?* Paper for the Centre for Development and Enterprise, March 26, 2001. http://www.cde.org.za/focus/labour.htm.

[8] *The Nature of Mass Poverty*, Out of print as a Harvard University Press hardback, 1970. Made available as an iUniverse.com print-on-demand book, March 2001, through Barnes & Noble's online bookshop http://www.barnesandnoble.com.

[9] This is the substance of a remark Einstein made about Piaget, who discovered that the intelligence of children is, in principle, different to that of adults.

consumed nearly 400 times as much of the Earth's resources as a citizen of Mali, for example. This meant, the calculation revealed, that if everyone had to advance to the civilisational level of America, the approximate equivalent of three and a half planets Earth would be needed to sustain the consumption of natural resources that such a state of humanity would entail.

The implications are sobering — and their absorption by the global development community has been slow. It's not hard to see why. The central implication invalidates the unspoken premise of development: that we strive for a world in which everyone enjoys the same standard of opportunities and rewards ... and that those standards are set by the developed world. It cannot ever be.

What this means for development is that the targets have to be changed. More importantly, the definition of development has to be changed. And that is precisely what is happening.

In a place such as South Africa, much of the agony in the misunderstanding of inequality would be alleviated if this were to become more clearly lodged in the conscious perceptions of society. It means that great, and probably growing, disparities in humanity are an inevitability. It means that, for the foreseeable future, sectors of the South African population are going to go through the civilisations upheavals described by Rattray Taylor in his depictions of 17th and 18th Century England; it means that yet other sectors are going to be experiencing industrialisation, and the social realties that attend on that economic experience; it means, too, that another sector of the population will be in the advanced, information-based economy of the developed world.

If — and this is a critical "if" — the disparities are not to lead to intensifying conflict, then a visible and credible process of improvement must be created to allay the resentment of those on the lower rungs of the development ladder. Each South African, no matter where he or she may be on the ladder, must feel there is a path upward ... and assistance and encouragement for the climb is readily available. When this belief dies, and it is dying, the social and political consequences will be significant.

But they are not inevitable. There are two factors that define the positive possibilities of the future. The first is that communities have integrated matrist characteristics and passed through industrialisation before. We have experiences and lessons from the past to guide us, and to blunt the cutting edges of the experiences. It takes deep study, careful thought and wise government, but it works.

The second factor is the emergence of another mental framework in which to understand, and deal with, the development disparity — and it is one that we have already examined. It is a changing tide of values, a shift from an excessively materialistic culture to Arie de Geus's "humanistic capitalism". In this value shift will be found a way to recognise human worth that is not counted in coin. Working with the World Bank's ethos of "power, voice, and security", a new consciousness may arise ... no, *must* arise ... to arrest the otherwise irretrievable break-up of the human family.

The recognition of this view is encouragingly widespread, and spreading.

A congressional study in Washington in 2000 found that the West's bid to turn Russia from communism to a successful *laissez faire* economy through the application of money alone failed. A *New York Times* account of the study says:

> A cumulative $66 billion in aid from the United States, Europe and the leading international lending agencies did prevent communists from returning to power and kept the nation from descending into anarchy. But the aid programs failed to build robust capitalist institutions or produce sustained economic growth in Russia, which produces roughly one third less now than it did a decade ago.[10]

It is now possible to see, more and more, that a sharpened perception is developing of the difference between wealth and quality of life. In no small measure this flows from the West's own disenchantment with the hollow benefits of the riches it has created. In his book *The World in 2020,* Hamish McRae makes the point vividly when he compares the effects rising crime, and people taking short holiday breaks in luxury hotels, or staying married:

> It costs roughly the same to keep someone in a high security prison as it does to stay in a top-flight hotel. Building a new prison or a new hotel appears as economic activity and so adds to GDP. Each extra night spent in either also increases GDP. In that sense both are a form of economic growth; but one decreases welfare, while the other increases it. This flaw is equally well illustrated by the divorce rate in a country. If it rises there will be additional activity for the lawyers who agree the settlements — that shows up as an increase in GDP. But the standard of living in the country has not risen as a result of the rise in the number of divorces; indeed, it has almost certainly fallen. A country may *appear* richer if its GDP rises, but the crude measurement of wealth of GDP per head makes no allowance for the way the GDP is generated.[11]

---

[10] Joseph Kahn, "Why West's billions failed to give Russia a robust economy", *New York Times*, November 2, 2000.

[11] Hamish McRae, *The World in 2020 — Power, Culture and Prosperity: A Vision of the Future.* Harper Collins, London, 1995.

This is not merely a clever notion. McRae uses OECD figures to show that between 1970 and 1990, when GNP per head rose about 30% in the USA, living standards hardly budged.

The guru of global development, Jeffrey Sachs, director of the Centre for International Development and professor of international trade at Harvard University, has been arguing for a rethink on globalisation.[12] He says the rich countries have never been richer. This is thus the best they have been placed to look beyond their immediate needs and, by implication, ensure their continued prosperity by making more of the world's people part of it. Sachs makes it clear this will entail a change of attitude in the West. At present, the richest country is also the smallest donor to international development: Americans muster only a paltry $5 per head per year for foreign aid.

Sachs bases his revised globalisation strategy on three main points. In the first he reflects the new thinking by nominating attention to public health and population as the primary concerns.

> The burden of disease on poor countries, especially in sub-Saharan Africa, is simultaneously a humanitarian catastrophe, a daunting barrier to development, and (through its effects on population) a first order threat to critical regions of high biodiversity. Foreign investors shun the worst-affected economies, and the burdens of ill-health block development in other ways, too. Sick children often face a lifetime of diminished productivity because of interrupted schooling together with cognitive and physical impairment.

He calculates an effective campaign for health in the developing world will cost $10 billion a year — that is, $10 per year from each of the one billion people in the developed world.

Secondly, Sachs believes, the marginalised regions of the world need to be networked to a far greater extent. He means networked with one another — opening intriguing visions of nations at similar stages of development focusing on trade with one another, rather than being crushed in competition with the developed world ... setting the stage for a multi-strata global economy — and networked with the developed world. He advocates flexible tax strategies and joint ventures between governments and corporations as the way to achieve this.

Lastly, Sachs states: "At the core of the global divide is the vast inequality in innovation and diffusion of technology." He contrasts the $50 million the World Bank spends a year on tropical agriculture research with the

---

[12] Jeffrey Sachs, "Sachs on globalisation: a new map of the world", *The Economist*, June 24, 2000.

pharmaceutical company Merck's research budget of $2.1 billion in 1999. Sachs notes that American universities, alone, receive more than $25 billion a year in philanthropic and foundation giving (the whole of national government in South Africa runs on about $10 billion a year). Part of this money should be used to internationalise the best education, through the creation of international campuses. This is an idea that has been advocated also by Manuel Castells.[13] Sachs advocates, too, that international should not target countries, as such, but rather terrains of the human experience — like education.

None of these ideas and trends of thought is unfamiliar in South Africa. In deed, people like Sachs and Castells are not infrequent visitors to South Africa and its senior government persons.

What remains unknown is whether the ideas and trends of thought will be realised in action. If they are, South Africa will find itself with an opportunity to retell the world a story that began 350 years ago with the start of colonialism. Then, the explorers of the old world found here a new one, which contributed greatly to the advancement of their lives and their societies. Now, the same would be the case — the old world, reaching for renewal of its jaded spirit, would find a new world here. But this time, because the new is, in truth, a hybrid of the old and the new, the advancement would enrich us all.

---

[13] Manuel Castells, op. cit.